Constitutionalizing Criminal Law

Constitutionalizing Criminal Law

COLTON FEHR

© UBC Press 2022

All rights reserved. No part of this publication may be reproduced, stored in a retrieval system, or transmitted, in any form or by any means, without prior written permission of the publisher, or, in Canada, in the case of photocopying or other reprographic copying, a licence from Access Copyright, www.accesscopyright.ca.

31 30 29 28 27 26 25 24 23 22   5 4 3 2 1

Printed in Canada on FSC-certified ancient-forest-free paper (100% post-consumer recycled) that is processed chlorine- and acid-free.

Library and Archives Canada Cataloguing in Publication

Title: Constitutionalizing criminal law / by Colton Fehr.
Names: Fehr, Colton, author.
Description: Includes bibliographical references.
Identifiers: Canadiana (print) 20210319712 | Canadiana (ebook) 2021032404X |
    ISBN 9780774867665 (hardcover) | ISBN 9780774867672 (paperback) |
    ISBN 9780774867689 (PDF) | ISBN 9780774867696 (EPUB)
Subjects: LCSH: Criminal law – Canada – Interpretation and construction. |
    LCSH: Constitutional law – Canada.
Classification: LCC KE8809 .F44 2022 | LCC KF9220.ZA2 F44 2022 kfmod |
    DDC 345.71 – dc23

Canadä

UBC Press gratefully acknowledges the financial support for our publishing program of the Government of Canada (through the Canada Book Fund), the Canada Council for the Arts, and the British Columbia Arts Council.

The publication of this book has been made possible in part by funding from Simon Fraser University.

Printed and bound in Canada by Friesens
Set in Sabon Next LT Pro and Myriad Pro by Apex CoVantage, LLC
Copy editor: Dallas Harrison
Proofreader: Judith Earnshaw
Cover designer: Alexa Love

UBC Press
The University of British Columbia
2029 West Mall
Vancouver, BC V6T 1Z2
www.ubcpress.ca

For Marian and Avery

Contents

1 Choosing among Rights / 3

2 Principles of Criminal Law Theory / 17

3 Principles of Instrumental Rationality / 58

4 Enumerated Principles of Criminal Justice / 102

5 A Normative Approach to Constitutionalizing Criminal Law / 140

6 Lessons from the Canadian Experience / 173

Notes / 179

Bibliography / 233

Index / 253

Constitutionalizing Criminal Law

Choosing among Rights   1

In *Reference re Section 94(2) of the Motor Vehicle Act*,[1] the Supreme Court of Canada was asked to determine the constitutionality of a law imposing a mandatory seven-day jail sentence for anyone caught driving without a licence or with a prohibited licence. The legislation specifically excluded any requirement that the state prove that the accused intended to drive without a valid licence.[2] This law was contrary to the common law presumption that all criminal and quasi-criminal offences require proof of fault to commit an offence.[3] Common law presumptions, however, are subject to clear legislative displacement. The impugned provision was therefore consistent with established law at the time subject to its compliance with the newly adopted *Canadian Charter of Rights and Freedoms*.

The *Motor Vehicle Act Reference* presented the Supreme Court with its first opportunity to interpret section 7 of the Charter. That provision provides that "everyone has the right to life, liberty, and security of the person and the right not to be deprived thereof except in accordance with the principles of fundamental justice."[4] Because the impugned law in the *Motor Vehicle Act Reference* imposed mandatory imprisonment, the subject's liberty interest was engaged. This raised a novel question: Was this deprivation of liberty inconsistent with the "principles of fundamental justice"?[5]

In answering this question, the Supreme Court was asked to interpret the phrase narrowly. There were textual, political, and historical arguments in favour of a narrow interpretation. Textually, the phrase "principles of fundamental justice" was borrowed from section 2(e) of Canada's statutory Bill of Rights. The interpretation of that provision could not be definitive, however, of how "fundamental justice" should be interpreted under the Charter. Section 2(e) provides that "no law of Canada shall be construed or applied so as to ... deprive a person of the right to a fair hearing in accordance with the principles of fundamental justice for the determination of his rights and obligations."[6] The specific reference to "a fair hearing" made it obvious that the provision was meant to be reserved for procedural protections.[7] The absence of such language in section 7 of the Charter implied a broader role for the term "fundamental justice."

Politically, it was argued that allowing section 7 of the Charter to protect substantive principles of justice would convert the Supreme Court into a "super-legislature" empowered with the ability to decide both law and policy.[8] To this contention, Justice Lamer responded that "the historic decision to entrench the *Charter* in our Constitution was taken not by the courts but by the elected representatives of the people of Canada."[9] Because the people had entrusted the courts with interpreting the Constitution, he was confident that a broad, substantive interpretation of section 7 would not be undemocratic if it were supported textually. For Justice Lamer, if the government wanted section 7 to provide procedural protections only, then it could have used clearer language by substituting the long-accepted term "natural justice."[10]

Justice Lamer maintained this position despite historical evidence supporting the view that section 7 was intended to provide only procedural protections. Commentators have since uncovered significant evidence of intent from some of the drafters of the Charter supporting a narrow, procedural rights interpretation of section 7.[11] It was this evidence that drove leading Canadian constitutional law scholar Peter Hogg to predict that it was "unlikely that [the] section 7 phrase 'principles of fundamental justice' can be pushed beyond procedural safeguards."[12] This view had also initially received support in the lower courts.[13]

Contrary to these earlier opinions, the Supreme Court concluded that evidence of the drafters' intent was of limited weight.[14] As Justice Lamer wrote, "the *Charter* is not the product of a few individual public servants, however distinguished, but of a multiplicity of individuals who played major roles in the negotiation, drafting and adoption of the *Charter*."[15] As a result, he asked "how can one say with any confidence that within this enormous multiplicity of actors, without forgetting the role of the provinces, the comments of a few federal civil servants can in any way be determinative?"[16] For the Supreme Court, placing too much emphasis on this evidence would allow ministers to legislate indirectly that which they could not negotiate in the political arena.[17]

The Supreme Court ultimately did not accede to the arguments supporting a narrow reading of section 7 of the Charter. Instead, it held that "the principles of fundamental justice ... are to be found in the basic tenets of our legal system."[18] Such principles are essential to the beliefs on which Canada is founded. They include a "belief in 'the dignity and worth of the human person' (preamble to the *Canadian Bill of Rights* ...) and in 'the rule of law' (preamble to the ... *Charter*)."[19] Given this broad interpretation of "fundamental justice," the court concluded that any law that engages an individual's life, liberty, and security of the person interests must conform to both procedural and substantive principles of justice.[20]

The law at issue in the *Motor Vehicle Act Reference* contravened a basic tenet of substantive justice: the "morally innocent" should not be deprived of liberty.[21] This violation followed from the law's potential to convict and imprison an accused person even though that person has not done anything wrong. For instance, the person might have received a suspended licence because of a missed payment resulting from a clerical error. Although preventing such an individual from serving a mandatory jail sentence would appear to be just in the eyes of most people, how the Supreme Court chose to strike down the law had much broader implications. The fact that the court did not place any significant limitations on which types of principles of justice might qualify as "fundamental" provided a broad form of substantive review, unprecedented in modern constitutionalism.[22]

In the ensuing years, the Supreme Court has used section 7 to constitutionalize two distinct types of substantive principles. First, it has constitutionalized a variety of moral philosophical principles. Because the vast majority of cases under section 7 implicate criminal law,[23] the principles constitutionalized derive primarily from criminal law theory. These principles are far-reaching, including prohibitions against convicting the morally innocent,[24] a requirement that offences exhibit proportionality between the *mens rea* of an offence and the moral blameworthiness of the actor,[25] and prohibitions against convicting accused persons for physically[26] and morally involuntary conduct.[27]

Second, the Supreme Court has constitutionalized principles of "means-end" or "instrumental" rationality.[28] This method of review assesses whether a law's effect is adequately connected to its objective or strikes an inappropriate balance between its objective and its effect.[29] It employs three main principles: arbitrariness, overbreadth, and gross disproportionality.[30] A law is arbitrary when its effect bears no connection to its objective,[31] overbroad when its effect fails to achieve its objective in some circumstance,[32] and grossly disproportionate when its effect is "totally out of sync" with its purpose.[33] As the Supreme Court's interpretation of section 7 progressed, the court increasingly preferred the instrumental rationality principles in testing whether criminal laws are in accordance with fundamental justice.[34]

The relationship that developed between criminal law and constitutional law under the Charter is notable for one further reason: it prioritized section 7 review at the expense of specifically enumerated Charter rights. To the dismay of some commentators,[35] rights such as freedom of expression,[36] the prohibition against cruel and unusual treatment or punishment,[37] and the right to equal treatment before the law[38] have taken on a secondary, and mostly modest, role in constitutional litigation of substantive criminal law issues.

Choosing among Rights

The existence of multiple avenues to challenge the constitutionality of criminal laws raises four key questions. First, to what extent is there overlap among these methods of substantive review? Although trial and appellate courts typically answer all rights questions raised at trial, the Supreme Court generally abstains from striking down criminal laws on multiple grounds. Instead, the court almost always applies one right and deems it "unnecessary" to decide the merits of the remaining rights claims. If there are significant overlaps among the methods of constitutional review, then it is highly likely that the court is explicitly choosing from among the methods when striking down a criminal law.

Second, if the Supreme Court is choosing from among competing methods of substantive review, then what are the benefits and detriments of employing each method? To date, the court has not explained why it tends to favour the instrumental rationality principles over the principles of criminal law theory despite appearing to have made such an explicit choice on several recent occasions. Moreover, the court has not explained why it often avoids considering the merits of enumerated rights claims in constitutional cases implicating the substantive criminal law. To understand and critique these decisions better, it is necessary to pare back each method of substantive review to determine its overall purpose and its effect on the development of criminal law.

Third, is there any utility in preserving all three rationales for constitutionally challenging criminal laws? With a better understanding of the ends sought by each method, as well as the ability of each method to achieve its ends, it becomes possible to assess whether it is necessary to preserve all three methods of review. For instance, it is possible that there is complete overlap between the application of section 7 and other enumerated rights. It is also possible that enumerated rights serve purposes similar to those underlying each method of section 7 review. If so, then the democratic objection to section 7 review canvassed briefly above (and in more detail in later chapters) would favour abandoning substantive review under section 7 of the Charter. If, however, section 7 and enumerated rights do not apply with equal breadth and serve different purposes, then it becomes necessary to balance the ability of each method to attain its objective when employing the Charter to shape criminal law.

Fourth, what lessons might be drawn from the Canadian experience of constitutionalizing criminal law for other jurisdictions? Although section 7 of the Charter provides Canadian courts with unprecedented powers of substantive review, several other jurisdictions have similar provisions that could be interpreted as providing similarly broad substantive rights.[39] Should these jurisdictions follow the Canadian path to constitutionalizing criminal law? What differences in comparable countries' constitutional frameworks would favour or reject the Canadian approach?

Argument of the Book

The fact that Canada is among the jurisdictions with the most experience in constitutionalizing criminal law makes it a natural choice for studying the relationship between criminal law and constitutional law.[40] The question for Canada and other countries with a similar constitutional design is whether allowing for the full constitutionalization of criminal law – principles of criminal law theory, instrumental rationality, and enumerated rights – is a prudent path to criminal justice. Answering this question requires significant empirical inquiry, a task yet to be undertaken comprehensively in the Canadian context. Equally important, answering this question requires a concrete understanding of the purpose underlying each of Canada's three methods of substantive review.

I agree with Victor Ramraj that constitutionalizing principles of criminal law theory affords courts the opportunity to create greater coherence in criminal law.[41] This is a laudable aim since legislatures, faced with majoritarian pressures to be "tough on crime," are unlikely to focus on defendant-friendly considerations when crafting criminal law. Constitutionalizing criminal law theory principles thus provides a valuable check on majoritarianism by allowing courts to constitutionalize a fair, balanced, and consistent theory of criminal law. I further contend that moral philosophical principles drawn from criminal law theory are theoretically better able to create coherence in criminal law than enumerated rights since the former provide more precise guidance to future courts and legislatures about the appropriate scope of criminal law.

Yet it is imprudent to assume that courts, by virtue of being courts, will constitutionalize a coherent theory of criminal law. Courts are imperfect actors with limited resources and expertise. The latter is especially true for generalist apex courts such as the Supreme Court of

Canada. A detailed review of its jurisprudence and the ensuing academic commentary shows that the court has constitutionalized a number of principles of criminal law theory in an incoherent manner. In essence, the court has constitutionalized several principles that are inconsistent (or refused to constitutionalize principles that are consistent) with the bedrock principles that the court maintains underpin criminal law. The court's inability to constitutionalize a coherent theory of criminal law suggests that allowing generalist courts to constitutionalize their own substantive principles of criminal justice can distort our understanding of criminal law.

The principles of instrumental rationality serve a different end. Unlike the vast majority of laws struck down based on principles of criminal law theory, instrumental rationality cases tend to elicit a substantive response from Parliament.[42] As Peter Hogg and Allison Bushell explain, when courts and legislatures engage in such "dialogue" about the scope of rights, this softens the criticism that courts act undemocratically when they strike down laws.[43] As opposed to legislatures being told what they cannot do, as occurs when courts employ principles of moral philosophy, judicial use of instrumental rationality allows legislatures to choose from among a broad range of policy responses as long as in pursuing those objectives the impugned law does not have illogical or severe effects. Employing the principles of instrumental rationality is therefore designed to increase the legitimacy of judicial review. As a result, this method of review leaves it primarily to the legislature to develop the principles underlying the substantive criminal law.

The Supreme Court's development of section 7 of the Charter suggests that neither method of review fully achieves its aim. The court's constitutionalization of criminal law theory principles has led to some extent to greater coherence in criminal law. It remains unknown, however, whether the court could have improved its structuring of criminal law under section 7 of the Charter as it discontinued constitutionalizing principles of criminal law theory. The reason for this retreat was likely due to criticism from those who maintain that this form of judicial review is undemocratic.[44] Building on these criticisms, I contend that allowing courts to constitutionalize their chosen moral philosophical principles aggravates the traditional counter-majoritarian critique since doing so imposes rights as opposed to applies rights explicitly adopted in the Charter. The need to maximize the legitimacy of judicial review therefore militates against allowing courts to strike down laws based on principles of criminal law theory that the court thinks are "fundamental" to justice.

Although utilizing the instrumental rationality principles increases dialogue between courts and legislatures, the Canadian experience reveals that employing these principles typically does not give rise to healthy dialogue. Parliament frequently responds to judicial decisions in a politically charged manner that does not address core rights issues. This is possible because the legislature can claim to have "rebalanced" the effects of a law vis-à-vis the impugned law's now (typically) overblown objective. Legislatures therefore can pass laws with identical effects and, importantly, do so without proving that the new law substantially furthers the social good that it claims to accomplish. As a result, instrumental rationality review softens the counter-majoritarian critique by providing legislatures with fewer concrete barriers to passing laws. However, this method of review comes at a high price: complex, costly, and time-consuming relitigation of important rights issues.

Alternatively, courts could fall back on enumerated rights to constitutionally structure criminal law. There are at least two reasons to prefer enumerated rights to those constitutionalized by a court. First, employing enumerated rights is more democratic since those rights utilize the most precise language on which the polity agreed to challenge democratically enacted laws constitutionally. Utilizing terms such as "fundamental justice" invites courts to imbue the law with its own subjective sense of justice. Second, preferring enumerated rights limits generalist judges' ability to venture into areas of moral philosophy where there is little prospect of agreement. Without the explicit wording of an enumerated right, judges simply will be forced to pick from the principles that counsel maintains would forward the case if constitutionalized.

Preferring one of these methods to the exclusion of the others is nevertheless unlikely to satisfy the competing objectives underlying the constitutionalization of criminal law: creating greater coherence in criminal law while maintaining the legitimacy of judicial review. As I contend, the enumerated rights of the Charter do not apply in numerous situations in which the Supreme Court has struck down an unjust law under section 7 of the Charter. The court therefore faces a choice in such circumstances – allow a clearly unjust criminal law to remain in force or sacrifice some legitimacy in conducting judicial review by allowing courts to constitutionalize their own principles of substantive justice under section 7 of the Charter.[45]

To balance these competing objectives, I maintain that the Supreme Court should render constitutional decisions implicating the substantive criminal law based on enumerated rights where possible. This approach is not only the most democratically legitimate but also allows courts to achieve substantively just results in many cases. However, I also maintain that the Supreme Court was not wrong to constitutionalize other substantive principles of criminal law theory. Constitutionalizing those principles can serve two purposes. First, it can serve a gap-filling role by providing a means for constitutionally challenging criminal laws that are unjust but do not implicate the Charter's enumerated rights; second, it can serve a limited communicative function. Put differently, the principles of criminal law theory should be used *in addition to* an enumerated right where they provide guidance to Parliament and courts that can aid them in resolving future legal issues likely to come before them for legislative reform.[46]

Although concerns will remain that courts will provide "overprotection" of rights under section 7, these concerns can be assuaged for two reasons. First, the opportunity for courts to constitutionalize overly broad principles of justice is limited if they prioritize enumerated rights review. Given the significant overlap between enumerated rights and the principles of criminal law theory, I argue that many of the principles of criminal law theory that the Supreme Court constitutionalized were unnecessary. Second, the structure of the Charter provides Parliament with the option of justifying an infringement of rights under section 1 or invoking the section 33 notwithstanding clause. Although the court has been reluctant to justify infringements of section 7 of the Charter,[47] I maintain that this choice was unprincipled. Moreover, strong support for "tough on crime" policies suggests that criminal law is an area where legislatures should be able to garner majority support to override rights. Should political support not be forthcoming, it is because the Canadian polity generally trusts its courts to make fair decisions about the scope of criminal law.

I also contend that the instrumental rationality principles ought to be abandoned as a method of judicial review. I come to this conclusion for two reasons. First, as I explain in Chapter 3, the Supreme Court has had significant difficulty developing the instrumental rationality principles. Originally, these principles mirrored the section 1 test for justifying infringements of Charter rights. After "individualizing" these principles, they applied so broadly that they allowed for any bright-line rule that engaged any individual's life, liberty, or security interests to result in a breach of fundamental justice. Although I maintain that these principles can be repaired, the fact that the court failed to develop them coherently illustrates a generalist court's ability to constitutionalize its own principles of justice.

Second, and more importantly, the instrumental rationality principles are unlikely to achieve their laudable end of creating sustained and meaningful dialogue between courts and legislatures. The structure of these rights, properly conceived, communicates only narrow instances of unconstitutionality. This, in turn, allows legislatures to respond without meaningful restrictions. Any increased legitimacy that results from using the instrumental rationality principles is therefore offset by the uncertainty for rights bearers resulting from instrumental rationality decisions. Because I find that the combination of the principles of criminal law theory and enumerated rights applies as broadly as the instrumental rationality principles, the latter principles can be abandoned without any cost to criminal justice.

Several lessons can be derived from the Canadian experience constitutionalizing criminal law. Although constitutionalizing principles of fundamental justice allowed the Supreme Court to rid the law of many unjust criminal law doctrines, doing so also added confusion to the conceptual underpinnings of criminal law. This fact supports the view that a generalist court such as the Supreme Court of Canada should use section 7–like review only as a last resort. Instead, similarly situated courts should employ enumerated rights where possible to increase the legitimacy of judicial review. Given the more specific language inherent in the text of enumerated rights, decisions based on those rights are also less likely to add confusion to the law when using the Constitution to strike down a criminal law.

It is also important that the structure of the Charter allows legislatures to justify or override constitutional rights. Although section 1 has yet to be used by the Supreme Court to justify an infringement of section 7, the Supreme Court recently signalled that it is willing to revisit this position.[48] Similarly, I argue that the moribund nature of section 33 is of no concern in the criminal law context. Given the majoritarian biases implicit in criminal law, legislatures should have little difficulty convincing a majority of the public to override controversial decisions implicating substantive criminal justice. Parliament, I maintain, has simply refused to try to persuade the public that the notwithstanding clause ought to be used as a response to alleged judicial overreach in the criminal justice context. By providing such a means to check judicial overreach, the Canadian model of judicial review preserves a better balance between the need to ensure fairness to criminal accused and legitimacy in judicial review. Jurisdictions without a similar power have one less tool to preserve this balance and are therefore relatively less justified in allowing courts to constitutionalize their own principles of justice.

A final factor in favour of allowing courts to constitutionalize limited substantive principles of criminal justice arises from the fact that Canadians exhibit a high level of trust in their courts as the de facto arbitrators of rights. As the empirical evidence shows, even when Canadians are unlikely to agree with the reasoning underlying a particular Supreme Court decision, frequently they still agree with the result because judicial review is viewed overall as a necessary check on state power.[49] In other words, Canadians are much less concerned with rights "overprotection" than they are with rights "underprotection." If a polity holds similar beliefs, I maintain that its courts will be relatively more justified in constitutionalizing their own principles of justice, at least in circumstances in which enumerated rights are not applicable.

Structure of the Book
In Chapter 2, I review the Canadian experience constitutionalizing principles of criminal law theory. This review shows that the Supreme Court has rid Canadian criminal law of a variety of outdated and unjust forms

of criminal liability. Yet I also find that the court has caused significant confusion when constitutionalizing principles of criminal law theory. First, and most concerning, at times the court has misunderstood the principles that it has constitutionalized. Second, it has become hesitant to build on its previous rulings, leaving litigants and lower courts guessing about how the law will develop in future cases. This hesitancy has derived from the court's increased awareness of the questionable legitimacy of constitutionalizing its preferred principles of moral philosophy. These findings suggest that the court might not have sufficient expertise or willingness to engage in constitutionally entrenching a complete theory of criminal law.

In Chapter 3, I detail the Supreme Court's development of the principles of instrumental rationality and its trajectory in replacing the principles of criminal law theory as the primary method of substantive review. As the court itself has observed, its initial foray into constitutionalizing the principles of instrumental rationality illogically mirrored the proportionality test for justifying a rights infringement under section 1 of the Charter. As this approach imposed the government's justificatory burden on the accused, the court rightly switched course. In so doing, however, it failed to ask whether its new "individualistic" principles of instrumental rationality qualified as principles of fundamental justice. Such an inquiry reveals that the court has constitutionalized at least one principle that cannot, on any account, qualify as fundamental to justice.

I also find that the principles of instrumental rationality have failed to achieve their aim of facilitating productive dialogue between courts and legislatures. The structure of the Supreme Court's principles of instrumental rationality instead allows for legislatures to respond to rights violations by passing a substantively similar law while making unfounded claims that its law achieves a vague but important objective such as furthering substantive equality or protecting vulnerable groups. The dialogue between courts and legislatures has instead turned into more of a shouting match in which the legislature forces the court to reconsider its initial assessment of a law's constitutionality without having responded seriously to the often severe effects that the legislature's law has on people's life, liberty, and security of the person interests.

In Chapter 4, I answer one of the questions left unanswered by the preceding chapters: Could the explicitly enumerated provisions of the Charter related to substantive criminal justice give rise to protections equal to those provided for under section 7 of the Charter? In considering this question, I use alternative arguments provided in lower courts and other novel applications of enumerated rights to test whether the results would be similar to those that arose under the court's section 7 jurisprudence. Although there is significant overlap between the court's moral philosophical and instrumental rationality methods of substantive review, I find that enumerated rights do not apply to several unjust criminal laws.

In Chapter 5, I then consider whether the various costs and benefits of each method of substantive review support the Supreme Court's current approach of using all three methods but heavily favouring instrumental rationality. Employing enumerated rights is defendable under several theories of judicial review. The democratic objection to judicial review, however, is qualitatively different under section 7 of the Charter. Although the text of section 7 is worded broadly enough to allow the court to constitutionalize substantive principles of justice, I contend that prioritizing section 7 review over enumerated rights is tantamount to a judicial rewriting of the provisions of the Charter affecting criminal justice. The court should acknowledge this objection and respond by using section 7 only as a last resort.

In deciding which principles of fundamental justice to constitutionalize, I also contend that the court should utilize principles of criminal law theory over principles of instrumental rationality. Although the court has constitutionalized several questionable principles of criminal law theory, the cost to the coherence of criminal law must be weighed against any cost imposed by the principles of instrumental rationality. The benefit of employing the principles of instrumental rationality is that they allow courts to rid the law of unprincipled doctrines of criminal liability without constitutionalizing potentially confusing theoretical principles. However, the principles of instrumental rationality also invite Parliament to respond to judicial rulings by ignoring their substance, thereby allowing Parliament to impose its own interpretation of the Charter over that of the court. In my view, the cost imposed on rights bearers by this coordinate construction approach to judicial review is far greater than any potential confusion arising from the court's occasional constitutionalization of an incoherent principle of moral philosophy.

I conclude in Chapter 6 by distilling the lessons learned from the Canadian experience constitutionalizing criminal law. I find that the relative specialization of a country's apex court, the structure of its bill of rights, and the degree of trust that the citizenry holds in its top court all affect whether courts ought to be allowed to constitutionalize their own principles of substantive justice. Even where these factors favour providing courts with such discretion, I nevertheless contend that it would be preferable for legislatures to consider explicitly constitutionalizing more substantive criminal law principles when enacting a bill of rights. Legislatures, as opposed to courts, have sufficient time and resources to prepare a coherent set of principles to guide judicial decision making. A section 7–like provision might nevertheless often need to be included in a bill of rights since gathering support to enact the types of substantive rights at the heart of criminal law might prove to be politically unfeasible. In such a scenario, I suggest that the enacting legislative body make it clear that a section 7–like provision is applicable only where the Constitution's enumerated rights are inapplicable.

Principles of Criminal Law Theory 2

George Fletcher has identified Canada as "one of the leading jurisdictions in the world in applying constitutional provisions to the general part of criminal law."[1] Yet prominent Canadian criminal law scholars observe that the interaction between substantive criminal law doctrine and section 7 of the *Canadian Charter of Rights and Freedoms* "has proved as likely to limit change and entrench the old as to offer a lever for enlightened reform."[2] Such critiques are not without merit. However, the analysis on which they are based is far from comprehensive, and therefore any generalization about the merits of constitutionalizing principles of substantive criminal law theory in Canada under section 7 of the Charter should be approached with caution.

In this chapter, I maintain that the Supreme Court's constitutionalization of principles of criminal law theory has purged a variety of unjust criminal laws. In other instances, however, it has led to considerable confusion about the principles underlying criminal law. Despite these inconsistencies, Charter doctrine allows the court to right the course. The reason that the court has not attempted to do so concerns the perceived illegitimacy of constitutionalizing principles of criminal law theory. This concern, I maintain, resulted in the court abandoning the project of constitutionalizing criminal law theory principles and replacing it with a different method of substantive review, that of instrumental rationality.

Before proceeding, it is prudent to comment on my organization of the Supreme Court's jurisprudence. There is obviously significant disagreement about whether certain issues fall under the headings of *actus reus, mens rea,* justification, excuse, sentencing consideration, and so on. Like any other criminal law theorist, I have my opinion on the appropriate structure of criminal law, but I ask the reader to put these questions to one side, knowing that questions of theoretical coherence can be answered in different ways. Instead, I want to focus on whether the court has misunderstood the principles that it has constitutionalized and whether its chosen principles generally fit within a coherent theory of criminal law.

Actus Reus

The Supreme Court has concluded that it is a constitutional requirement that criminal law treat citizens as "rational, autonomous and choosing agents."[3] This basic premise raises two core questions about the relationship between the *actus reus* of a crime and the principles of fundamental justice. First, what does it mean to say that a person committed a criminal act? This question was answered during litigation of the common law rules governing the voluntary intoxication "defence."[4] Second, which types of acts can qualify as criminal offences? The court answered this question when it considered whether the principle of "respect for human dignity" and John Stuart Mill's "harm principle" qualified as principles of fundamental justice.

Intoxication and Physical Voluntariness

The plea of self-induced intoxication has been applicable historically only to specific intent offences.[5] Such offences, in contrast to general intent offences, require more complex thought and reasoning processes.[6] As an example, the offence of murder is a specific intent offence because it typically requires intent to kill another human being and, in the case of first-degree murder, planning and deliberation with respect to the killing.[7] Manslaughter, conversely, is a general intent offence since it requires only that the offender killed another person through the use of force or some other unlawful act. The manslaughter offence is therefore distinguishable from murder based on the minimal mental acuity required for its commission.[8]

An accused who successfully pleads self-induced intoxication will be acquitted of the more serious specific intent offence but nevertheless convicted of a lesser included general intent offence.[9] However, self-induced intoxication historically did not result in an acquittal of a general intent offence even if the intoxication was at the level at which the accused did not have the capacity to form the intent to perform basic actions. As explained in *R v Leary*,[10] although the act was involuntary, the fault for becoming voluntarily intoxicated would substitute for the minimal intent required to perform the *actus reus* of the offence.[11]

The Supreme Court considered the constitutionality of the voluntary intoxication rule in *R v Daviault*.[12] The accused was charged with sexually assaulting a paralyzed elderly woman confined to a wheelchair. Daviault knew the complainant and was asked to run an errand for her the night of the offence. He accordingly arrived at the complainant's house with a forty-ounce bottle of brandy. The complainant had one drink and fell asleep in her wheelchair. During the night, she woke up to go to the bathroom but was taken back into her bedroom and raped. The complainant subsequently discovered that the bottle of brandy was empty. At trial, the accused submitted expert evidence showing that he was in an extremely intoxicated state akin to automatism during the sexual assault.[13]

The Supreme Court concluded that an extreme form of intoxication that puts the accused in a state akin to insanity or automatism prevented the crown from proving the *actus reus* and *mens rea* of the offence.[14] As the majority observed, "the requisite mental element or *mens rea* cannot necessarily be inferred from the physical act or *actus reus* when the voluntariness or consciousness of that act is put in question by the extreme intoxication of the accused."[15] Convicting someone for an act that is physically involuntary because of intoxication, the court reasoned, violated the foundational principle of criminal law that only those capable of choosing to commit an offence be subject to criminal liability.[16] Given this reasoning, the court also implicitly provided a constitutional "defence" for other forms of automatism such as those arising from somnambulism[17] or "psychological blows."[18]

That the intoxication defence resulted in the acquittal of a man who "committed" a sexual assault against a disabled and vulnerable female victim understandably caused much public uproar.[19] This in turn prompted the government to pass section 33.1 of the *Criminal Code of Canada* shortly after *Daviault* was decided. That section provides that an individual who commits a general intent offence in a manner that displays a "marked departure" from the standard of care of a reasonable person cannot plead the intoxication defence.[20] A "marked departure" is defined in the legislation as any crime involving a threat to the bodily integrity of another person.[21] Thus, section 33.1 reversed *Daviault* to the extent that it allowed extreme intoxication to be pleaded for an offence that includes an element of violence.

Despite the provision's clear inconsistency with *Daviault*, courts have been divided on whether section 33.1 is constitutional. Surprisingly, until recently, no appellate court had ruled on the constitutionality of section 33.1 even though the provision had been passed over a quarter of a century earlier.[22] Although courts have unanimously held that the provision violates section 7 of the Charter, several trial courts have upheld the provision as a justifiable infringement of rights under section 1.[23] Application of the justificatory provision is surprising since the Supreme Court had held that breaches of section 7 would be justified "only in cases arising out of exceptional conditions, such as natural disasters, the outbreak of war, [and] epidemics."[24]

Respect for Human Dignity

In *Rodriguez v British Columbia (Attorney General)*,[25] the applicant challenged the constitutionality of the prohibition against assisted suicide found in section 241(b) of the *Criminal Code*. The applicant was diagnosed with a fatal neurodegenerative disease known as amyotrophic lateral sclerosis. The disease causes the person progressively to lose bodily functions and eventually results in death.[26] The prohibition against assisted suicide posed a dilemma for terminally ill patients: either they take their lives while physically capable of doing so, often by violent means, or they die from natural causes in a slow and agonizing manner.[27]

The physical and psychological pain arising from the state's imposition of this choice was enough to engage the applicant's security of the person interests, thereby giving rise to the question of whether this infringement was consistent with the principles of fundamental justice.[28]

The applicant argued that the state's duty to respect the human dignity of individuals constituted a principle of fundamental justice under section 7 of the Charter.[29] Because the prohibition against assisted suicide subjected the applicant to needless suffering, she maintained that the provision robbed her of autonomy in deciding how to live her life and took away her dignity by requiring her to live through intolerable suffering.[30] Although respect for human dignity underlies many Charter rights, the Supreme Court rejected the contention that this principle qualified as a principle of fundamental justice.[31] In the majority's view, acceding to the applicant's submission would collapse the two stages of section 7 analysis. If an act impinges on human dignity, then the law will engage the security of the person interest. To conclude that infringing a person's human dignity is also sufficient to breach the principles of fundamental justice would render the latter stage of the analysis redundant.[32]

The Supreme Court's conclusion therefore does not deny that human dignity serves an important constitutional role, as exemplified by constitutional jurisprudence in other jurisdictions.[33] Nor should the court be interpreted as endorsing the view that the principle of human dignity must be explicitly constitutionalized before it can lead to principled application.[34] Constitutionalizing a principle that underpins the threshold interest of security of the person does not communicate anything about the content of the principles of fundamental justice. Given the general role played by dignity at the threshold stage of the section 7 analysis, the court acted prudently in requiring that the applicants propose a narrower aspect of the broader human dignity principle when challenging the constitutionality of a law under section 7.

The Harm Principle

In *R v Malmo-Levine*,[35] the applicant argued that John Stuart Mill's harm principle ought to qualify as a principle of fundamental justice. The harm principle provides that only conduct that harms another person ought to be subject to state sanction.[36] The harm principle is typically contrasted with the theory of legal moralism, which purports that criminal law may be used to express society's disapproval of a practice deemed morally objectionable by society.[37] Whether the harm principle or legal moralism properly delineates the boundaries of criminal law was famously debated by H.L.A. Hart and Lord Patrick Devlin.[38] Hart is widely thought to have won this debate, thereby solidifying the pivotal role of the harm principle in the eyes of many criminal law theorists.[39]

Despite unanimity among provincial appellate courts,[40] the majority of the Supreme Court found that the harm principle failed to pass the two most fundamental criteria for qualifying as a principle of fundamental justice.[41] First, the principle must be adequately precise. This requirement ensures that "vague generalizations about what our society considers to be ethical or moral" do not become the basis for striking down democratically enacted laws.[42] With the insistence on a high degree of precision, the principles of fundamental justice can provide meaningful guidance to legislatures, courts, and the public when assessing the permissible scope of the law.

The Supreme Court observed that there is a general consensus that the notion of harm is too vague to provide meaningful guidance on the legitimate scope of criminal law. The harm principle's indeterminacy is connected to the aftermath of the Hart-Devlin debate. In his work, Devlin offered two distinct responses to the harm principle's proposed delineation of the appropriate boundaries of criminal law. First, he defended the traditional legal moralist position that immorality as such was sufficient to attract criminal sanction. Second, and more importantly, Devlin suggested that immoral acts are likely to cause *social* harms that might justify the use of criminal sanctions.[43]

Building on his second retort, criminologists began to investigate the various social harms implicit in nearly all conduct possibly classified as "immoral." Prohibitions underlying pornography and sex work are illustrative. These activities have been argued to undermine women's equality and dignity interests because of their portrayal of women as both inferior to and controlled by men.[44] Other "disorderly conduct" – such as loitering, panhandling, and squeegeeing – was also linked to social disintegration, which in turn is likely to cause public harm.[45] Implicitly relying on such studies, the Supreme Court in *Malmo-Levine* agreed that "claims of harm have become so pervasive that the harm principle has become meaningless."[46] The simple notion of harm came to serve only as a gateway to the debate about how best to balance competing claims of harm. On that question, however, the harm principle is silent.[47]

Second, a principle of fundamental justice must obtain sufficient societal consensus that it is vital to the legal system. This requirement invokes the "shared assumptions upon which our system of justice is grounded."[48] As the Supreme Court observed, these assumptions "find their meaning in the cases and traditions that have long detailed the basic norms for how the state deals with its citizens" and are principles that "society views ... as essential to the administration of justice."[49] This framework does not, however, endorse an empirical investigation of what citizens believe ought to qualify as a principle of fundamental justice. Instead, the decisive question is what role the principle plays in a legal order committed to the values expressed in the Charter.[50]

Despite the Supreme Court's recognition that Mill's conception of harm is frequently the target of criminal prohibitions,[51] the fact that it was not able to capture all offences was sufficient to find an absence of societal consensus under section 7 of the Charter.[52] The court cited several instances in the *Criminal Code* where harm to other individuals does not underpin a criminal prohibition to support this view: cannibalism (does not harm another sentient being),[53] bestiality (harm to animals),[54] duelling (activity of consenting adults),[55] and incest (where consent is given).[56] These instances were adequate to deny the harm principle the status of principle of fundamental justice even though most criminal offences cause harm in the Millian sense.

The Supreme Court's conclusion that the harm principle has become too amorphous to provide *any* guidance is overstated.[57] A law that makes it a crime to go to the beach would plainly violate the harm principle. To use a more plausible example – that underpinning the Hart-Devlin debate – it is highly unlikely that criminalizing homosexual sex could be proven to prevent harm. Although some advocate that homosexuality causes public harms linked to the spread of HIV/AIDS, this empirical claim is frail at best and unlikely to be accepted by a modern court in constitutional jurisprudence.[58] Hart made a similar point, observing that such a proposition "is entitled to no more respect than the Emperor

Justinian's statement that homosexuality was the cause of earthquakes."[59] This example thus shows that the harm principle is still capable of performing *some* function in delineating the scope of criminal law. This narrower application of the harm principle also suggests that it is sufficiently precise, for only those offences that do not cause any harm, broadly construed, violate the harm principle.[60]

The fact that the harm principle cannot account for a variety of criminal offences poses a greater challenge to its status as a principle of fundamental justice. It is nevertheless arguable that the Supreme Court was too strict in its application of the societal consensus requirement. Although the court identified several offences that do not come within the ambit of the harm principle, the fundamental role of the principle with respect to the vast majority of offences arguably ought to be sufficient to satisfy the societal consensus requirement.

Alternatively, the Supreme Court could have found that other principles operate alongside the harm principle in determining which acts are sufficient to qualify as crimes. The most notable of these principles – Joel Feinberg's offence principle – received only passing mention by the court. That principle provides that objectively offensive conduct – such as cannibalism or bestiality – is a proper object of criminal prohibition.[61] As Feinberg concludes in a lengthy treatise that need only be summarized here, "harm and offense prevention are far and away the best reasons that can be produced in support of criminal prohibitions, and the only ones that frequently outweigh the case for liberty."[62]

The Supreme Court could have constitutionalized both the harm principle and the offence principle as forming the foundation of which acts are sufficiently wrong to qualify as criminal offences. This approach was impeded because the accused did not plead that the harm and offence principles together qualify as a principle of fundamental justice. Typically, Canadian courts only assess constitutional arguments raised by counsel. Yet nothing prevents a court from discussing potential solutions to limitations that it finds in a constitutional challenge in its *obiter* reasons. The fact that the court did not engage in such a discussion suggests that it was unaware of or unopen to the potential to broaden the litigant's constitutional argument.

The Supreme Court's limited engagement with criminal law theory in *Malmo-Levine* is also not justified based on other constitutional restrictions on the scope of criminal law. Most notably, the federal criminal law power found in section 91(27) of the *Constitution Act, 1867*,[63] provides that any criminal prohibition that does not possess a valid criminal law purpose will be declared *ultra vires* Parliament. Such purposes include the furtherance of "public peace, order, security, health and morality."[64] In *Malmo-Levine*, the court read the term "morality" narrowly to exclude any potential for a criminal law based on legal moralism, thus suggesting that there was no need to provide further constitutional protections under section 7 of the Charter.[65]

As Justice Arbour observed, however, Parliament is not barred from relying on other federal powers to criminalize an act. Most notably, the federal government has a residual power to govern where it is necessary for "peace, order, and good government." This "POGG" power allows Parliament to create rules related to any "new problem which did not exist at the time of Confederation and clearly cannot be put in the class of '[m]atters of a merely local or private nature.'"[66] The subject matter at issue in *Malmo-Levine* was illustrative – the prohibition against possessing and trafficking in marijuana – since its authorizing legislation had been interpreted to fall within the POGG power.[67] Thus, even if the federal criminal law power incorporated the harm and offence principles, Parliament could use alternative powers to uphold its drug legislation as well as other similarly problematic laws. The majority explicitly abstained from deciding whether to overrule its past interpretation of the POGG power, suggesting that there was merit to Justice Arbour's critique.[68]

Mens Rea

The Supreme Court's jurisprudence constitutionalizing aspects of *mens rea* under section 7 of the Charter has gone further than that in any other jurisdiction.[69] This jurisprudence has nevertheless received mixed reviews from criminal law scholars. Some have criticized the court for incoherently developing the law of *mens rea*, and others have maintained that the court improperly used the Charter to reduce common law protections. Still others have lauded the court for ridding criminal law of several unjust doctrines of liability. Although I endorse the latter view,

I maintain that the court's jurisprudence requires some adjustment to respond to the former criticisms.

Absolute Liability

In *Beaver v The Queen*,[70] the accused were caught selling an illegal drug to an undercover police officer. They were subsequently charged with possession and distribution of illegal narcotics under the *Opium and Narcotic Drug Act*.[71] The accused maintained that they thought the package contained sugar or powdered milk; however, the trial judge did not put that theory to the jury. Instead, he directed that, if the jury members were satisfied that the accused possessed and sold the package to the undercover officer, then as long as there was proof that the substance was illegal, they would be guilty of possession of and trafficking in illegal narcotics. The question of whether the accused had any knowledge of what the substance was or whether they believed that it was harmless was irrelevant.[72]

In overturning this ruling, the Supreme Court adopted a common law presumption of subjective fault for all crimes. Relying on earlier common law holdings, Justice Cartwright observed that it "is contrary to the whole established law ... to say that a person can be guilty of a crime in England without a wrongful intent."[73] Absent a constitutional bill of rights, however, this presumption of subjective fault was subject to legislative displacement.[74] Fortunately for the accused, the impugned legislation was unclearly drafted, thus leaving room for the court to impose a subjective requirement of fault.[75]

This common law presumption was extended to the field of public welfare or "regulatory" offences in *R v Sault Ste Marie*.[76] The city had been charged with illegally dumping garbage into a river. As with many regulatory offences at the time, the offence was argued by the crown to be one of absolute liability, requiring conviction upon proof of the *actus reus* of an offence.[77] The Supreme Court held that regulatory offences are subject to a presumption in favour of "strict liability." This presumption allows defendants to prove, on a balance of probabilities, that they had taken all reasonable steps to avoid committing the offence or were making a reasonable mistake in committing the prohibited act.[78] Again, however, the court qualified its ruling by observing that this common law presumption was subject to legislative displacement.

These common law rules set the stage for the constitutionalization of fault under section 7 of the Charter. In the *Motor Vehicle Act Reference*,[79] the Supreme Court considered the constitutionality of an offence imposing a mandatory minimum seven days of imprisonment upon proof that the accused was driving with a suspended or prohibited licence. As Justice Lamer wrote for the majority, "a law that has the potential to convict a person who has not really done anything wrong offends the principles of fundamental justice and, if imprisonment is available as a penalty, such a law then violates a person's right to liberty under s. 7 of the *Charter*."[80] This broad prohibition against depriving the morally innocent of life, liberty, and security of the person ensured, at a minimum, that absolute liability and imprisonment could not be combined.[81]

The Supreme Court's decision did not spell the death, however, of absolute liability offences. It is a basic principle of section 7 of the Charter that if a law does not engage the life, liberty, and security of the person interests of an individual, then the law need not comply with the principles of fundamental justice.[82] Laws that do not engage these threshold interests can therefore still impose absolute liability.[83] The *Motor Vehicle Act Reference* also endorsed the view that strict liability – which requires that the accused be afforded the opportunity to prove that her conduct was duly diligent – is the *minimal* fault requirement for offences that engage section 7 of the Charter.[84] Whether the principles of fundamental justice required a higher form of *mens rea* for more serious crimes was left to be decided another day.

High-Stigma Offences

In *R v Vaillancourt*,[85] two accused entered a pool hall to commit a robbery. Vaillancourt was armed with a knife, and his accomplice possessed a handgun. Vaillancourt testified that he had specifically told his co-accused to empty the gun before the robbery and believed that the co-accused had complied. During the robbery, however, the accomplice engaged in a physical altercation with a patron of the pool hall during which his gun fired and killed the patron. Vaillancourt was subsequently tried for second-degree murder under (then) section 213(d) of the *Criminal Code*. That section provided a list of offences – including robbery – that, if committed while using or possessing a weapon, would constitute murder if death resulted from the commission of the offence. Although the accused did not directly commit the murder, he was liable as a party to murder under section 21(2) of the *Criminal Code*.

Section 213(d) effectively adopted the doctrine known as "felony murder." This controversial mode of liability allows for a murder conviction if death ensues during the commission of an enumerated offence. Intent to cause death is irrelevant. The Supreme Court was asked to strike down this law by constitutionalizing the common law rule that subjective fault attached to all criminal offences.[86] The court passed on the opportunity to answer the question so broadly. Instead, it determined that, for certain "high stigma" offences, "the principles of fundamental justice require a *mens rea* reflecting the particular nature of that crime."[87] Murder was among those offences. In the court's view, a murder conviction required *at least* objective foreseeability of death. Substituting the intent to commit a robbery for the objective foreseeability of death therefore violated the principles of fundamental justice.[88]

The Supreme Court broadened this conclusion in *R v Martineau*.[89] The accused committed a robbery of a domestic residence with a co-accused, and in so doing the co-accused shot and killed the residents of the house. The shooting was done explicitly to prevent the witnesses from identifying the accused.[90] Causing bodily harm where death ensues during the commission of a robbery for the purpose of committing the crime or facilitating escape was a mode of constructive murder under (then) section 213(a) of the *Criminal Code*. Because this offence again did away with the requirement to prove foresight of death, it was struck down under section 7 of the Charter. In so doing, however, the court held that *subjective* foresight of death was required by the principles of fundamental justice to sustain a murder conviction.[91]

In *R v Logan*,[92] the Supreme Court affirmed that the standard of fault devised in *Martineau* for murder was also constitutionally required for the offence of attempted murder. The court reasoned that the same opprobrium attached to a person who intended to kill as attached to those who actually killed. As the court observed, "the attempted murderer is no less a killer than a murderer: he may be lucky – the ambulance arrived early, or some other fortuitous circumstance – but he still has the same killer instinct."[93] Despite the seemingly principled nature of this conclusion, imposing a constitutional standard of subjective foreseeability of death was actually a lower form of *mens rea* than that imposed under the common law: intent to cause death.[94]

In *Logan*, the majority also reiterated that "the principles of fundamental justice require a minimum degree of *mens rea* for only a very few offences."[95] Since *Logan*, the Supreme Court has required subjective fault for only two other criminal offences: commission of war crimes and crimes against humanity.[96] In *obiter*, the court has also found that the offence of theft attaches sufficient stigma to warrant subjective fault.[97] Not even the constitutionality of the new terrorism offences was resolved on the basis of whether the provisions imposed a constitutionally acceptable degree of fault.[98] The court has otherwise been comfortable imposing objective forms of fault for a range of criminal offences.

Objective Fault

In *Vaillancourt*, Justice Lamer wrote for a plurality of the Supreme Court that "it may well be that, as a general rule, the principles of fundamental justice require proof of a subjective *mens rea* with respect to the prohibited act, in order to avoid punishing the 'morally innocent.'"[99] Justice Lamer therefore was open to the possibility of constitutionalizing the common law fault standards developed in *Beaver* and *Sault Ste Marie*. Other members of the court were cautious of this approach and explicitly stated that whether subjective *mens rea* would be constitutionally required for all criminal offences was to be left for another day.[100]

The Supreme Court's decision in *R v Wholesale Travel Group Inc*[101] witnessed a near-immediate retreat from Justice Lamer's proposal. The court was asked to decide the constitutionality of the regulatory offence of false advertising under the *Competition Act*.[102] The offence allowed for conviction despite absence of intent or knowledge that the advertisement was deceitful. It also allowed for a maximum five-year term of imprisonment, thereby engaging the liberty interest of the accused.[103] Although the offence allowed the accused to avoid conviction by proving due diligence, this option was available only if the accused retracted the ad immediately after publication.[104] This raised the prospect of convicting an accused who showed due care by retracting the ad within a reasonable amount of time. The law therefore raised the prospect of convicting the morally innocent and was thus struck down based on the rationale in the *Motor Vehicle Act Reference*.[105]

The defendant further argued that the law's potential to result in imprisonment required subjective intent even though the provision was a regulatory offence.[106] This argument triggered a broader consideration of the appropriate *mens rea* for criminal and regulatory offences. Although the case generated a plethora of judgments, there was a general reluctance to exclude negligence from the scope of criminal liability.[107] A year later in *R v Nova Scotia Pharmaceutical Society*,[108] a unanimous Supreme Court explicitly adopted this dictum and held that objective forms of liability may be upheld under section 7 of the Charter.[109] The court's acceptance of negligence as a constitutional form of *mens rea* nevertheless left undecided whether various forms of objective fault in the *Criminal Code* would be constitutional.

The first decision to consider this issue was *R v DeSousa*.[110] The Supreme Court was asked to determine whether the prohibition against unlawfully causing bodily harm violated the principles of fundamental justice. The offence requires subjective intent in relation to the unlawful act but only objective foreseeability that the bodily harm caused as a result of the unlawful act would occur.[111] The court determined that subjective intent in relation to the consequences of an act was not necessary to prevent the innocent person from being convicted. As the court put it, "neither basic principles of criminal law, nor the dictates of fundamental justice require, by necessity, intention in relation to the consequences of an otherwise blameworthy act."[112]

In *R v Creighton*,[113] the Supreme Court considered the constitutionality of a provision that arguably carried adequate stigma to require a higher degree of fault: unlawful act manslaughter.[114] The accused had consensually injected cocaine into another user, causing her to overdose and die. The unlawful act (trafficking illegal drugs) required intent, but the court was divided on whether, in order to prove manslaughter, the crown had to establish that the consequences of the unlawful act required reasonable foreseeability of death or merely reasonable foreseeability of bodily harm that is neither trivial nor transitory.[115] A narrow majority of the court found that the stigma and punishment attached to manslaughter did not necessitate imposing the higher standard.[116] To hold that reasonable foreseeability of death was constitutionally required would have abandoned the common law principle that an aggressor must "take a victim as he finds him," also known as the "thin skull principle."[117]

Finally, in *R v Hundal*,[118] the Supreme Court considered whether the principles of fundamental justice required a subjective *mens rea* for the offence of dangerous driving. As the court observed, "to insist on a subjective mental element in connection with driving offences would be to deny reality."[119] The fact that driving is a licensed activity ensures that those who drive are familiar with the rules of the road and fit to operate a motor vehicle.[120] Driving also typically involves automatic, reflexive response, making it unlikely that the activity is intended in any meaningful sense.[121] It is therefore reasonable to use criminal law to ensure that appropriate care is taken when performing an act that poses a significant risk to the public.[122] As a result, a modified objective standard requiring that the defendant displayed a "marked departure" from the standard of a reasonable person was sufficient to satisfy section 7 of the Charter.[123]

The Supreme Court's jurisprudence was nevertheless unclear whether all criminal offences constitutionally required a *marked* departure from the standard of care to sustain a conviction. In *R v Durham*,[124] the Ontario Court of Appeal concluded that the civil standard of negligence was constitutionally permissible for the offence of using, handling, or storing a firearm or ammunition in a careless manner found in section 86(2) of the *Criminal Code*. Justice Arbour concluded that insufficient stigma attached to the offence to compel any higher *mens rea* requirement.[125] This decision was subsequently overturned by the Supreme Court in *R v Finlay*.[126] Although the court found that the *mens rea* requirement for careless storage of a firearm did not carry adequate stigma to demand subjective *mens rea*, it confirmed that true crimes require the crown to prove at least a marked departure from the standard of care.[127]

Symmetry between Actus Reus *and* Mens Rea

In *R v Rees*,[128] the accused was convicted of encouraging a youth to become a delinquent, contrary to the *Juvenile Delinquents Act*.[129] The issue arose regarding whether the offence required knowledge that the person was a delinquent. The statute provided that the offence must be committed *knowingly*, but lower courts had determined that the use of this word did not apply to all aspects of the offence. As a result, the crown did not need to prove that the defendant actually knew the person's age. This determination was found to be inconsistent with the common law presumption of symmetry between all aspects of the *actus reus* and *mens rea* of an offence. Absent clear parliamentary intent, the word *knowingly* therefore was required to apply to each aspect of the *actus reus*.[130] Although this decision is dated, it was affirmed two years before the adoption of the Charter in *R v Pappajohn*.[131]

In *DeSousa*, however, it was found that symmetry between the *actus reus* and *mens rea* of an offence did not qualify as a principle of fundamental justice. Such a distinction, the Supreme Court concluded, was unnecessary to avoid convicting the morally innocent. This followed given the sufficiency of the moral blameworthiness that flowed from the accused's commission of the unlawful underlying act.[132] The court was also influenced by the fact that requiring intention in relation to every consequence would bring a large number of offences into constitutional question.[133] For these reasons, the court upheld "a general principle in Canada and elsewhere that, in the absence of an express legislative direction, the mental element of an offence attaches only to the underlying offence and not to the aggravating circumstances."[134]

The Supreme Court affirmed in *Creighton* that there is no constitutional requirement that overlap exist between the consequence of the prohibited act and the *mens rea* for the offence. As the court observed, the general rule that *actus reus* and *mens rea* overlap is "just that – a rule – to which there are exceptions."[135] Since the rule does not have universal application, the court held that it cannot qualify as a principle of fundamental justice.[136] In the view of the majority, "it is important to distinguish between criminal law theory, which seeks the ideal of absolute symmetry between *actus reus* and *mens rea*, and the constitutional requirements of the *Charter*."[137] As the court cryptically emphasized, "the Constitution does not always guarantee the 'ideal.'"[138]

Intoxication and Specific Intent Offences

In *DPP v Beard*,[139] the House of Lords determined that evidence of intoxication rendering the accused incapable of forming the specific intent for an offence could lead to an acquittal for that crime and instead result in a conviction for a less serious general intent offence.[140] Controversially, however, the House of Lords also required that the evidence of intoxication prove *incapacity* to form the intent necessary to commit the crime.[141] Put differently, the accused was required not only to disprove specific intent but also the ability to form any degree of intent. In *R v Robinson*,[142] the Supreme Court found that the latter requirement violated sections 7 and 11(d) of the Charter. As the court observed, "the *Beard* rules put an accused in jeopardy of being convicted despite the fact that a reasonable doubt could exist in the minds of the jurors on the issue of actual intent."[143]

The Supreme Court also applied its jurisprudence requiring that the *mens rea* for an offence must be proportionate to the moral blameworthiness of the act. If intoxication raised a reasonable doubt about whether the accused committed a specific intent offence such as murder, then the accused might still be convicted if she did not also prove an incapacity to form intent. The ability to convict an accused for a serious offence such as murder despite the blameworthiness of the accused's actions being similar to the lesser included offence of manslaughter resulted in a clear violation of the proportionality principle between fault and stigma. Hence, judges faced with an intoxication "defence" for a specific intent crime are now permitted to instruct the jury only to consider actual intent and may not reference capacity.[144]

A (Partial) Defence of the Supreme Court's Constitutionalization of Mens Rea

The "slippage" between common law and constitutional fault standards constitutionalized under section 7 of the Charter has received significant criticism.[145] In line with the above review, Kent Roach observes that the presumption against absolute liability was narrowed from a general presumption against absolute liability offences to the prohibition against absolute liability only when the law engaged the threshold interests of life, liberty, and security of the person. The common law presumption of subjective fault was also abandoned, in turn allowing objective standards of fault for all but a few "high stigma" offences. The constitutionally required *mens rea* for attempted murder was further lowered from intent to cause death to subjective foreseeability of death. Finally, the Supreme Court refused to constitutionalize the common law presumption requiring overlap among all aspects of the *actus reus* and *mens rea* of an offence.[146]

Despite the narrowing of fault standards under the Charter, Roach recognizes that the Supreme Court's abandonment of its common law presumptions can be defended as a matter of criminal law theory. Most importantly, the court's refusal to constitutionalize a presumption of subjective fault might simply reflect a recent theoretical interest in the use of objective forms of liability.[147] Citing the work of Ulrich Beck and David Garland, Roach agrees that "there is a general uneasiness with individualistic demands for subjective fault in modern societies where there is increased knowledge about and regulation of risk and an increased willingness to use the criminal sanction to demand that all individuals regulate their own risky behaviour."[148] This realization overrode the strong support that subjective fault commanded near the middle of the twentieth century.[149]

It is possible that these early courts did not contemplate the same risks inherent in modern society when crafting the common law presumptions of fault. More plausibly, the Supreme Court was simply overcompensating when acting under the common law because it knew that its decisions could be overturned by regular legislation. Erring on the side of upholding rights was sensible because Parliament could amend the criminal law at will.[150] After section 7 of the Charter was interpreted to provide substantive protections, the tables were turned, and the caution had to be directed toward ensuring that Parliament had sufficient room to manoeuvre. Constitutionalizing stringent criminal law theory principles meant that the legislature would have to justify infringements of rights under section 1 or override the court's decisions under section 33 of the Charter.[151]

Although Roach acknowledges this line of argument, he contends that the Supreme Court ought to have constitutionalized a presumption of subjective fault. He suggests as a middle ground, however, that section 1 ought to be more readily available to justify infringements of section 7.

In *Canada (Attorney General) v Bedford*,[152] the court recently held that the previous strict standard for justifying breaches of section 7 must be relaxed,[153] although it remains to be seen if section 1 will be applied more generously to justify infringements of all principles of fundamental justice.[154] Putting aside for now the view that section 1 justifications of section 7 rights are "troubling,"[155] Roach's suggestion allows for the constitutionalization of subjective fault and allows Parliament to impose reasonable forms of objective fault under section 1 of the Charter.

In my respectful view, this approach unnecessarily complicates the relationship between constitutional theory and criminal law theory. Importantly, Roach's critique does not include a strong argument about why the Supreme Court's use of objective fault should constitute a violation of "fundamental justice."[156] Since there are many exceptions to the presumption of subjective fault, it is unlikely that there would be adequate societal consensus for the presumption of subjective fault to qualify as a principle of fundamental justice.[157] Equally important, there are other ways of constitutionalizing fault that do not require straddling the relationship among principles of criminal law theory, Charter rights, and justifications for breaches of rights. A better approach is the one adopted in the court's jurisprudence: requiring some sense of *proportionality* between the stigma underlying an offence and the *mens rea* requirements imposed for different types of criminal acts.[158]

The Supreme Court, however, has equivocated on the meaning of its proportionality principle. In *Martineau*, the court found that it is a "fundamental principle of a morally based system of law that those causing harm intentionally be punished more severely than those causing harm unintentionally."[159] In the same paragraph, however, the court maintains that the constitutionalization of fault requires "a proportionality between the stigma and punishment attached to a[n] [offence] and the moral blameworthiness of the offender."[160] As Alan Brudner observes, the latter "cardinal" conception of proportionality is empty of normative content.[161] Take the court's application of this principle in *Creighton*. The majority and the minority debated whether the stigma of unlawful act manslaughter required objective foreseeability of harm or death. How is the court supposed to choose between these two methods without an objective way of measuring how much stigma attaches to each act?[162]

The first or "ordinal" conception of proportionality does not require such speculation. Instead, it simply requires that those who are less blameworthy be stigmatized and punished less severely than those who are more blameworthy.[163] According to Brudner, stigmatizing an offender who causes death where only bodily harm is foreseeable in the same way as a person who objectively foresees death collapses two distinct levels of fault. For instance, convicting a person who causes death by punching someone in the nose of the same offence as a person who causes death by hitting another person with a baseball bat ignores a glaring moral difference between the two acts and thus inappropriately stigmatizes the former offender.[164] This ordinal conception of proportionality is coherent since it forgoes the need for courts to speculate about what level of stigma is appropriate without any reasonable foundation to answer that question. It simply requires courts to use discernible facts to rank the seriousness of various ways of committing an offence. Unfortunately, the Supreme Court has not explained how the ordinal conception of proportionality ought to be employed. This has caused some confusion about what the principles of fundamental justice require in terms of *mens rea*.

The proportionality approach to *mens rea* is also capable of addressing another common criticism of the objective fault requirements. This criticism cautions that using objective fault will inevitably ensnare people who are significantly less capable of acting in accordance with the reasonable person standard.[165] An inexperienced driver, for instance, will be held to the same standard as an experienced driver even though experience is necessary to realistically meet the reasonable person standard.[166] Leaving aside the obvious point that driving is a licensed activity requiring that all drivers meet a threshold of competence, the proportionality approach to constitutionalizing *mens rea* responded by imposing a marked departure standard. In my view, this standard sets the floor low enough to adjudicate fairly both experienced and inexperienced drivers, thus imposing a fair and proportionate form of *mens rea*.[167]

More difficult questions arise when considering the fairness of utilizing objective standards of *mens rea* with accused persons who bear characteristics that affect their ability to appreciate risk.[168] Accused persons with fetal alcohol syndrome disorder (FASD) are illustrative.[169] FASD causes brain dysfunction that can result in "inconsistent memory and recall, slower and inconsistent cognitive and auditory processing, difficulty in managing/filtering sensory stimuli from the environment, poor motor coordination, [and] inability to read social cues or predict outcomes."[170] FASD also makes it exceedingly difficult for those with the disorder to learn from past mistakes.[171] It is not difficult to imagine such an accused person having difficulty meeting even the marked departure standard of objective fault.

Whether the minimal capacity to meet the modified objective standard is present in a person with FASD might be better left to the context of claims of unfitness to stand trial and mental disorder. An early example arose in *R v WALD*,[172] in which Judge Whelan found that an accused with FASD "had no concept of the roles played by the crown, defense counsel, and judge in the courtroom and there was real doubt as to his ability to receive information and communicate his instructions to his counsel on even the most basic level."[173] She also relied on expert testimony showing that the accused was "unlikely to gain much information from what he hears."[174] Since there was a clear lack of fitness to stand trial, the question of whether the accused would be able to meet the objective *mens rea* test became moot. In less clear cases, the appellate jurisprudence to date unfortunately has focused on the impact of FASD on the accused's moral blameworthiness in sentencing without seriously considering the impact of FASD on the mental disorder defence.[175] However, it could be argued that this is the mistake, not the unwillingness of the Supreme Court to fit FASD within objective standards of fault.

Defences

The Supreme Court's jurisprudence constitutionalizing the moral principles underlying criminal defences has been limited. The court has refused to constitutionalize the principle that those who act under duress or out of necessity are "morally blameless."[176] Instead, the court has preferred George Fletcher's concept of normative or "moral involuntariness" as the constitutional basis for the duress and necessity defences.[177] Contrary to the court's jurisprudence, commentators have also built on the principle of fundamental justice that the morally innocent not be deprived of liberty as a basis for constitutionalizing justification-based defences.

Moral Involuntariness

The defence of duress is partially codified in section 17 of the *Criminal Code*. Since the wording of the provision does not apply to parties, the common law has served to fill in the gap left by Parliament's legislation.[178] Over time, the statutory and common law duress defences have come to adopt the same underlying principles,[179] with limited exceptions pertaining to whether some offences are excluded from the purview of the statutory defence.[180] The necessity defence has not received explicit statutory recognition. As such, it remains a common law defence under the authority of section 8(3) of the *Criminal Code*, which preserves common law defences to the extent that they are not inconsistent with the *Criminal Code*.[181]

In a series of cases, the Supreme Court developed the "excuses" of duress and necessity (and later included mental disorder) within Fletcher's principle of normative or "moral involuntariness."[182] As Fletcher explains, this principle prohibits convicting those who act without "free choice."[183] "Free choice," however, is not understood literally. Instead, it is understood as a lack of "realistic choice." In *Perka v The Queen*,[184] the court concluded that such morally involuntary conduct requires the accused to prove that her circumstances were "so emergent and the peril ... so pressing that normal human instincts cry out for action and make a counsel of patience unreasonable."[185]

In *R v Ruzic*,[186] the Supreme Court considered whether the moral involuntariness principle qualified as a principle of fundamental justice. The accused was a resident of then war-torn Yugoslavia. She had been verbally, physically, and sexually harassed for approximately two months by a man who had been an assassin during the Yugoslav Wars. Ruzic was told that, if she did not import a significant amount of heroin into Canada, her mother would be harmed or killed. She subsequently boarded a plane carrying the heroin and a false passport. She was caught on arrival in Canada and charged with importing illegal narcotics and using false identification. Despite the extreme pressures on Ruzic to commit these crimes, section 17 of the *Criminal Code* prevented her from pleading duress in two ways. First, it required that the threatening party be physically present during the offence. Second, it required that the threat be immediate.[187]

In opposing the constitutionalization of the moral involuntariness principle, the crown argued that the content of criminal defences was owed special deference. The crown maintained this position because it thought that criminal defences are an inherently "policy-driven exercise" that involves complex and conflicting value judgments.[188] This argument had some grounding in the common law. In *Perka*, the Supreme Court rejected the idea that duress and necessity could be pleaded as justification-based defences since it was outside the legitimate role of the courts to impose their views of when a person is justified in violating the law. That task, the Supreme Court reasoned, was reserved solely for Parliament.[189] The court in *Perka* maintained this position despite recognizing that duress and necessity fit philosophically into both the justification category and the excuse category.[190]

The Supreme Court, however, ultimately found no reason to differentiate between constitutionalizing criminal defences and other aspects of the substantive criminal law under section 7 of the Charter. As the court maintained, "statutory defences do not warrant more deference simply because they are the product of difficult moral judgments. The entire body of criminal law expresses a myriad of policy choices. Statutory offences are every bit as concerned with social values as statutory defences."[191] Given the prominence of the moral involuntariness principle to the court's common law conceptualization of excuse-based criminal defences, the court elevated moral involuntariness to the status of a principle of fundamental justice.[192]

The presence and immediacy requirements in section 17 of the *Criminal Code* were struck down as a result.[193] Ruzic's case illustrated how those requirements could result in a conviction for morally involuntary conduct. The relevant threat from a third party could come to fruition regardless of whether the threatening party was in her presence. The threat also need not be immediate to be taken seriously. Yugoslavia was in a near-lawless state after the Yugoslav Wars. Hence, it was highly unlikely that Ruzic could have taken measures, such as calling the local police, to protect her mother. Relaxing the presence and immediacy requirements was therefore necessary for Ruzic to plead the duress defence.[194]

Moral Blamelessness

Counsel for Ruzic offered an alternative principle of criminal law theory to conceptualize the duress and necessity defences: moral blamelessness.[195] This principle provides that a person who commits a crime while under extreme pressure is not to be blamed for her conduct. The Supreme Court concluded that the moral blamelessness principle failed to qualify as a principle of fundamental justice. In its view, unlike a person who commits an act without proof of *mens rea*,[196] the person who acts under duress or out of necessity is not necessarily morally blameless for her actions. The court offered two arguments in support of this position. First, it maintained that not all morally involuntary conduct could also be said to be morally blameless.[197] Moral involuntariness therefore better captured excuse-based defences. Second, moral involuntariness was consistent with the court's conception of duress and necessity as excuses that serve by definition as defences for *wrongful*, and thus blameworthy, conduct.[198]

The Supreme Court used the common hypothetical scenario of the lost alpinist who breaks into a cabin to preserve her life to elaborate its first position. Although the court was not explicit on this point, it is important to pay attention to the word *lost*. In other words, it is necessary to consider why the alpinist was lost. Did she wander off because of a self-induced impairment? Did she lose her map because of carelessness? Did she severely overestimate her abilities as a cartographer? In these scenarios, can she be said to be *entirely* free of blame for her circumstances? If not, then it is reasonable to conclude that she was not *entirely* free of blame when she broke into the cabin to preserve herself. This is a reasonable way of explaining the court's conclusion that "conduct that is morally involuntary is *not always intrinsically* free of blame."[199]

Compare the lost alpinist with the *stranded* alpinist. The tragic circumstances of the survivors of Uruguay Air Force Flight 571, as documented by Piers Paul Read in his novel *Alive*,[200] provide a useful hypothetical scenario. If the survivors of the plane crash were on the verge of death because of the elements and had come across a cabin, weighing the property interests of the cabin owner against the value of their lives (in jeopardy through no fault of their own), then it would be reasonable to conclude that their conduct was blameless. This follows for two reasons.

First, the survivors cannot be faulted for being in their perilous circumstances. Second, the choice to preserve their lives over the property interests of the cabin owner, from a utilitarian standpoint, is a rightful and therefore justified act. As several commentators have observed, it is incongruous to identify a rightful act as somehow blameworthy.[201] If true, then it is possible for some accused who plead duress and necessity to be blameless, whereas others are not.

The Supreme Court's second argument pertaining to the appropriate conceptualization of the duress and necessity defences was far less persuasive. Although the court in *Perka* conceptualized these defences as excuses, it did so for public policy reasons and despite recognizing that the duress and necessity defences fit conceptually within the excuse and justification categories. In the court's view, it was inappropriate for a court to use the common law to conclude that an accused was justified in committing an act prohibited by Parliament.[202] Under the Charter, however, the court had constitutionalized a general prohibition against convicting the morally innocent. This raised the question of why this, or some similar justification-based rationale,[203] could not extend to the realm of criminal defences.

Moral Innocence

The Supreme Court's rationale in *Ruzic* for rejecting moral blamelessness as a constitutional basis for criminal defences had implications for whether the court would constitutionalize justification-based defences. As the court observed, "the undefinable and potentially far-reaching nature of the concept of moral blamelessness prevents us from recognizing its relevance beyond an initial finding of guilt in the context of s. 7 of the Charter."[204] If this is true, then it is improbable that the Supreme Court will constitutionalize justification-based defences. This follows because the court has consistently described such defences as connoting "rightful" acts.[205] If any act qualifies as a morally innocent and thus blameless act, it is a rightful act.[206]

The Supreme Court's insistence on constitutionalizing excuses but not justifications is incoherent. Whatever rationale there might be for failing to uphold common law justifications,[207] that rationale dissipated when the court subjected the substantive criminal law to constitutional scrutiny. Since the court has concluded that excuses connote wrongful but morally involuntary conduct, it would be paradoxical for justifications, which connote rightful conduct, not also to receive constitutional protection.[208] For this reason, various authors have suggested that there must be a constitutional rationale for justification-based defences despite the court's implicit view to the contrary in *Ruzic*.[209] To date, however, Canadian courts have not constitutionalized any moral principles underlying justification-based defences.

Moral Involuntariness, Proportionality, and the Role of Blamelessness

The Supreme Court's constitutionalization of the moral involuntariness principle resulted in two further critiques. The first, espoused by Benjamin Berger, questioned the appropriateness of constitutionalizing a principle that focuses exclusively on the effect that an accused person's emotions have on her will.[210] With such a focus, the values underlying those emotions are hidden "behind the veil of the voluntarist account."[211] The danger of such an approach, Berger maintains, is that it constitutionalizes the right to permit morally inappropriate emotions to form the basis of a criminal defence.[212] For instance, conduct might become morally involuntary if the accused person succumbs to "homosexual panic."[213] To the contrary, Berger suggests that the moral blamelessness principle, rejected as a principle of fundamental justice in *Ruzic*, allows the law to exclude wrongheaded emotions by focusing on the moral quality of the accused person's emotional response.

As Stanley Yeo and I have observed separately, this criticism fails to account for the meaning of the adjective *moral*.[214] As Yeo puts it, the adjective "stipulates that social policy and values form an integral part of [the moral involuntariness] concept."[215] Building on this observation, I contend elsewhere that interpreting the adjective as a screening device for emotional responses deemed wrongful by society is logically consistent with the function of the moral involuntariness principle.[216] Indeed, this explains why the Supreme Court requires that accused persons who plead duress and necessity act in accordance with how society would expect a reasonable person to act in the circumstances.[217] Viewed in this manner, I contend that Berger's concerns are assuaged.

A second and more forceful critique arose from the Supreme Court's determination that a utilitarian proportionality requirement is implicit in the moral involuntariness principle.[218] Although the court maintained that the proportionality requirement derived from Fletcher's original description of the moral involuntariness principle, this was plainly incorrect. The court relied on the following passage: "If the gap between the harm done and the benefit accrued *becomes too great*, the *act is more likely to appear voluntary* and therefore inexcusable."[219] The italicized words do not suggest that proportionality is anything more than a contextual factor to be considered in the analysis. To require proportionality, then, is contrary to Fletcher's conception of moral involuntariness.

Scholars also questioned the inclusion of proportionality in the moral involuntariness principle on normative grounds. This critique is illustrated by considering the classic kill-or-be-killed duress scenario. If the accused kills one person to save her life, then her actions are proportionate. However, if the accused kills two people to preserve her life, then her actions are disproportionate. Yet the effect on her will is the same in both circumstances, for the accused has no more of a "realistic choice" to preserve herself in either scenario. To conclude otherwise imposes a moral requirement on the moral involuntariness principle that is inconsistent with its conceptual basis: excusing wrongful conduct.[220] The inclusion of a proportionality requirement, then, has resulted in the moral involuntariness principle being treated "in terms more readily analyzable as ... [a] justification."[221]

This inconsistency also gives rise to a critique of the Supreme Court's insistence on constitutionalizing moral involuntariness as the principle underlying criminal defences while recognizing that some defensive acts might also be morally blameless. Recall the circumstances of the stranded alpinist. The conclusion that she is morally blameless derives from two facts. First, she was placed in her perilous position through no fault of her own. Second, she made the *rightful* choice (from a utilitarian standpoint) by choosing her life over the property interests of the cabin owner. Yet such rightful acts are the realm of justification-based defences. It is illogical for the law of excuses to fill the conceptual space of what is clearly a justification-based defence.[222]

This point is also illustrated by considering the classic self-defence case in which the accused kills an attacker to preserve her life. According to *Ruzic*, the accused acts in a morally involuntary manner because she is faced with a kill-or-be-killed scenario.[223] Yet she also acts in a justified manner since self-defence is conceptualized elsewhere by the Supreme Court as a rightful act.[224] If moral involuntariness is not restricted to wrongful acts, then the principle ventures into the conceptual space of justifications despite the court's insistence that it underlies excuse-based defences. The court's unwillingness to draw this distinction was the result either of a misunderstanding of the function of justification- and excuse-based defences or of the court's reluctance to use the Constitution to enter a realm that it viewed as better suited to Parliament. The latter explanation, however, is inconsistent with the court's jurisprudence. As the court held in *Ruzic*, "statutory defences do not warrant more deference [than statutory offences] simply because they are the product of difficult moral judgments."[225]

Sentencing

The main constitutional tool for ensuring fair sentences is the same in Canada as in many constitutional democracies: the prohibition against cruel and unusual punishment.[226] Notably, this provision has been used in Canada to challenge the constitutionality of a variety of mandatory minimum sentences.[227] However, the Supreme Court has also considered whether several other foundational principles of sentencing might qualify as principles of fundamental justice under section 7 of the Charter.

Reduced Moral Blameworthiness for Youth

In *R v DB*,[228] the Supreme Court was faced with a challenge to part of the sentencing scheme in the *Youth Criminal Justice Act*.[229] Section 2(1) required that courts presumptively sentence young persons as adults for the crimes of murder, attempted murder, manslaughter, and aggravated sexual assault. The court concluded that this presumption violated the principle of fundamental justice that young persons are entitled to a presumption of diminished moral blameworthiness.[230] As the court observed, youth must be treated differently because they have "heightened vulnerability, less maturity and a reduced capacity for moral judgement."²³¹ As a result, the reverse onus provision was struck down for being inconsistent with the principles of fundamental justice. The decision also had much broader implications since it constitutionally entrenched the need to have a separate criminal justice system for youth. This is important because, in the lead-up to the adoption of the *Youth Criminal Justice Act*, some politicians were still advocating the abolition of a separate youth justice system.²³²

Proportionality in Sentencing

The proportionality principle in sentencing provides that any sentence must be proportionate to the gravity of the offence and the moral blameworthiness of the offender.²³³ Under its common law sentencing jurisprudence, the Supreme Court determined that proportionality in sentencing was an organizing principle of sentencing.²³⁴ This followed given the principle's direct relationship with the fundamental purpose of sentencing, "the maintenance of a just, peaceful and safe society through the imposition of just sanctions."²³⁵ For this reason, the court in *R v Ipeelee*²³⁶ concluded that "proportionality in sentencing could aptly be described as a principle of fundamental justice under s. 7 of the *Charter*."²³⁷ Justice LeBel's comments in *Ipeelee* were repeated two years later in *R v Anderson*.²³⁸ Leading commentators also concurred with the application of section 7 offered in *Ipeelee* and *Anderson*.²³⁹

Given the *obiter* nature of the comments in these cases, the Supreme Court was asked to consider directly whether the proportionality principle qualified as a principle of fundamental justice in *R v Safarzadeh-Markhali*.²⁴⁰ The constitutional challenge arose as a result of restrictions placed on the practice of granting enhanced credit for time spent in pretrial custody under section 719(3.1) of the *Criminal Code*.²⁴¹ Enhanced credit historically has been granted for two reasons. First, time spent in pretrial detention is not applicable toward parole eligibility in Canada. Second, the conditions under which pretrial detention is served are often much more onerous than regular prison conditions.²⁴² Credit was typically granted on a 2:1 basis, although the Supreme Court allowed credit to be granted at a higher rate in some cases.²⁴³ The Conservative government deemed this approach imprudent and passed the impugned legislation allowing for a maximum credit of 1.5:1. Importantly, the enhanced credit was not applicable if the judge stated on the record that the primary reason for denying bail was related to the accused person's criminal record.[244]

The accused maintained that the impugned provision was inconsistent with the proportionality principle in sentencing.[245] This followed because the rationale for credit to be denied was based on an arbitrary distinction between offenders' criminal records. Consider two offenders with identical records. The first applies for bail and is denied. The judge provides an endorsement that bail was denied primarily because of that person's record. The second offender does not apply for bail. Hence, there is no opportunity for a judge to explain why the accused is remanded for trial. Only the latter person would be eligible for enhanced credit.[246] Handing similar offenders different sentences based on a consideration (whether they applied for bail) that has nothing to do with the moral blameworthiness of the offender's conduct constituted a clear breach of the proportionality principle in sentencing.

Surprisingly, the Supreme Court reversed course and found that the principle of proportionality in sentencing was not a principle of fundamental justice.[247] The Ontario Court of Appeal had found that proportionality in sentencing entitles an offender "to a *process* directed at crafting a just sentence" and "prevents Parliament from making sentencing contingent on factors unrelated to the determination of a fit sentence."[248] The Supreme Court's main reason for overruling that decision was that sentencing is governed under the prohibition against cruel and unusual punishment found in section 12 of the Charter, which applies a standard of *gross* disproportionality. The court reasoned that any constitutionalization of mere proportionality would therefore be inappropriate.[249]

This argument confuses the purpose of prohibiting cruel and unusual punishment with the purpose underlying the proportionality principle in sentencing. The former analysis is directed at the *quantum* of a sentence.[250] Thus, any law that requires a judge to impose a grossly disproportionate sentence runs afoul of section 12 of the Charter. The proportionality principle in sentencing requires courts to ensure that the *factors* used to devise a sentence relate to the offender's moral blameworthiness.[251] It is impartial to the resulting sentence as long as the process for determining the sentence was fair. There is no principled reason why both of these rationales cannot play separate constitutional roles.

Even more worrisome is the fact that the Supreme Court did not consider whether the proportionality principle in sentencing met the test for qualifying as a principle of fundamental justice.[252] If the court had done so, then the proportionality principle would have readily qualified.[253] First, the proportionality principle has long been recognized as a legal principle and is even codified in section 718.1 of the *Criminal Code*.[254] Second, the court recognized in *Ipeelee* and other cases that the proportionality principle is the driving force that allows for "the maintenance of a just, peaceful and safe society through the imposition of just sanctions."[255] This strongly suggests that there would be adequate societal consensus that the proportionality principle qualifies as a principle of fundamental justice. Third, the proportionality principle is sufficiently precise since judges have been able to apply it with consistency "for over a hundred years."[256] The Supreme Court's refusal to constitutionalize proportionality again strongly implied that it misunderstood the relevant principle or was simply uncomfortable with constitutionalizing principles of criminal law theory under section 7 of the Charter.

Parity in Sentencing

In *Carter v Canada (Attorney General)*,[257] the Supreme Court was asked to constitutionalize the principle of parity in sentencing.[258] The principle provides that offenders with similar criminal backgrounds who commit similar offences receive similar sentences.[259] The accused argued that the prohibition on assisted suicide found in section 241 of the *Criminal Code* violated the parity principle because it imposed the highest possible sanction on those who assist people in committing suicide (murder) while exempting comparable end-of-life practices such as a person's choice to commit suicide from criminal sanction.[260]

As the Supreme Court observed, "parity *in the sense invoked* by the appellants has not been recognized as a principle of fundamental justice in this Court's jurisprudence to date."[261] The emphasized words convey why the court was correct to reject the appellants' argument. The parity principle compares similar *offenders*, whereas the appellants asked the court to compare the consequences of physician-assisted suicide with a similar *activity*, such as committing suicide or receiving end-of-life treatment. Requiring the state to forgo criminalizing assisted suicide because similar conduct is legal would constitute a vast intrusion into the legislative realm. For instance, there is no principled difference between the argument advanced in *Carter* and the one unsuccessfully advanced in *Malmo-Levine* requiring that various drugs causing harms similar to those caused by alcohol not be prohibited because alcohol is legal.[262]

Whether the parity principle ought to receive constitutional status therefore remains an unanswered question. It is notable, however, that Hamish Stewart concludes otherwise. In his view, the parity principle cannot be constitutionalized for substantively the same reasons that the proportionality principle failed to qualify as a principle of fundamental justice.[263] However, this argument depends on whether the proportionality principle was properly rejected as a principle of fundamental justice. Stewart's point, then, is correct from a doctrinal perspective but is less persuasive when considered alongside the merits of the Supreme Court's reasons for rejecting proportionality as a principle of fundamental justice.

Indigenous Status

In *R v Anderson*,[264] the accused attempted to constitutionalize a principle that would require the crown to consider Indigenous status in determining whether to enforce a mandatory minimum punishment for impaired driving.[265] The *Criminal Code* imposes different mandatory minimum sentences based on the offender's number of prior impaired driving convictions.[266] To enforce these minimum sentences, the crown must serve a notice of intent to seek greater punishment.[267] It is common practice for the crown to agree not to submit this notice if there are significant gaps between a person's impaired driving convictions or for other sentencing-related reasons. The crown in this case, however, objected to being constitutionally required to consider an offender's Indigenous status before tendering a notice of intent to seek greater punishment. Instead, it maintained that its exercise of discretion is subject to review only when its actions are so repulsive as to constitute an abuse of process.[268]

The lower courts accepted the accused's proposed principle of fundamental justice.[269] The basis for constitutionalizing the principle requiring the crown to consider Indigenous status before mandating a sentence of imprisonment rested in Parliament's decision to pass section 718.2(e) of the *Criminal Code*, which requires that all sanctions other than imprisonment that are reasonable and just in the circumstances be considered "for all offenders, with particular attention to the circumstances of Aboriginal offenders." The section was enacted to address the injustice arising from the gross overincarceration of Indigenous people in Canada.[270]

The lower court decisions were unanimously overturned by the Supreme Court.[271] In its view, section 718.2(e) cannot be translated into a constitutional requirement to override crown discretion.[272] As Justice Moldaver observed, such a conclusion "is contrary to a long-standing and deeply rooted approach to the division of responsibility between the Crown prosecutor and the courts."[273] Prosecutors operate within an adversarial system and, where they have powers that are otherwise constitutional, requiring a judge to scrutinize those powers for anything more than an abuse of process would prevent the judge from playing the role of neutral arbitrator required by the adversarial system of justice.[274]

Marie Manikis nevertheless rejects the Supreme Court's conclusion that the proposed principle of fundamental justice in *Anderson* fails to meet the societal consensus requirement.[275] She bases this position on a misunderstanding of this central element for determining whether a principle qualifies as a principle of fundamental justice. To begin, she maintains that there was a similarly low level of agreement about the court's constitutionalization of fault in *Vaillancourt*.[276] As my review above illustrates, however, the court's constitutionalization of fault did not contradict a foundational principle of the adversarial system of justice. Manikis also relies on a comment from Peter Hogg to the effect that the societal consensus requirement is "not intended to be taken seriously."[277] A closer reading of Hogg's article suggests that the societal consensus requirement, in the *empirical* sense, is not to be taken seriously. Societal consensus in the *normative* sense is described by a leading scholar as the most important consideration for determining whether a principle qualifies as a principle of fundamental justice.[278]

In making this critique, I am not suggesting that the *Gladue* principle is not worthy of constitutional status. The Supreme Court in *Anderson* did not consider this broader question since it was asked only whether the *Gladue* principle should bind the decision-making authority of the *prosecution*. If Parliament were to bar consideration of Indigenous status during sentencing, then it would remain open for litigants to challenge such a law. Since the *Gladue* principle is a fundamental aspect of the proportionality principle in sentencing,[279] the Supreme Court's rejection of the proportionality principle implies that the court might not be willing to constitutionalize that principle. For the reasons noted above, however, the court erred in *Safarzadeh-Markhali* when it refused to constitutionalize the proportionality principle in sentencing. If the court reversed its decision, then there would be ample constitutional space for the *Gladue* principle.

Constitutionalizing Criminal Law Theory: A Promising Venture or a Failed Experiment?

As should be evident from the above review, many unjust doctrines of criminal liability were expelled from criminal law by constitutionalizing principles of criminal law theory. At the same time, noticeable gaps and inconsistencies arose in the Supreme Court's jurisprudence. The extent to which the court was incapable of developing and/or unwilling to develop the relationship between criminal law and constitutional law should raise various concerns about the merits of allowing courts to constitutionalize principles of criminal law theory.

Coherence

The Supreme Court's attempt to bring more coherence to the substantive criminal law under section 7 of the Charter relied heavily on three bedrock principles of criminal law: choice, proportionality, and innocence.[280] First, the court maintained that those who are physically incapable of choosing their actions cannot be held criminally responsible. Despite the controversial facts underlying *Daviault*, the court followed this bedrock principle. The court also used the prohibition against convicting accused persons for physically involuntary conduct to bolster its case for constitutionalizing the moral involuntariness principle.[281] That principle, however, was required to do too much heavy lifting. As opposed to simply providing a rationalization for excuse-based defences, the Supreme Court – largely because of its misunderstanding of proportionality's role in excuse-based defences – confusingly allowed moral involuntariness to provide the theoretical basis not only for excuses but also for justifications.

Second, the Supreme Court gave proportionality pride of place in the substantive criminal law's expression under section 7 of the Charter.[282] Its development of the law of *mens rea* using the proportionality principle provided a workable approach that was reasonably adopted over calls to constitutionalize common law standards of subjective fault. The court's use of the proportionality principle in relation to *mens rea* was nevertheless problematic in some contexts. Notably, the court insisted on characterizing limited offences – murder, attempted murder, war crimes, crimes against humanity, and theft – as "high stigma" offences.[283] As several authors have observed, this list is both over- and underinclusive. Although the opprobrium attached to theft (dishonest) is significant, so is the opprobrium attached to many other crimes, such as assault (violent), sexual assault (rapist), impaired driving (drunk), possession of child pornography (pedophile), and manslaughter and criminal negligence causing death ("killer").[284] Surely the opprobrium associated with such convictions is equally if not more serious than the opprobrium underlying theft, yet the court has not recognized a requirement for subjective *mens rea* in these other contexts.[285]

At no point has the Supreme Court said, however, that if Parliament reduced the *mens rea* for the aforementioned offences that it would not also violate the proportionality principle. It is not difficult to devise scenarios in which it would be unprincipled for Parliament to impose objective liability for many of the offences listed above. It is possible, then, that the problem with the court's jurisprudence is its suggestion that only "high stigma" offences require proportionality between *mens rea* and blameworthiness of the offence. Viewed in this way, a more general requirement of proportionality allows for a workable and principled approach to determine the constitutionality of any given fault element of a criminal offence.

The Supreme Court's decision in *Creighton* refusing to categorize unlawful act manslaughter as a "high stigma" offence revealed a more theoretical incoherency. The court's cardinal conception of proportionality proved to be empty of normative content. Despite the best efforts of the court, it sought in vain to determine a generally appropriate level of opprobrium to attach to crimes such as unlawful act manslaughter. The ordinal conception of stigma is nevertheless capable of yielding a more predictable and coherent result. The current manslaughter provision captures a wide variety of conduct and thus equally stigmatizes those who kill with objective foreseeability of death and those who cannot objectively foresee death because of the victim's "thin skull."[286] Constitutionally requiring Parliament to draw a distinction between these means of committing manslaughter – and ideally imposing different degrees of maximum punishment for each – provides a principled approach to constitutionally challenging the unfair stigma imposed by the current manslaughter provisions.

The Supreme Court's jurisprudence on the relationship between sentencing principles and section 7 of the Charter was also incoherent. The court's refusal to constitutionalize the proportionality principle in sentencing was particularly perplexing. Since this principle clearly met the court's basic requirements for qualifying as a principle of fundamental justice, the court's reasoning left the law of sentencing with protections related only to the quantum of sentencing that, under section 12 of the Charter, need only result in a sentence that is not grossly disproportionate to the moral blameworthiness of the offender's actions. The court's decision to constitutionalize a separate system of justice for youth is nevertheless commendable. This decision ensures that justice for youth – which inherently consists of less blameworthy conduct – must be subject to sentencing rules different from those of the justice system for adults.

Third, the Supreme Court's reliance on a general principle prohibiting the conviction of the morally innocent was applied with moderate success. The court initially provided a strong endorsement of the moral innocence principle in the *Motor Vehicle Act Reference*. Yet the court got cold feet when it came to using section 7 of the Charter to define the outer parameters of what conduct qualified as morally innocent. In particular, the court's refusal to constitutionalize the harm and offence principles left a gap in its constitutional structure for criminal law. The Supreme Court's refusal to use the innocence principle in the context of criminal defences was also puzzling. Overall, the court expressed an unwillingness to extend the idea of innocence to conceptualize justification-based defences. Although rejecting the idea that those acting under duress and necessity are *always* "morally blameless" was reasonable, the court's implicit decision to forgo constitutionalizing justification-based defences failed to live up to its explicit recognition that offences and defences are equally concerned with questions of social values.

Given the above review, it is fair to conclude that every area of substantive criminal law that the Supreme Court has constitutionalized using principles of criminal law theory has resulted in incoherent doctrinal development. These issues were partially the result of the court's misunderstanding of the relevant criminal law principles. As I explain below, however, the court's failure to coherently constitutionalize principles of criminal law theory can also often result from another factor: judicial hesitancy to constitutionalize substantive principles of criminal law theory out of concern that doing so is democratically illegitimate. Before turning to that consideration, it is necessary to determine whether the court's decisions constitutionalizing principles of criminal law theory increased the overall fairness of the substantive criminal law.

Fairness
Although the Supreme Court's jurisprudence constitutionalizing criminal law theory principles created some conceptual confusion, the court did purge Canadian criminal law of a number of unjust laws. The first of these laws fell as a result of the court's decision in *Daviault* to abandon the common law rule allowing for proof of extreme intoxication akin to automatism to substitute for the minimal volition requirement to prove the *actus reus* of an offence. Similarly, the court's decision in *Robinson* ensured that intoxication short of incapacity could be pleaded as a means of raising a reasonable doubt about whether an accused intended to commit a specific intent offence. Without the court's constitutionalization of the physical voluntariness principle and proportionality principle related to fault, both of these common law rules likely would have continued to result in convictions for crimes that accused persons did not intend to commit.

The felony murder provisions are another example of an unjust law struck down for violating section 7 of the Charter. Convicting a person for murder – one of the most serious crimes known to criminal law – absent any intent to cause death has long been criticized as unfair.[287] Although the rule has its defenders, the Canadian felony murder provisions went beyond most versions of the felony murder rule, such as the applicable rule in Texas requiring that the defendant actually be the one who "commits" a felony "clearly dangerous to human life."[288] Given the exceptionally broad scope of the rule, Canada's felony murder laws rightly received criticism for being "the harshest in the common law world."[289]

With the exception of the Supreme Court's refusal to find that manslaughter did not require a higher form of *mens rea*, the court's conclusion that objective *mens rea* is commensurate with the moral blameworthiness of various criminal acts was reasonable. Similarly, the court acted reasonably in refusing to constitutionalize a requirement that the *actus reus* and *mens rea* overlap in relation to all elements of an offence, including any aggravating circumstances. Accepting either that objective liability is impermissible or that there must always be overlap between the *actus reus* and the *mens rea* of an offence would effectively do away with a long-accepted principle that one must take the victim as found. Without a persuasive critique of this "thin skull" principle, the Supreme Court acted reasonably in refusing to use section 7 of the Charter to dispose of it. As outlined above, however, imposing the same stigma on someone who kills as a result of a minor degree of harm and someone who objectively ought to have known that her conduct would cause death is unprincipled and could have been addressed by preferring an ordinal conception of proportionality in relation to the stigma underlying a criminal offence.

The constitutionalization of the moral involuntariness principle also partially rid the law of a perplexing and unjust statutory duress defence. In addition to requiring the threatening party to be present and the threat immediate in all circumstances, section 17 of the *Criminal Code* categorically prevents pleading duress to such varied offences as "robbery, assault with a weapon or causing bodily harm, aggravated assault, unlawfully causing bodily harm, [and] arson." Several of these restrictions have been struck down by lower courts applying the moral involuntariness principle constitutionalized in *Ruzic*.[290] It stretches rationality to suggest that a person must sacrifice her life to avoid something like causing bodily harm – defined as harm that is not trivial or transient – to another person. Although other offences such as murder might be properly excluded from the duress defence,[291] the restrictions in the current provision are so broad as to cause profound injustice.[292]

The law of sentencing was also made fairer as a result of constitutionalizing sentencing principles. Most notably, the *Youth Criminal Justice Act* was rid of a reverse onus on youth to show why they ought not to be sentenced as adults for various serious crimes. As the Supreme Court observed, "heightened vulnerability, less maturity and a reduced capacity for moral judgement" made this presumption contrary to basic understandings of youth cognition.[293] The court's retraction of its *obiter* statement that the proportionality principle in sentencing qualified as a principle of fundamental justice failed to ensure that offenders were sentenced exclusively based on factors relevant to their moral blameworthiness. As I detail in the next chapter, however, the court did strike down this law for violating the principles of instrumental rationality.

The Supreme Court in *Anderson* did not constitutionally require the crown to consider the status of Indigenous people when deciding to enforce a mandatory minimum sentence that limits a judge's discretion in sentencing. Although the plight of Indigenous people requires significant criminal justice reform, the court's decision is reasonable given its wider implications for the criminal justice system. As the court observed, the principle of fundamental justice proposed by counsel would limit whether the crown could "bring the prosecution of a charge laid by police; whether to enter a stay of proceedings ... ; whether to accept a guilty plea to a lesser charge; whether to withdraw from criminal proceedings altogether; and whether to take control of a private prosecution."[294] This constitutes a significant incursion into the function of the adversarial system that in turn is unlikely to attract societal consensus that the proposed principle is vital to the criminal justice system.[295]

The Politics of Constitutionalizing Criminal Law Theory

The Supreme Court's decision in the *Motor Vehicle Act Reference* to constitutionalize substantive principles of fundamental justice is notoriously controversial.[296] As Kent Roach and Jamie Cameron observe, "the

Court's caution in [constitutionalizing criminal law] may be related to doubts about the project of interpreting the guarantees of the principles of fundamental justice in section 7 of the *Charter* to include more than procedural fairness."[297] This caution derives in no small part from the unique nature of how laws are struck down under section 7 of the Charter. A judge might reasonably believe that devising her own conception of "substantive justice" is a less legitimate form of judicial review than interpreting an enumerated right in the text of the Charter. The latter type of right was enacted with a democratic mandate, whereas the former allows a judge to impose her own sense of justice in overturning democratically enacted laws.

The Supreme Court's jurisprudence constitutionalizing principles of substantive criminal law supports this view. The court often justified delimiting its approach to constitutionalizing criminal law principles by appealing to the "policy" nature of the principles that it was being asked to constitutionalize. For instance, in *Logan* Justice Lamer rejected constitutionalizing the principle that parties and principal offenders must have the same type of criminal fault. In so concluding, he observed that, "[although] as a matter of policy ... [this rule] seems more equitable than not, I am not ready to characterize it as a principle of fundamental justice."[298] A similar rationale was offered in *Creighton* for rejecting subjective fault for the offence of criminal negligence causing death.[299] In *DeSousa*, the Supreme Court was expressly concerned with the fact that "to require intention in relation to each and every consequence would bring a large number of offences into question."[300] A similar rationale was offered in *Vaillancourt*[301] and *Ruzic*[302] for rejecting, respectively, the constitutionalization of the common law presumption of subjective fault and justification-based defences.

These concerns about not deciding "policy" matters suggest that the Supreme Court was strongly influenced by criticisms of the separation of powers and judicial overreach into the legislative realm.[303] Yet it is not clear whether these concerns alone ought to have resulted in the court halting its foray into constitutionalizing principles of criminal law theory. Criminal law is an area in which majoritarian politics are particularly prone to result in unjust laws imposed on often vulnerable groups.[304] Even though the court made a variety of mistakes, it also purged many unjust criminal laws using section 7 of the Charter. Moreover, the court did provide some concrete guidance to future courts and legislatures on the basic principles underlying criminal law even if just as often it caused confusion about the principles that it used to constitutionally structure criminal law.

Conclusion

Although the Supreme Court's constitutionalization of criminal law theory has rid the law of various unjust doctrines of criminal liability, it has also created confusion about the constitutional principles underlying Canadian criminal law. The latter effect was frequently the result of the court's misunderstanding of the principles that it sought to constitutionalize. At other times, however, it was the result of the court's reluctance to use substantive review under section 7 of the Charter to strike down laws enacted by democratically accountable legislatures. These concerns in turn resulted in the court experimenting with a different form of substantive review under section 7 of the Charter: instrumental rationality.

Principles of Instrumental Rationality 3

The Supreme Court of Canada began to alter its approach to substantive review shortly after the turn of the twentieth century. Instead of constitutionalizing principles of criminal law theory,[1] the court increasingly decided the constitutionality of criminal laws by considering their "means-ends" or "instrumental" rationality.[2] A law can violate the instrumental rationality principles in three main ways. A law will be arbitrary where the means chosen to achieve a legislative objective are in no way connected to the law's objective.[3] A law will be overbroad where the means chosen by the legislature go further than necessary to achieve its objective.[4] Finally, a law that achieves its objective at too high a cost to the threshold interests of life, liberty, and security of the person will violate the gross disproportionality principle.[5]

I begin this chapter by identifying the various substantive criminal laws that have been challenged using the principles of instrumental rationality. This review serves two purposes. First, it will illustrate that the Supreme Court has had difficulty conceptualizing its instrumental rationality principles of fundamental justice. Not only did the court begin by illogically developing arbitrariness, overbreadth, and gross disproportionality as mirror images of the proportionality test under section 1 of the *Charter of Rights and Freedoms*, its decision to "individualize" the instrumental rationality principles resulted in every bright-line rule that engages the life, liberty, or security of the person interests violating section 7 of the Charter.

Second, my review will show that the Supreme Court often chooses the principles of instrumental rationality as the means to strike down a law despite viable alternative principles of criminal law theory available under section 7. I will explain the court's preference by appealing to the different rationales that underlie each method of substantive review. Constitutionalizing principles of criminal law theory can create greater coherence in criminal law, whereas principles of instrumental rationality aim to increase the legitimacy of substantive review by entering into democratic dialogue with Parliament about the legitimate scope of criminal law. Although the latter method softens the counter-majoritarian critique, my review will show that Parliament often enters into this dialogue in an unproductive, politically charged manner.

Two Approaches to Instrumental Rationality

The plain wording of section 7 of the Charter suggests that it applies if anyone is affected in a manner that is inconsistent with a principle of fundamental justice. Despite this wording, the unique focus on means-ends rationality inherent to the instrumental rationality principles initially resulted in the Supreme Court's assessment of whether a law was suitably tailored to its ends in a holistic manner. With this approach, the applicant was required to weigh the actual ability of the law to further its objective against the negative effects of the law on the life, liberty, and security of the person interests of all affected individuals.[6]

The holistic approach effectively mirrored the section 1 test for justifying infringements of rights.[7] Laws that infringe Charter rights may be upheld under section 1 if the government proves on a balance of probabilities that the law is rationally connected to its objective, minimally impairs its objective, and balances its salutary and deleterious effects.[8] The instrumental rationality principles had an uncanny resemblance to this "proportionality" test. An arbitrary law was not rationally connected to the objective of the law; an overbroad law was connected to the law's objective but not minimally impairing since it caught more conduct than was reasonably necessary; and a grossly disproportionate law failed to appropriately balance a law's salutary and deleterious effects.[9]

The holistic approach to instrumental rationality was problematic not only because it rendered the principles underlying the justificatory test for infringements of rights redundant[10] but also because it reversed the burden of proof in Charter proceedings. As opposed to the state offering justificatory reasons for infringing a Charter right, litigants were required to submit significant amounts of evidence explaining why the government's law failed to strike a reasonable balance between legitimate policy objectives and the law's effects. Intuitively, the burden of proving the positive effects of a law belonged to the state.[11]

As a result of these inconsistencies, the Supreme Court abandoned the holistic conception of the instrumental rationality principles in *Canada (Attorney General) v Bedford*.[12] The novelty of the court's "individualistic" approach was that it required litigants to prove only an arbitrary, overbroad, or grossly disproportionate effect on a single individual.[13] In addition, the litigant was not required to address how well the law achieved its objective. Instead, the law was presumed to achieve its objective.[14] If the litigant could prove an arbitrary, overbroad, or grossly disproportionate effect on even a single hypothetical person, then the government would be required to submit evidence justifying its infringement on rights.

Presuming that a law achieves its objective is arguably necessary for the individualistic analytical structure to serve its broader purpose. Without this presumption, it would be necessary to consider whether the law is capable of meeting its objective at the section 7 stage of the analysis. Yet this is precisely the type of evidence that the Supreme Court wished to consider only under section 1. As the court reasoned in *Bedford*, "unlike individual claimants, the Crown is well placed to call the social science and expert evidence required to justify the law's impact in terms of society as a whole."[15] As the court continued, "to require s. 7 claimants to establish the efficacy of the law ... would impose the government's s. 1 burden on claimants under s. 7. That cannot be right."[16] By limiting the amount of evidence needed to prove a section 7 violation, the court realigned the burden of proof in a way that is sensitive to the appropriate role of each party.

In the following review of the Supreme Court's jurisprudence, I will differentiate between the court's use of the holistic and the individualistic conceptions of instrumental rationality as much as possible.

If my chronological review is unclear at any point, then the reader should note that *Bedford* was decided in 2013. Thus, all decisions before that point were made under the holistic conception of instrumental rationality. Exactly which conception is pleaded, however, has been of little relevance so far. With one notable exception at a provincial appellate court discussed below,[17] all laws that have violated either understanding of the instrumental rationality principles have been struck down under the Charter.

Arbitrariness

Although the test for arbitrariness historically has been stated in numerous ways, an arbitrary law, at base, is one that displays no rational connection between its means and its ends.[18] In other words, to hold that a law is arbitrary is to declare that the legislature was acting in a completely irrational manner.[19] Understandably, courts have been reluctant to impute this level of irrationality to a legislature. As such, only a few substantive criminal laws have been struck down for violating the arbitrariness principle.[20]

Abortion

The arbitrariness principle was constitutionalized in *R v Morgentaler*.[21] Henry Morgentaler and his co-accused had been charged under section 251 of the *Criminal Code* with performing an abortion without following the prescribed procedure.[22] Section 251(4) required that an abortion be performed only by a "qualified medical practitioner" in "an accredited or approved hospital" following the hospital's "therapeutic abortion committee" providing a "certificate in writing [stating] that in its opinion the continuation of the pregnancy ... would or would be likely to endanger her life or health."[23]

The Supreme Court concluded that section 251(4) violated the principles of fundamental justice but diverged in its reasoning. Chief Justice Dickson (Justice Lamer concurring) found that the law violated section 7 because it provided an illusory defence that rendered the law "manifestly unfair."[24] The need to have four physicians available to approve and perform an abortion rendered the defence unavailable to a quarter of hospitals because of low staff levels.[25] More than half of hospitals also did not meet the criteria for being qualified as "approved" facilities.[26] Of those eligible hospitals, half elected not to set up abortion clinics.[27] Provinces were also able to place additional restrictions on maintaining abortion clinics, such as increasing the number of staff required to provide abortions.[28] Finally, some doctors interpreted the word *health* in section 251(4) narrowly, erecting a further obstacle to receiving an abortion.[29]

Justice Beetz (Justice Estey concurring) similarly found that the procedure imposed by Parliament created "manifestly unfair [delays] because they are not necessary to assure that [Parliament's] objectives are met."[30] Justice Wilson was the most critical of the substantive criteria restricting women's ability to receive an abortion: endangering the mother's life or health.[31] However, she also agreed with the majority justices that the barriers preventing women from receiving an abortion were disconnected from the impugned law's objective.[32] As such, the law may fairly be said to have violated a general principle that a law must display some degree of connection to its purpose.[33]

Euthanasia

In *Rodriguez v British Columbia (Attorney General)*,[34] the applicant challenged the prohibition on assisted suicide in section 241(b) of the *Criminal Code*. The majority found that the objective of the provision was "the protection of the vulnerable who might be induced in moments of weakness to commit suicide."[35] The majority also found that this purpose was "grounded in the state['s] interest in protecting life" and in the state's belief that "human life should not be depreciated by allowing life to be taken."[36] With this framing, the majority was able to conclude that a complete ban on assisted suicide was likely to ensure that *some* individuals would be prevented from committing suicide in moments of weakness. Although other people might reasonably desire assistance in committing suicide, the Supreme Court maintained that allowing all people access to assisted suicide would "open the floodgates" and result in many unnecessary deaths.[37]

Three dissenting justices nevertheless found the prohibition against assisted dying to violate a yet to be refined arbitrariness principle.[38] As Justice McLachlin wrote, under section 241(b) it was legal for a physically capable person to commit suicide, but a physically incapable person was prohibited from being aided by another person in committing suicide.[39] She maintained that this distinction was arbitrary.[40] The "floodgate" argument, she concluded, was properly considered as a section 1 justification for violating Charter rights.[41] For Justice McLachlin, the notion that a person might desire to end her life to avoid significant suffering was within a reasonable range of perspectives on the value of life. To scapegoat such people despite the availability of alternative procedures for protecting vulnerable persons from being pressured into committing suicide was unjustifiable under section 1 of the Charter.[42]

Possession/Distribution of Marijuana

In *R v Malmo-Levine*,[43] the accused challenged the constitutionality of the offences of possession for the purposes of trafficking and possession of marijuana.[44] The accused argued that these general prohibitions were incapable of achieving the law's objective of protecting vulnerable persons from being exposed to marijuana. However, the trial judge found that prohibiting marijuana was likely to take the drug out of the hands of vulnerable users who might not be identifiable in advance.[45] Young persons in particular are susceptible to developmental delay and psychosis resulting from marijuana use.[46] As a result, the majority of the Supreme Court found that there was at least a rational connection between the effects of the law and its objective.[47]

The accused also argued that Parliament's choice to prohibit marijuana but not alcohol (a substance with similar or worse harms) was arbitrary.[48] In other words, the accused maintained that Parliament acted arbitrarily if its choice to prohibit one harmful act but not a similarly harmful act could not be rationalized as a matter of policy. The Supreme Court held that this argument – similar in principle to the dissenting reasons in *Rodriguez* – misconstrued the proper role of courts and legislatures. Accepting the appellant's argument would "involve the courts in not only defining the outer limits of the legislative action allowed by the Constitution but also in ordering Parliament's priorities within those limits."[49] In rejecting this argument, the court clarified that the effects of a challenged law must simply be measured against the objective of the law to determine if it exhibits a rational connection.[50]

Safe Injection Sites

Section 56 of the *Controlled Drugs and Substances Act* (*CDSA*)[51] allows for the federal government to grant exemptions to its enforcement for various purposes, including the operation of safe injection sites. The federal government and the BC government had used this provision as the basis for opening a safe injection site known as Insite. After the exemption expired, the federal government – which in the meantime had changed to a Conservative Party government – refused to renew the exemption. Without it, the staff at Insite were required to cease operations or face the prospect of being charged with possession and trafficking of illegal narcotics under the *CDSA*.

As with any exercise of state discretion, a minister's decision must comport with the principles of fundamental justice where a citizen's life, liberty, [or] security of the person interest is engaged.[52] As a result, the applicant in *Canada (Attorney General) v PHS Community Services Society*[53] argued that the minister's decision to refuse renewal of the exemption violated the arbitrariness principle. The Supreme Court determined that the purpose of the minister's decision was to forward the basic objectives of the *CDSA:* enhancing public health and safety.[54] Yet the effect of that decision was to halt a program that had saved lives and to reinstate enforcement of the *CDSA*, which the trial judge had found did not deter drug use in the area where Insite was located.[55] As a result, the decision was found to undermine its inferred goal of increasing health and public safety.

Medical Marijuana

In *R v Smith*,[56] the Supreme Court considered whether a prohibition on non-dried forms of medical marijuana violated the arbitrariness principle. Regulations under the *CDSA* permitted the use of marijuana for treating medical conditions. However, the rules prohibited the use of non-dried forms of marijuana, which in effect required users to inhale marijuana, typically by smoking.[57] The accused, an authorized provider, nevertheless sold both dried and non-dried forms of marijuana at his store.[58] The police became aware of this activity and subsequently charged the accused with possession of marijuana and possession for the purpose of trafficking contrary to sections 4(1) and 5(2) of the *CDSA*.[59]

The Supreme Court found that there was no connection between the law's objective of protecting health and safety and allowing possession of dried but not non-dried forms of medical marijuana.[60] For some users, non-dried forms in fact are more effective in treating their symptoms.[61] Moreover, the prohibition on non-dried forms of marijuana required users to accept the clear health risks resulting from inhaling marijuana smoke.[62] As the court concluded, "it follows from these findings that the prohibition on non-dried medical marihuana undermines the health and safety of medical marihuana users by diminishing the quality of their medical care."[63] Given the clear disconnect between the purpose of the regulation and its effects, the law was found to violate the arbitrariness principle.[64]

The "Individualistic" Conception of Arbitrariness

The *Smith* decision is the only post-*Bedford* case to strike down a law for violating the arbitrariness principle. Yet the analysis conducted in both the pre- and the post-*Bedford* cases does not appear to be affected by the "individualization" of the instrumental rationality principles. This is likely because the Supreme Court subsequently realized that the arbitrariness principle is unworkable under the individualistic conception of instrumental rationality. Since a law is arbitrary if it displays no rational connection between its objective and its effects, Hamish Stewart rightly contends that a court will require evidence of a law's overall effectiveness to determine whether the law is arbitrary.[65] It is therefore necessary for the accused to show that the law could not have its intended effect on every person, not just a hypothetical individual. To conclude otherwise would collapse the main distinction between the arbitrariness and overbreadth principles.

Overbreadth

Unlike the arbitrariness principle, the Supreme Court's decision in *Bedford* to "individualize" the overbreadth analysis profoundly altered the scope of the principle. The individualistic conception of overbreadth has been used subsequently in a variety of scenarios as the basis for striking down substantive criminal laws.[66] I nevertheless maintain that the *Bedford* conception of overbreadth remains contrary to the court's jurisprudence outlining the basic prerequisites for qualifying as a principle of fundamental justice.

Vagrancy

In *R v Heywood*,[67] the Supreme Court was asked to strike down the vagrancy prohibition found in section 179(1)(b) of the *Criminal Code*. The section prohibited those convicted of sexual assault and other sexual offences from "loitering in or near a schoolground, playground, public park, or bathing area." The accused had been convicted of two counts of sexual assault against adults and was subsequently found loitering near a playground and public park on two occasions.[68] Both times the appellant possessed a camera, and, on being arrested for the second offence, a search of the camera revealed pictures of the genital areas of several children.[69] The accused was subsequently charged with vagrancy.

The accused claimed successfully for the first time that a criminal law was overbroad since the scope of the law was not reasonably necessary to achieve the objective of the legislation.[70] Given that the objective of the vagrancy law was to protect children from sexual predators,[71] the Supreme Court determined that the prohibition was overbroad in three ways. First, it was geographically overbroad since it applied to places where children were unlikely to be found, such as vast wilderness parks.[72] Second, the prohibition was temporally overbroad since it lasted for life without any possibility of review. This prevented people who ceased to be a threat to children from having the ban lifted.[73] Third, the ban applied to anyone convicted of a sexual offence. Since one can be convicted for sexual offences against an adult without being a threat to children, the law was completely divorced from its objective as it applied to many offenders.[74]

Fitness to Stand Trial

The overbreadth principle was dormant for a decade until the Supreme Court's decision in *R v Demers*.[75] The accused was charged with sexual assault but successfully pleaded that he was unfit to stand trial because of an intellectual disability caused by Down syndrome.[76] After being declared unfit to stand trial, the accused was required to undergo a disposition hearing pursuant to Part XX.1 of the *Criminal Code*.[77] The court or board hearing the disposition had to impose one of the dispositions set out in section 672.54. That provision, however, did not allow for an absolute or unconditional discharge for persons found permanently unfit to stand trial. Moreover, section 672.81(1) required that those found unfit to stand trial be subject to an annual review hearing to determine their fitness or whether it is necessary to take any other measures to protect the public.

The combined effect of sections 672.54 and 672.81(1) was to require an accused person to remain under the disposition body's jurisdiction subject to a limited exception in which the crown was no longer capable of establishing a prima facie case against the accused.[78] Parliament's objective in enacting this legislation was to provide ongoing treatment or assessment of the accused person in order to aid the accused in becoming fit for an eventual trial while respecting the accused's liberty and dignity interests.[79] The accused, however, was a clear example of a person who would never become fit to stand trial. Despite a permanent state of unfitness, people such as the accused were "subject to anxiety, concern and stigma because of the criminal proceedings that hang over them indefinitely."[80] As a result of this clear inconsistency with the objective of the legislation, the impugned laws were declared overbroad.[81]

Participating in or Facilitating Terrorism

In *R v Khawaja*,[82] the accused maintained that the offence of participating in or contributing to terrorism as found in section 83.18 of the *Criminal Code* is overbroad. Section 83.18(1) makes it an offence for anyone "knowingly [to] participate in or contribute to, directly or indirectly, any activity of a terrorist group for the purpose of enhancing the ability of any terrorist group to facilitate or carry out a terrorist activity." Section 83.18(2) makes it clear that the offence can be committed whether or not 1) a terrorist activity is actually facilitated or carried out; 2) "the participation or contribution of the accused actually enhances the ability of a terrorist group to facilitate or carry out a terrorist activity"; or 3) the accused knows of "the specific nature of any terrorist activity."[83]

The accused in this case maintained that the *mens rea* requirement in section 83.18 can catch conduct not intended to promote terrorism. As the accused observed, "in the absence of some explicit disassociation from the group's terrorist ideology, participating in *any activity* of the group could be viewed as intending to enhance the group's abilities to carry out terrorist activities."[84] This view received support from at least one commentator, who argued that a lawyer or doctor who provides services to a terrorist could be convicted under section 83.18.[85] Without explicit disassociation from the relevant terrorist group, the act of defending a terrorist from criminal charges or bringing a terrorist to good health could help the terrorist to materially continue her activity.[86]

The Supreme Court rejected this interpretation of section 83.18. In its view, the provision imposes a significantly more demanding *mens rea* requirement. This follows since the provision requires not only that the accused "knowingly" participate in or contribute to the relevant terrorist activity but also that the person do so "'for the purpose' of enhancing the ability of the terrorist group to facilitate or carry out a terrorist activity."[87] The combination of these two subjective forms of *mens rea* resulted in the crown having to prove that the accused intended to aid a terrorist group, not serve an otherwise innocent purpose.[88]

The *actus reus* for the offence found in section 83.18(2)(b) of the *Criminal Code* appears to set a significantly lower bar for committing an offence related to terrorism. The section provides that "an offence may be committed ... whether or not ... the participation or contribution of the accused actually enhances the ability of a terrorist group to facilitate or carry out a terrorist activity." Given this wording, the accused maintained that relatively innocuous conduct could be caught by the provision. The accused cited as an example "a person who marches in a non-violent rally held by the charitable arm of a terrorist group, with the specific intention of lending credibility to the group and thereby enhancing the group's ability to carry out terrorist activities."[89] Although the person does not contribute to terrorism in a material way, she could be convicted under section 83.18 of participating in terrorism since the activity need not "enhance" the capacities of the terrorist group under consideration.[90]

The Supreme Court's response to this problem was typical in Canadian jurisprudence: reliance on what the "reasonable person" would view as materially enhancing the abilities of a terrorist group.[91] This approach required that the *actus reus* of the offence be something beyond *de minimis*.⁹² Yet this interpretation is plainly contrary to the wording of section 83.18(2)(b), which states that whether or not the activity "actually enhances" the terrorist group "to facilitate or carry out" its desired activity is irrelevant.⁹³ As Hamish Stewart observes, the court's reluctance to interpret the impugned offence in this manner (and thus find that the legislation overshot its objective of preventing terrorist attacks) was illustrative of a troubling trend in Charter jurisprudence: as opposed to interpreting the offence in light of its wording, the Supreme Court stretched the meaning of the statute to apply only to constitutional cases.⁹⁴

Living on the Avails of Sex Work

The popularity of the overbreadth principle increased significantly after the Supreme Court's decision in *Canada (Attorney General) v Bedford*.⁹⁵ The applicants provided a multi-pronged section 7 challenge to the laws governing sex work. Although sex work was legal, several *Criminal Code* provisions made almost every activity related to it illegal. Section 210 made it an offence to be an inmate of a bawdy house, to be found in a bawdy house without lawful excuse, or to be an owner, landlord, lessor, tenant, or occupier of a place and knowingly permit it to be used as a bawdy house. Section 212(1)(j) made it an offence to live on the avails of another's sex work. Finally, section 213(1)(c) made it an offence to communicate or attempt to communicate with someone in public for the purpose of engaging in sex work. The overall effect of these provisions was to restrict sex work to out-calls and street work.

This legislation was upheld in 1990 despite arguments that the impugned laws unjustifiably infringed sections 2(b) (freedom of expression) and 7 of the Charter.⁹⁶ The major differences between past and present constitutional challenges were in both the nature of the evidence submitted and the principles of fundamental justice pleaded.⁹⁷ First, the accused in *Bedford* amassed 25,000 pages of evidence – including studies, reports, newspaper articles, legislation, Hansard statements, and other documents – proving that restricting sex work to out-calls and street work made it substantially more dangerous.⁹⁸ Second, the accused expanded the scope of the constitutional challenge by pleading the full gamut of instrumental rationality principles.⁹⁹ Previously, the Supreme Court had only considered whether the legislation violated section 7 by being unconstitutionally vague.[100]

The Supreme Court held that only one of the impugned sex work laws violated the overbreadth principle, although it did not rule out this possibility for all three laws.[101] The court determined that the objective of the prohibition on living on the avails of sex work was to denounce exploitative relationships between sex workers and their pimps.[102] The provision had been interpreted as applying to those who provide a service or good to a sex worker *because* she is a sex worker, thus excluding grocers, doctors, and the like.[103] Yet the provision still caught those who provide services connected to sex work, such as drivers, bodyguards, and receptionists.[104] Since these types of workers do not exploit but protect sex workers, the legislation was found to be overbroad.[105]

Euthanasia Revisited

The Supreme Court reconsidered its decision to uphold the prohibition against assisted suicide in *Carter v Canada (Attorney General)*.[106] Similar to the applicant in *Rodriguez*, one of the applicants, Gloria Taylor, suffered from amyotrophic lateral sclerosis, a degenerative muscle disease that results in the body failing "piece by piece" until the victim eventually succumbs to the disease and dies.[107] Since the applicant did not have the financial means to acquire assistance in committing suicide abroad, she was faced with the "'cruel choice' between killing herself while she was still physically capable or giving up the ability to exercise any control over the manner and timing of her death."[108]

The Supreme Court affirmed that the objective of Parliament's prohibition on assisted suicide was the same as in *Rodriguez:* to protect citizens from committing suicide in moments of weakness.[109] Contrary to now–Chief Justice McLachlin's dissenting reasons in *Rodriguez*, the court concluded that the complete ban on assisted suicide helped to achieve this goal and therefore did not violate the arbitrariness principle.[110] The legislation was overbroad, however, since it caught applicants such as Taylor who were clearly not vulnerable and simply desired to stop their suffering at a point of their choosing.[111] Whether it was reasonably necessary to uphold the complete ban on assisted suicide to protect vulnerable people from committing suicide in moments of weakness was relevant only to whether the law was justifiable under section 1 of the Charter.[112] Since screening procedures could readily be put in place to minimize this risk, the legislation was found not to be minimally impairing and therefore was declared unconstitutional.[113]

Human Smuggling

In *R v Appulonappa*,[114] the accused were charged with smuggling people into Canada contrary to section 117 of the *Immigration and Refugee Protection Act* (*IRPA*).[115] The Supreme Court interpreted the objective of the legislation to be the prevention of "smuggling of people into Canada in the context of organized crime."[116] Parliament had explicitly recognized during the legislative process that its legislation was broad enough to allow for the conviction of those who helped undocumented immigrants to settle in Canada for humanitarian purposes.[117] However, the crown maintained that the requirement in section 117(4) of *IRPA* that all prosecutions be approved by the attorney general would ensure that humanitarian aid cases would not be prosecuted.[118]

Consistent with its jurisprudence in other contexts,[119] the Supreme Court concluded that even a strong likelihood that discretion would be exercised to avoid prosecuting those who helped undocumented migrants to settle in Canada was irrelevant to the overbreadth analysis.[120] As the court observed, "so long as the provision is on the books, and so long as it is *not impossible* that the Attorney General could consent to prosecute," prosecutorial discretion is no response to a finding of overbreadth.[121] Since convicting people for aiding undocumented immigrants for humanitarian purposes would not further the legislative objective of thwarting organized crime, the court found that the legislation was overbroad.[122] As opposed to striking down the impugned law, the court "read down" the provision so that it was "not applicable to persons who give humanitarian, mutual or family assistance."[123]

Sentencing Credit

The Supreme Court in *R v Safarzadeh-Markhali*[124] faced a challenge to restrictions placed on the practice of granting enhanced credit for time spent in pretrial custody pursuant to section 719(3.1) of the *Criminal Code*.[125] Enhanced credit was not available if the judge stated on the record that her primary reason for denying bail was related to the accused's criminal record.[126] As such, an offender who applied for bail, was denied, and subsequently had the judge provide a section 719(3.1) endorsement would receive lower credit than an offender who committed a similar crime with an identical criminal record who chose not to apply for bail.[127]

Although the Supreme Court refused to constitutionalize the proportionality principle in sentencing, it found that restricting the practice of granting enhanced credit based on a factor such as bail eligibility rendered the law overbroad. In so concluding, the court found that the objective of the legislation was to "enhance public safety and security by increasing violent and chronic offenders' access to rehabilitation programs."[128] Yet the scope of the provision applied in circumstances that had nothing to do with enhancing safety and security. For instance, a person with multiple convictions for failing to appear in court might be denied bail despite no reason to suspect that the person posed a threat to public safety or security.[129]

The language used by the Supreme Court for finding an overbreadth breach in *Safarzadeh-Markhali* is also notable. The court stated that a law is overbroad where it goes "further than *reasonably necessary* to achieve its legislative goals."[130] Yet the court also relied on the statement from *Bedford* that an overbroad law "goes too far and interferes with *some* conduct that bears no connection to its objective."[131] The former statement is best framed as an inadvertent mistake as opposed to an attempt to adjust the *Bedford* approach three years after it was adopted. To conclude that a law violates the overbreadth principle only where it goes "further than reasonably necessary" effectively readopts the holistic conception of instrumental rationality. As the court observed in *Bedford*, this approach is imprudent given the undesirability of constitutionalizing elements of the section 1 proportionality test as principles of fundamental justice.

Rethinking Overbreadth

Despite the infrequent use of the overbreadth principle during the first thirty years of the Charter, overbreadth has been much more frequently invoked by litigants post-*Bedford*.[132] This frequent use is unsurprising since the Supreme Court's individualistic conception of overbreadth makes it relatively easy to argue that a law violates the principles of fundamental justice. A litigant must simply define the objective of the legislation and then find one hypothetical instance in which the law applies in a manner that does not forward the objective of the legislation. As several commentators have observed, this approach renders many regulatory and criminal laws in breach of the overbreadth principle.[133]

Despite this foreseeable consequence, the Supreme Court in *Bedford* failed to ask whether its individualistic conception of the instrumental rationality principles qualified as principles of fundamental justice.[134] Put in clear light, the court was now saying that it is a principle of fundamental justice that any law that engages the life, liberty, and security of the person interests must be crafted perfectly and be aligned with its objective in all circumstances. Few people, I think, would agree that such a principle is imperative to whether a law is fundamentally just. This follows for at least one reason: using bright-line rules is a necessary part of modern governance.

There is an extensive debate about when bright-line rules ought to be used in place of a standard. As one author summarizes, with bright-line rules "the Court can buy itself uniformity, predictability, and low decision costs, at the expense of rigidity, inflexibility, and [at times] arbitrary-seeming outcomes. With standards, it can buy itself nuance, flexibility, and case-specific deliberation, at the expense of uncertainty, variability, and high decision costs."[135] The literature debating the merits of employing rules over standards and vice versa is voluminous.[136] For present purposes, however, bright-line rules are clearly accepted as one of two main rule types that are widely used in modern governance.

The need for bright-line rules arises from human fallibility. If given a standard to follow, some people will inevitably fail to further the ends of the law because of errors in judgment. Where human fallibility is particularly acute and prone to serious consequences, bright-line rules are used in place of standards to protect the broader community. These rules are thus tailored to recognize that the law must be drawn broadly so as not to miss any seriously harmful conduct. In so doing, however, bright-line rules typically catch conduct divorced from its objective. As such, these rules can be expected to violate the overbreadth principle as a matter of course if the impugned rule engages an individual's life, liberty, or security of the person interests.

The post-*Bedford* case law illustrates how far the overbreadth doctrine reaches with the individualistic approach. In *R v Michaud*,[137] the Ontario Court of Appeal was asked to decide whether Ontario's *Highway Traffic Act* (*HTA*),[138] and its associated regulations,[139] violated section 7 of the Charter. The relevant provisions required that speed limiters be placed on large vehicles.[140] The accused set his vehicle's speed limiter 4.4 kilometres per hour higher than allowed under the *HTA* and its regulations. The applicant successfully maintained that the speed limiter would jeopardize his life interests in narrow circumstances in which it is necessary to increase speed to avoid an accident. As such, the law was disconnected from its objective of making the roads safer in readily defined circumstances and was therefore declared overbroad.[141]

The Court of Appeal did not mince words in expressing its dissatisfaction with this finding. Writing for the court, Justice Lauwers observed that it was "strangely incongruous to consider highway safety regulation, or any safety regulation, as 'depriving' anyone of 'security of the person' or of engaging the 'principles of fundamental justice' in the sense demanded by s. 7."[142] Justice Lauwers continued by noting that "[regulators may choose] a pro-active bright-line rule in preference to a general behavioural standard, even though such a rule is usually over-inclusive and errs on the side of safety."[143] In the court's view, determining that such a choice breaches "fundamental justice" risks trivializing the concept.[144] As a result, the court suggested resorting to the holistic approach to instrumental rationality in instances in which a regulatory law engages the life, liberty, or security of the person interests of any individual.[145]

It is nevertheless unclear why such trivialization ought to be tolerated at all given the high likelihood that overbreadth will have similar effects in other areas of the law.[146] Criminal law is the next most obvious candidate. Since penal sanctions typically are available when an offender violates a criminal law, the liberty interests of the accused will be engaged, thereby requiring the law to be consistent with the principles of fundamental justice.[147] Any bright-line rule related to a criminal law therefore violates section 7 regardless of whether the use of a standard would inadequately serve the purpose of the legislation.

Section 150.1(1) of the *Criminal Code* is illustrative.[148] That provision sets the age of consent to sexual activity at sixteen. Although there are several exceptions to this rule,[149] the provision would allow for the conviction of a twenty-one-year-old person in a non-exploitative relationship with an emotionally mature teenager who is fifteen years and eleven months old. The teenager's liberty interests are engaged as a result of the state's choice to restrict her sexual conduct. The adult's liberty is engaged given the possibility of imprisonment upon conviction. Since the purpose of the law is to protect young persons from *premature* sexual activity, this hypothetical scenario clearly runs contrary to the purpose of the law. The law is therefore overbroad.[150]

Requiring the truck driver in *Michaud* to "drive safely" or adults to engage in sexual relations only with "sufficiently mature" teenagers provides unclear guidance to those who might cause the serious harms at the heart of these broader prohibitions. For this reason, the Ontario Court of Appeal in *Michaud* viewed the Supreme Court's individualistic conception of overbreadth as "trivializing" the idea of "fundamental justice." The appeal court, however, would have done better to state this conclusion using section 7 language: the individualistic conception of overbreadth is unlikely to attract significant *societal consensus* given the numerous instances in which bright-line rules are necessary tools of modern governance.

This conclusion is not meant to discount the result of each case that applies the individualistic conception of the overbreadth principle. The fact that the laws in *Bedford, Carter,* and *Safarzadeh-Markhali* were not minimally impairing of the liberty and security of the person interests at issue suggests that there is indeed something constitutionally suspect about these laws. A similar conclusion can be drawn with respect to the overbreadth cases decided under the holistic approach to instrumental rationality. Although the reasoning at the section 7 stage of the analysis is unprincipled, the fact that these laws are unjustifiable under section 1 raises clear constitutional concerns. As I contend below, the instrumental rationality defect in all of these laws is more readily framed as a breach of the gross disproportionality principle.

Gross Disproportionality

Although the gross disproportionality principle originated outside the criminal law context,[151] it was developed substantially in the Supreme Court's decision in *Malmo-Levine*. As the court observed, the principle provided an alternative method for constitutionally assessing harm. As opposed to asking whether *any* harm existed, the gross disproportionality principle asked a more determinate question: Are a law's effects grossly disproportionate when compared to its objective?

Possession/Distribution of Marijuana

In addition to arguments pertaining to the arbitrariness and harm principles, the accused in *Malmo-Levine* maintained that the offences of possession for the purpose of trafficking and possession of marijuana violated the gross disproportionality principle.[152] The basis for this challenge implored what criminologists had recognized for centuries: the process of criminal law causes (sometimes serious) harms.[153] If the negative consequences of invoking the criminal justice system are found to be grossly disproportionate to the objective underlying a criminal prohibition, then that law would violate the principles of fundamental justice.

Invoking the criminal justice process against a person causes several harms, many of which stem from the resulting criminal record. Most notably, a criminal record can affect a person's ability to travel and acquire employment and education.[154] The criminal justice process also compels the accused to attend court, which requires a significant time commitment that often results in missing work or incurring other expenses (travel, child care, and so on). These consequences can be especially onerous when the accused is from a lower socio-economic background.[155] The result of a criminal conviction, even for a less serious offence such as possession of marijuana, also requires the accused to bear the stigma of being a criminal.[156]

The accused in *Malmo-Levine* maintained that these consequences outweighed any harm caused by the impugned prohibitions on marijuana. This argument was based on the proposition that the prohibitions were entirely ineffective.[157] In the majority's view, it was inappropriate to speculate on the effectiveness of the impugned prohibitions. As the majority observed, "it remains important that some deference be accorded to Parliament in assessing the utility of its chosen responses to perceived social ills."[158] The majority continued, noting that "the so-called 'ineffectiveness' [of a law] is simply another way of characterizing the refusal of people in the appellants' position to comply with the law."[159] To allow a general willingness to ignore the law to affect the gross disproportionality analysis is plainly contrary to the rule of law.[160]

Although willingness to follow the law is an inappropriate factor in a gross disproportionality assessment, this consideration distracts from the central question of whether the objective of the law is grossly disproportionate when weighed against its effects on those convicted of possessing marijuana. In its sentencing jurisprudence, the Supreme Court recently determined that imposing a minimal mandatory victim surcharge constituted grossly disproportionate punishment under section 12 of the Charter.[161] If a minimal court fee could constitute grossly disproportionate punishment, then it is unclear why similar costs related to the justice system for a non-serious charge such as possession of marijuana could not also have grossly disproportionate effects. Although the subsequent legalization of marijuana has rendered this question moot,[162] the court's failure to engage in a more nuanced analysis is indicative of the court's difficulties applying the gross disproportionality principle in a consistent manner.

Safe Injection Sites
In addition to finding the federal minister's refusal in *PHS* to renew Insite's safe injection site exemption arbitrary, the Supreme Court also found that the decision violated the gross disproportionality principle. In so doing, the court departed from its usual practice of striking down unconstitutional laws by applying only one constitutional right. Although its reasons were brief, the court found that there was no evidence to suggest that safe injection sites such as Insite made society less safe or taxed public health resources.[163] To the contrary, Insite saved lives and was linked to a reduction in crime rates in areas known to be occupied by drug users.[164] Since the law was incapable of achieving its objective, these deprivations of the life, liberty, and security interests of the drug users at Insite, as well as the threat of criminal sanctions posed to staff who continued operations, were found to be "grossly

disproportionate to any benefit that Canada might derive from presenting a uniform stance on the possession of narcotics."[165]

Bawdy House and Communication Prohibitions

The applicants in *Bedford* challenged the constitutionality of three provisions of the *Criminal Code:* the prohibition against living on the avails of sex work, soliciting sex work in public, and keeping or working in a bawdy house.[166] The latter two provisions were struck down for violating the gross disproportionality principle. The prohibition against soliciting sex work in public prevented sex workers from screening clients. As the Supreme Court concluded, "face-to-face communication is an 'essential tool' in enhancing ... [sex workers'] safety."[167] In arriving at this conclusion, the court relied on testimony from sex workers stating that they were able to screen for intoxication and propensity for violence.[168] The provision also had the effect of displacing sex workers to less secure locations since they and their clients would head to more secluded areas to avoid detection by police.[169] These risks to the lives of sex workers were grossly disproportionate when compared to the nuisance-abatement objective of the law.[170]

The bawdy house provisions prohibited selling sex in any "place" that is "kept or occupied" or "resorted to" for the purpose of sex work. This made sex work materially more dangerous. The Supreme Court cited the notorious Canadian serial killer Robert Pickton as evidence of the heinous violence that sex workers face when pursuing their work in public places.[171] As the court observed, allowing sex workers to work from an established bawdy house would provide various safety benefits, including "proximity to others, familiarity with surroundings, security staff, closed-circuit television and other such monitoring that a permanent indoor location can facilitate."[172] Forgoing these basic safety measures was found to be grossly disproportionate compared to the nuisance abatement objective of the prohibition on bawdy houses, the maintenance of which the court found rarely gave rise to public complaints.[173]

Overlap between Overbreadth and Gross Disproportionality

In *Khawaja*, the Supreme Court observed that the overbreadth and gross disproportionality principles are at least *analytically* distinct.[174] However, the court also recognized that the interrelation between these concepts "may simply offer different lenses through which to consider a single breach of the principles of fundamental justice."[175] Similarly, in *Bedford*, the court recognized that there was "significant overlap" between the instrumental rationality principles.[176] The Supreme Court went further in *R v Clay*,[177] the companion case to *Malmo-Levine*, suggesting that "overbreadth ... addresses the potential infringement of fundamental justice where the adverse effect of a legislative measure on the individuals subject to its strictures is grossly disproportionate to the state interest the legislation seeks to protect."[178]

The appellate court decisions in *Bedford* and *Carter* illustrate how the overbreadth and gross disproportionality principles can overlap. Although Parliament maintained that the prohibition against living on the avails of sex work protected sex workers from exploitation, the provision also prevented them from hiring protective employees such as bodyguards, drivers, and receptionists. The law was therefore overbroad. As the Ontario Court of Appeal concluded in *Bedford*, a law that puts the lives of innocent citizens at risk without being capable of achieving its objective in readily definable scenarios has grossly disproportionate effects.[179]

In *Carter*, the goal of the law was to protect vulnerable persons from being tempted to commit suicide in moments of weakness. Yet people might reasonably request assistance in dying to avoid the cruel choice of ending their lives when capable of doing so or enduring a slow, agonizing death. In finding that the law breached both the overbreadth and the gross disproportionality principles, the British Columbia Court of Appeal similarly blended the analyses underlying the two principles.[180] As the court concluded, the potential of the law to result in premature deaths "is grossly disproportionate ... to the goal of protecting the vulnerable when such protections can be achieved through the regulation of physician-assisted dying."[181]

The conception of gross disproportionality utilized by the Ontario and British Columbia Courts of Appeal is unique because it compares the negative effects of the law to the inability of the law to achieve its objective in some circumstance. It is unsurprising that such a comparison yields a grossly disproportionate effect. By definition, every law assessed for consistency with the principles of fundamental justice infringes life, liberty, or security of the person. Given the importance of these interests, comparing them to a narrow, inefficacious application of the law will result, as a matter of course, in effects totally out of sync with the law's ability to achieve its objective in the impugned circumstance.

This conception of gross disproportionality arguably should not be adopted under the Supreme Court's individualistic approach to instrumental rationality. First, the approach would result in a complete overlap between the overbreadth and gross disproportionality principles. This is problematic for a simple reason: if the individualistic conception of overbreadth failed to qualify as a principle of fundamental justice for applying too broadly, then the same conclusion arguably should follow for an equally broad conception of the gross disproportionality principle. It is possible, however, that the gross disproportionality principle's mirror relationship to section 12 of the Charter provides sufficient support for the individualistic conception of gross disproportionality to keep its status as a principle of fundamental justice. Since section 12 prohibits grossly disproportionate punishments of any individual, it is not unreasonable to conclude that other actions that give rise to similar effects on an individual should also be constitutionally prohibited. Since the Supreme Court has interpreted the word *treatment* in section 12 narrowly, it is at least arguable that this other aspect of grossly disproportionate state action should be prohibited under section 7.[182]

Second, the approach utilized by the appellate courts in *Bedford* and *Carter* is doctrinally inconsistent since these cases predate the Supreme Court's requirement that the legislative objective be taken at "face value."[183] This requirement necessitates that courts *presume* that an impugned law achieves its objective at the section 7 stage of the analysis.[184] Presuming that a law achieves its objective nevertheless creates its own problem: it shields some grossly disproportionate laws from constitutional challenge.

The Supreme Court's decision in *PHS* is illustrative. Given the risks to life from illicit drug use, the government maintained that its decision to shut down Insite furthered public health and safety by deterring drug use. Assuming that the law accomplished this purpose, it is questionable whether proof that Parliament's decision also had the effect of endangering lives would be sufficient to demonstrate disproportionality, let alone gross disproportionality. Yet the ability of the law to deter drug use, especially by drug addicts, is tenuous at best.[185] As such, affording litigants the opportunity to challenge the law's ability to achieve its objective is necessary for at least some gross disproportionality challenges.[186] Such a challenge was possible in *PHS* because the Supreme Court was still applying the holistic, not individualistic, conception of instrumental rationality.

This issue with the gross disproportionality analysis can be addressed by considering the extent to which the law actually fulfills its objective at the section 7 stage. In so doing, however, it is also necessary to ensure that the burden of proof is not unfairly placed on the applicant. To achieve these ends, the applicant could begin by showing that the law has a grossly disproportionate effect on a single person when compared to the ability of the law to achieve its objective in a particular circumstance. The applicant could then be required to show that the government's objective likely is not fully realized in practice and that a lesser achievement of its objective could tip the balance in favour of a holistic finding of gross disproportionality. With such proof, the government could be required to provide the court with evidence of the extent to which the government's objective is fulfilled in practice. By adopting this strategy, the Supreme Court would be well placed to weigh the actual effect of the law on individual rights against the true benefits of the law, without placing an unduly onerous burden of proof on the applicant.

This approach would lead to a different result in the most problematic case decided under the individualistic conception of the instrumental rationality principles: the Ontario Court of Appeal's decision in *Michaud*. The accused could have provided evidence demonstrating that there are instances when requiring a speed limiter for large vehicles does not achieve its objective and endangers the life of one hypothetical individual. The accused then could have argued that, if such a scenario were to arise often enough, it could lead to grossly disproportionate effects depending on the extent to which the law achieves its objective. The state could then provide evidence demonstrating the extent to which the speed limiter realizes its aim. At that point, a court would be able to assess, in a holistic manner, whether the law results in a grossly disproportionate effect. Since speed limiters prevent far more accidents than they cause,[187] a comparison of the lives saved with those lost would avoid any finding that the law violated the gross disproportionality principle.

This approach is also workable in circumstances in which the applicant must concede that the law achieves its aim but maintains that it should do more to protect the threshold interests in section 7. The *Carter* case is illustrative. The applicant could prove that a non-vulnerable person reasonably would desire assistance in committing suicide. The applicant could then show that many people are in a similar position, thereby demonstrating the potential for a grossly disproportionate effect depending on the extent to which the state's law achieves its objective. The crown could then be required to prove not only that the law achieves its objective but also that it is a reasonably necessary means to do so. Given the ease with which procedural safeguards can be instituted to ensure that vulnerable persons do not commit suicide in moments of weakness, the state would be unable to disprove gross disproportionality.

This blended approach to the instrumental rationality principles nevertheless preserves two of the three main concerns about the holistic conception of instrumental rationality. First, mixing the individualistic and holistic conceptions of instrumental rationality renders the section 1 analysis redundant. The fact that other rights are also unjustifiable under section 1, however, mitigates this concern to some extent.[188] Second, the blended approach is inconsistent with the wording of section 7. Recall that the plain wording of section 7 suggests that it applies if *anyone* is affected in a manner inconsistent with a principle of fundamental justice. The reconceptualized principles offered above assess the effects of the law as it applies to *all* affected parties. Whether this inconsistency is worth preserving depends largely on whether the instrumental rationality principles serve their broader purpose of creating constructive dialogue between courts and legislatures about the scope of rights.

Theorizing Instrumental Rationality

In its recent jurisprudence, the Supreme Court has stated that the instrumental rationality principles are now its preferred principles of substantive review.[189] This observation solidified what some scholars already suspected: the court was moving away from constitutionalizing principles of criminal law theory.[190] This switch in method of section 7 review raises two questions. First, what purpose do the principles of instrumental rationality serve that the principles of criminal law theory do not? Second, will the court's preference for using the instrumental rationality principles have a narrower, broader, or similar impact on the substantive criminal law?

Instrumental Rationality and Legislative Dialogue

As detailed in the preceding chapter, the Supreme Court's aim in constitutionalizing principles of criminal law theory was to create greater coherence and fairness in the substantive criminal law. This is a laudable goal since legislatures are likely to disregard minority interests in the criminal law setting given majoritarian pressures to be "tough on crime." At the same time, the court was cognizant that its decision to allow for substantive review under section 7 of the Charter was controversial from a democratic standpoint. Allowing courts to choose from its favoured philosophical principles when striking down democratically enacted laws provides them with much more power than simply allowing them to strike down laws based on rights explicitly chosen by the drafters of the Charter.[191]

This controversy is worsened by the fact that the Supreme Court maintained for many years that breaches of section 7 can be justified only in uncommon circumstances.[192] As the court observed in the *Motor Vehicle Act Reference,* breaches of fundamental justice can be justified "only in cases arising out of exceptional conditions, such as natural disasters, the outbreak of war, [and] epidemics."[193] Although the court recently softened this view in *Bedford*,[194] it is unclear whether the court meant to allow for section 1 justifications outside the context of instrumental rationality.[195] If the court still opposes using section 1 to justify breaches of its moral philosophical principles, then it will continue to close the main vehicle for dialogue under this category of section 7 review.

In my view, it was this controversy that caused the Supreme Court to seek a more democratically legitimate method of substantive review.[196] As opposed to abandoning its decision that section 7 rights are effectively unjustifiable under section 1, the court placed significantly greater emphasis on the principles of instrumental rationality and developed them in a way that provided the legislature with more room to respond to judicial rulings. The instrumental rationality principles opened up legislative-judicial dialogue in three ways. First, the legislature may broaden the objective of its law, thereby aligning the effects of the law with its objective. Second, the legislature may narrow the scope of the law to avoid any negative effects identified by a court. Third, the legislature may place greater emphasis on law enforcement interests to ensure that the law strikes a more tolerable balance between law enforcement interests and individual rights.

It is notable at the outset that legislative responses to the Supreme Court's decisions to constitutionalize principles of criminal law theory that did more than simply accept the court's decisions were few and far between.[197] Most drastically, Parliament responded to the court's decision in *R v Daviault*[198] to modify the common law intoxication rule to allow accused persons to plead intoxication as a defence to general intent offences. Section 33.1 of the *Criminal Code* was passed to prevent intoxication from being pleaded to general intent offences of violence. This response stemmed from the controversial nature of the case, widely vilified for allowing men to use alcohol consumption to excuse sexual assaults against women.[199] Parliament's response has been upheld under section 1 by some trial courts, though the dominant view is that the provision violates section 7 in a manner that is unjustifiable under section 1 of the Charter.[200]

Parliament also responded to the Supreme Court's decision in *R v Wholesale Travel Group Inc*[201] by increasing the *mens rea* requirement for the offence of false corporate advertising.[202] The offence's constitutional defect was its ability to convict a corporation that otherwise acted in a duly diligent manner if it did not immediately correct its ad post-publication. Given the regulatory nature of the offence, it is unlikely that full *mens rea* is required to satisfy the principles of fundamental justice. Instead, it is likely that a due diligence defence typically provided for regulatory offences would suffice. Parliament's generous redrafting of this regulatory offence, however, is notably in the corporate context. Public choice theorists expect powerful corporations to achieve law reform to meet their interests given their ability to use wealth to influence political action.[203] Although difficult to prove, it is plausible that the generous redrafting of this provision arose for reasons related to public choice theory, not because the legislature took the court's concerns in *Wholesale Travel* seriously.

Several provincial legislatures also provided a response to the Supreme Court's decision in the *Motor Vehicle Act Reference*.[204] As detailed in the previous chapters, the impugned provision required a seven-day term of imprisonment if a person was caught driving without a licence. The provision also applied regardless of whether the actor possessed any fault for committing the offence. Although some legislatures responded by requiring an element of fault,[205] Alberta responded by restricting the punishment related to absolute liability offences to a fine, explicitly excluding any possibility of imprisonment or probation.[206] As a result, the law did not engage the life, liberty, or security of the person interests under section 7 and thus did not need to comply with the principles of fundamental justice.

The former and the latter legislative responses are explainable by observing that the constitutionalization of a principle of criminal law theory creates a strict "no-go zone" for a legislature. In turn, this forces the legislature either to work around the judicial ruling or explicitly to overrule the decision. Although the better route to overrule a decision might be to invoke the notwithstanding clause, it is understandable that Parliament would want to forgo admitting a Charter violation by justifying a section 7–infringing law with pressing and substantial policy reasons. However, the current approach of the Supreme Court to the relationship between sections 7 and 1 makes it unclear whether the court will accept such an argument.

Although legislative responses to the court's decisions to strike down criminal laws based on principles of criminal law theory were rare, such responses to recent decisions employing the instrumental rationality principles have occurred much more frequently.[207] Parliament replied to the Supreme Court's decision in *PHS* by modifying the rules governing whether safe injection sites would receive an exemption.[208] It also responded to *Bedford* by repealing the old sex work laws and designing a new regime with admirable expediency.[209] It took a similar course of action in response to *Carter*. Within less than two years, Parliament passed laws allowing limited access to medical assistance in dying.[210] And, when part of that law was struck down in the lower courts,[211] Parliament again swiftly began the process of devising a new law.[212] Parliament also responded quickly to the *Safarzadeh-Markhali* decision by repealing the unconstitutional limitation for refusing to grant sentencing credit for time served on remand but maintaining the lower 1.5:1 ratio for granting credit.[213]

Parliament even responded to recent cases employing the instrumental rationality principles before the Supreme Court was able to rule on the constitutionality of the provisions. In response to the lower court ruling in *Appulonappa*, Parliament amended the *Immigration and Refugee Protection Act*[214] to avoid the possibility of allowing prosecutions of people who help undocumented immigrants for humanitarian purposes.[215] More substantially, Parliament recently responded to two appellate court rulings striking down provisions of the *Corrections and Conditional Release Act (CCRA)*[216] permitting the use of solitary confinement.[217] The cases were subsequently granted leave to appeal to the Supreme Court and were scheduled to be heard in 2020.[218]

Although Parliament has recently shown much more willingness to respond to constitutional judgments striking down laws based on violations of the instrumental rationality principles, that does not mean that these responses engaged with the Supreme Court's reasoning in a "dialogical" manner. In their seminal article, Peter Hogg and Allison Bushell state that dialogue occurs when "a judicial decision striking down a law on *Charter* grounds can be reversed, modified, or avoided by a new law."[219] Importantly, however, not all responses count as genuine dialogues despite this broad definition. As Kent Roach observes, instances of what he aptly calls an "in-your-face" response do not count as democratic dialogue.[220] Legislative decisions that usurp judicial decisions by claiming that the reasoning was "wrong" should instead invoke the tool designed specifically for expressing such disagreement: the notwithstanding clause.[221]

The approach to dialogue against which Roach argues, and which I maintain has become common in response to the Supreme Court's recent instrumental rationality jurisprudence, is referred to more generally in the literature as "coordinate interpretation."[222] This approach maintains that both courts and legislatures have the power to interpret the Charter, and thus legislatures act legitimately when enacting laws that explicitly overturn judicial decisions.[223] For critics of dialogue, instances of coordinate interpretation count as actual instances of dialogue.[224] This follows because coordinate interpretation provides a more tangible response to the charge that judges act illegitimately when they strike down democratically enacted laws: it allows legislatures to overrule or modify decisions with which they disagree. For Roach, however, this understanding of dialogue is "dangerous"[225] for a powerful reason: allowing a legislature to assert that its response is constitutional with mere legislation "risks making a legislature a judge in its own majoritarian causes."[226]

Several of Parliament's recent responses discussed above illustrate a lack of dialogue in the sense described by Roach. The Conservative Party's response to the *PHS* decision was to enact the *Respect for Communities Act*.[227] This legislation – elsewhere described as "mean spirited" – imposed twenty-six strict criteria that must be followed before a safe injection site could be exempted from federal drug laws.[228] In effect, this deterred many cities from applying for safe injection sites and prevented many other applications from being successful.[229] As opposed to listening to the empirical conclusions of the Supreme Court, Parliament determined that scoring political points was more important than saving the lives of drug-addicted citizens. This was therefore an "in-your-face" response.[230]

Parliament's response to *Bedford* also failed to engage in dialogue since its new laws did not make sex work any safer than before.[231] The main innovation of the new sex work laws was to change their objective from nuisance abatement to denouncing and deterring sex work.[232] Sex work itself is also no longer legal, although it cannot be prosecuted.[233] Making sex work illegal and affirming the new law's more pressing and substantial objective constitute the main response to *Bedford*: it places significantly more weight on law enforcement interests. The legislation also purports to make engaging in sex work safer.[234] It claims to do so by replacing the bawdy house and living on the avails of sex work provision[235] and narrowing the scope of the former communications offence.[236]

Yet, as Hamish Stewart contends, these provisions do little, if anything, to improve the safety of sex workers.[237] The main prohibition against "materially benefitting" from sex work prohibits living off the avails of sex work subject to several exceptions. These exceptions, however, can exclude those working in a "commercial enterprise" that could feasibly prevent receptionists, drivers, and bodyguards from working for sex workers.[238] At the same time, Stewart argues that the material benefit offence makes it practically impossible to work indoors with anyone else present. It does so by requiring that sex workers own the property where the work takes place and prohibiting the workers from working in groups. It is therefore unlikely that sex workers will be able to work indoors for financial reasons, and if they do the law appears to require that they work alone.[239]

The inefficacy of these provisions leaves the new sex work laws open to challenge under section 7 of the Charter. Such a challenge could raise the fact that purporting to deter sex work is likely an impossible objective to attain in all instances. Indeed, it would not be difficult to find evidence that many sex workers enter the trade because of a lack of realistic choice.[240] The result is that the new restrictions are likely to put many sex workers in the same sorts of danger identified in *Bedford*. It is therefore possible that the material benefit offence will violate the gross disproportionality principle since it endangers the lives of many sex workers who had no realistic choice but to become sex workers.[241] Notably, however, this challenge requires abandoning the presumption that the law achieves its objective at the section 7 stage of analysis, which likely would require a significant overhaul of how a breach of the gross disproportionality principle is proven.

The case law challenging the new sex work laws is limited to date. In *R v Boodhoo*,[242] the Ontario Superior Court of Justice pithily dismissed an application to strike down the new sex work laws for violating section 7 of the Charter.[243] However, as subsequent case law has shown, the court's analysis was not informed by an adequate evidentiary record, in part because the constitutional issues were raised only after the conclusion of the jury trial.[244] The limited expert evidence presented in *Boodhoo* has also been criticized judicially for being biased in favour of the crown.[245]

The only other case considering the constitutionality of the new sex work laws found that they caused many of the same harms as the previous laws without substantially protecting or deterring sex workers, and they were struck down largely on that basis.[246] This case did not engage, however, with the doctrinal difficulties underlying the instrumental rationality principles and relied heavily on the overbreadth principle in its reasoning.[247] Regardless, the fact that judicial and academic commentators find the same harms in the new sex work laws without any of the benefits that the laws purport to achieve strongly suggests that Parliament is engaging in coordinate construction, not democratic dialogue.

With respect to Parliament's response to *Carter*, the Liberal Party's regulatory scheme for euthanasia contradicted *Carter* in at least one key respect.[248] It required reasonable foreseeability of death before authorizing euthanasia.[249] Yet the Supreme Court concluded that euthanasia was constitutionally available to anyone who "clearly consents to the termination of life and ... has a grievous and irremediable medical condition (including an illness, disease or disability) that causes enduring suffering that is intolerable to the individual in the circumstances of his or her condition."[250] There is no mention of reasonable foreseeability of death as a prerequisite for receiving euthanasia.

Parliament did not interpret the *Carter* decision as a rights floor below which the legislature must not go. Instead, it interpreted the decision narrowly as applying only to the balance struck under the previous complete ban on euthanasia. In other words, the crown maintained that the instrumental rationality principles allow for a rebalancing within Parliament's new legal context.[251] Although this interpretation is correct, it is difficult to reconcile this approach with the clear language in *Carter* constitutionally allowing for euthanasia in circumstances in which reasonable foreseeability of death is absent.[252] Indeed, this was precisely the conclusion arrived at by the first court ruling on the constitutionality of Parliament's response to *Carter*.[253]

It is unlikely that supporters of dialogue theory would view the *Carter* decision as an instance of dialogue.[254] As Peter Hogg observed during an appearance before the Senate, "[Ms.] Carter herself would not have satisfied the new conditions in the bill ... Parliament can't turn around and suddenly exclude from the right a group of people that have just been granted the right by the Supreme Court."[255] Hogg clearly did not view Parliament's response to be a legitimate form of dialogue. This view finds further support in the fact that Parliament did not attempt to justify its legislation as a form of dialogue under section 1 of the Charter. Instead, the government explicitly appealed to the concept of coordinate interpretation when justifying its law.[256]

A more evasive tactic was recently employed with respect to Parliament's rules regarding the practice of solitary confinement. Provisions under the *CCRA* allowed for prisoners to be placed in isolation for twenty-two hours a day.[257] These provisions constituted solitary confinement pursuant to the internationally adopted Mandela Rules.[258] Since the impugned laws did not place any limits on the length of time that a person could be detained, the *CCRA*'s scheme also authorized prolonged solitary confinement contrary to the Mandela Rules.[259] The Ontario and British Columbia Courts of Appeal found Parliament's solitary confinement scheme to be overbroad, to be grossly disproportionate, and to constitute cruel and unusual punishment.[260] In short, the use of solitary confinement was found to cause serious physical and mental harms to inmates contrary and grossly disproportionate to the impugned law's ability to achieve its aim of increasing institutional security.[261]

Despite being granted leave to appeal by the Supreme Court,[262] the crown abandoned its appeal. In so doing, it passed on an invaluable opportunity to gain constitutional guidance on Parliament's intermediary legislative response in Bill C-83.[263] As Adelina Iftene and her co-authors observe, the Liberal Party was likely concerned that the court would comment on the constitutionality of Bill C-83's new "structured intervention units."[264] These units do not end the practice of prolonged solitary confinement. Instead, they provide two additional hours per day of time outside solitary confinement during which the prisoner must have meaningful human contact. Since there is no evidence that these changes avoid the harsh consequences of solitary confinement, Iftene suggests that the Supreme Court likely would have commented on the constitutionality of these provisions.[265] By forgoing the appeal, the federal government not only ensured that a new round of litigation would be required but also strongly implied that it is not interested in participating in dialogue with the court about the constitutionality of its legislation.

It might be retorted that the responses to the instrumental rationality cases – in particular, *PHS*, *Bedford*, and *Carter* – are similar in principle to Parliament's response to *Daviault:* politically charged responses to controversial social issues. The difference, however, is that Parliament's response to *Daviault* was not seriously argued to be consistent with section 7 of the Charter. The argument – a longshot given the Supreme Court's stance on section 1 justifications of section 7 rights – was that Parliament's significant narrowing of the intoxication defence was justified under section 1. The legislative responses to the instrumental rationality cases were argued to be *consistent* with Charter rights despite sometimes having identical effects on the same vulnerable groups as their predecessor laws and providing no evidence that the new laws would achieve their lofty objectives. Such arguments are plausible because the structure of the instrumental rationality principles allows Parliament to modify the law's means or claim that a law serves an important objective without any scrutiny of its ability to achieve that objective at the section 7 stage of analysis.[266]

If the Supreme Court abandons the presumption that laws achieve their objectives at the section 7 stage of analysis, then it is possible, for the reasons explained earlier, to force the state to prove the extent to which the law actually achieves its objective. Even with this approach, however, Parliament can pass a criminal law with a slightly different objective and plausibly claim that it does not violate Charter rights since such a finding would turn largely on the empirical evidence supporting the extent to which the law achieves its objective and balances its effects. In my view, Parliament is much less likely to pass politically charged responses when it must admit a Charter violation. Admittedly, the empirical evidence for this claim is somewhat thin.[267] Nevertheless, this argument is supported by the fact that Parliament only responded to one criminal law theory ruling in a politically charged manner but has made a recent habit of so responding to the court's decisions applying the instrumental rationality principles.

Instrumental Rationality and Judicial Dialogue
Commentators have also criticized the Supreme Court's participation in the dialogue arising from employing the instrumental rationality principles.[268] As one author observes, "the rush to fit constitutional challenges into the new paradigm of 'overbreadth' [has resulted in an inability to] look at the actual impact of the legislation itself."[269] My review of the

court's overbreadth jurisprudence supports this contention. Nothing in the court's conception of overbreadth required a detailed assessment of the impugned law's impact on individual citizens. However, the gross disproportionality principle makes the impact of the law on individuals central to the analysis. If I am correct that this principle has crowded out overbreadth, then this criticism of the instrumental rationality principles is of little moment.

The critique that determining a singular legislative aim will often be contrary to legislative intent has much more bite.[270] The Supreme Court has recognized that legislation often "does not simply further one goal but rather strikes a balance among several goals, some of which may be in tension."[271] In the context of instrumental rationality, the court nevertheless reduces legislation to a singular purpose. Placing such high importance on a law's objective typically results in significant disagreements between the litigating parties. For instance, the court in *PHS* concluded that the purpose underlying the *CDSA* was the same as the minister's purpose in refusing to renew Insite's exemption: enhancing public health and safety.[272] Yet the provision authorizing the exemption permitted the minister to grant exemptions for broader purposes such as if "the exemption is necessary for a medical or scientific purpose or is otherwise in the public interest."[273] As Hart Schwartz observes, the minister's decision would not have been arbitrary or grossly disproportionate if the results of completing the safe injection experiment were unreliable or incomplete.[274]

In contrast to *PHS*, the Supreme Court in *Bedford* switched tactics and assessed the impugned provisions individually as opposed to ascertaining their purpose as a whole. This position undermined the crown's argument that the provisions were meant to deter sex work and prevent its commercialization to better uphold the dignity and equality interests of sex workers.[275] Instead, the court found that the narrower objectives of "nuisance abatement" and prevention of exploitation of sex workers underlie Parliament's previous sex work laws.[276] These narrower objectives made it relatively easy to find breaches of the overbreadth and gross disproportionality principles.[277]

The Supreme Court in *Carter* similarly refused to adopt the crown's understanding of the purpose of the law prohibiting assisted suicide. In the crown's view, the aim of the law was to "preserve life" by using the criminal law to deter any suicide attempt.[278] The court found, however, that the purpose of the law was simply to protect the vulnerable.[279] Given this narrower objective, it was impossible for a complete ban on euthanasia to comply with the instrumental rationality principles of fundamental justice. The court's insistence on finding a narrower legislative purpose than that proposed by the crown again preordained its conclusion under section 7 of the Charter.

In a series of post-*Carter* cases, the Supreme Court revised what had been described as its "summary" and "fast and loose" approach to determining legislative objectives in the constitutional context.[280] In terms of general guidance, the court made several observations. First, the text of the provision is not dispositive of legislative intent.[281] Second, courts must pitch the objective of a law at the appropriate level of generality. To find that a law forwards some "animating social value" or to restate the objective of the law in terms synonymous with the legislative text is therefore to be avoided.[282] Third, the objective must be stated in a manner that is "both precise and succinct" but also captures "the main thrust of the law."[283] Fourth, construing a law's objective must not be conflated with an assessment of the appropriateness or achievability of the objective. Instrumental rationality analysis takes the objective "at face value."[284]

In accordance with this guidance, the Supreme Court developed a multi-step approach to determine legislative purpose that relies on sources derived primarily from the legislative process. First, the court must look to statutory statements of purpose in the legislation and its preamble to discern legislative intent. Second, the court can aid its reasoning by observing the text, context, and scheme of the legislation. Third, the court can rely on relevant extrinsic evidence, such as speeches from the minister responsible for introducing the legislation.[285] Although each type of evidence is considered in a hierarchical manner, courts must consider the "full context" in determining the objective of a piece of legislation.[286]

This "rigorous approach" to interpreting legislative objectives has received praise from Marcus Moore.[287] The fact that the Supreme Court's new approach in the constitutional context mirrors that of statutory interpretation more generally lends credibility to the court's instrumental rationality principles of justice. As Moore observes, the process of determining legislative intention carries with it the possibility of frequent charges that courts are redrafting legislation.[288] Yet the Supreme Court's approach to statutory interpretation has been interpreted as "the epitome of a 'dry' exercise in neutral application of legal technique by specially-trained experts."[289] If the court's instrumental rationality principles mimic this approach, then concerns about the legitimacy of employing these principles will be diminished.[290]

This new approach to determining legislative objectives is nevertheless set to collide with Parliament's recent tendency to spell out broad objectives of a law in legislative preambles and purpose clauses.[291] For instance, one of Parliament's objectives in the new sex work laws can be described as an "animating social value,"[292] namely upholding the "dignity" and "equality" interests of sex workers. The new sex work laws' other objective of "deterring" sex work is also cast broadly. Since both of these objectives are clearly prescribed in the authorizing legislation, the Supreme Court will have to decide whether these broad purposes are permissible in light of their potential inconsistency with its new approach to determining legislative objectives. Alternatively, if the court adopts the approach to instrumental rationality that I outlined earlier, then it might simply require the state to prove the extent to which its legislation is capable of achieving its objectives at the section 7 stage of the analysis.

Overlap with Principles of Criminal Law Theory

If the myriad concerns about the Supreme Court's instrumental rationality principles can be addressed, then a second question arises: Do the instrumental rationality principles apply in a broader, narrower, or similar manner as the principles of criminal law theory constitutionalized under section 7 of the Charter? It is unproductive at this juncture to take a position on whether it would be a constitutional "good" if instrumental rationality led to a broader or narrower conception of substantive rights. For my purposes, determining whether the court's principles of criminal law theory and instrumental rationality overlap can aid in answering a more basic question: the extent to which judges choose from among competing principles of justice under section 7 when striking down substantive criminal laws.

The fact that alternative constitutional arguments were made in most of the Supreme Court's section 7 jurisprudence suggests that there is significant overlap between the principles of criminal law theory and instrumental rationality. This overlap, however, is not complete. Beginning with the court's jurisprudence on abortion, Justice Wilson in *Morgentaler* concluded that the right to choose whether to have an abortion is fundamental to the dignity and autonomy interests of women.[293] However, this argument was not distilled into a basic principle of fundamental justice. Instead, Justice Wilson came to this conclusion within the context of considering whether the threshold liberty interest in section 7 was engaged by a criminal prohibition against abortion. She went on to find that the law breached a separate provision of the Charter – the right to freedom of conscience in section 2(a) – which she adopted as a principle of fundamental justice to bolster her conclusion that the impugned law violated section 7.

Justice Wilson could nevertheless have followed the US Supreme Court's jurisprudence interpreting the analogous due process clause of the Fourteenth Amendment of the American Constitution. That clause prohibits the state from denying any person "life, liberty or property, without due process of law." Despite the procedural nature of this clause, the US Supreme Court has determined that certain aspects of liberty are so fundamental that no procedural protections or third-party interests can reasonably deny the pursuit of a fundamental liberty. In *Roe v Wade*,[294] the US Supreme Court found a limited right to abortion within this understanding of liberty.

The Canadian Supreme Court's interpretation of section 7 of the Charter differs from the due process clause of the Fourteenth Amendment. The dominant view is that liberty operates as a threshold interest that, upon being engaged, requires the impugned law to be consistent with the principles of fundamental justice. Although the "fundamental importance" of a given liberty interest is sufficient to engage section 7 of the Charter,[295] the court has not gone so far as to constitutionalize a right to any threshold liberty interest. Operating within this limitation, Justice Wilson's reasons in *Morgentaler* confusingly employed a principle of fundamental justice enumerated elsewhere in the Charter to find a breach of section 7, namely the right to freedom of conscience.[296] It is unclear why Justice Wilson did not simply apply the right to freedom of conscience to find the law unconstitutional. Without invoking freedom of conscience or some other enumerated principle as a principle of fundamental justice,[297] it is difficult to conceive how the impugned law would have violated the principles of fundamental justice.

Yet the Supreme Court has not foreclosed allowing the infringement of a threshold interest to constitute a breach of section 7 of the Charter. In *Gosselin v Quebec (Attorney General)*,[298] Justice Arbour observed in her dissenting reasons that the language of section 7 avails two distinct rights. Section 7 provides that "everyone has the right to life, liberty, and security of the person and the right not to be deprived thereof except in accordance with the principles of fundamental justice." The first clause arguably provides a free-standing "right to life, liberty, and security of the person" subject to section 1 justification. The inclusion of the "principles of fundamental justice" in the second clause can be read as an internal limitation on any infringements of the threshold interests, operating in a manner similar in principle to section 1.[299] The majority in *Gosselin* left open the possibility that such an interpretation could allow for even positive rights to derive from the "right" to life, liberty, or security of the person.[300]

Building on Justice Wilson's conclusion that choosing whether to have an abortion is of fundamental importance to a woman's liberty interest, one should ask whether any barrier to receiving an abortion is justifiable under section 1. Routine engagement of the liberty interest – typically arising from the potential to go to jail upon conviction of an offence – would be readily justified under section 1. However, when the liberty interest is of "fundamental importance,"[301] it is likely that the minimal impairment branch of the section 1 test would be substantially more difficult to meet. If no reasonable procedures could be implemented or competing interests identified to justify the complete ban on a fundamental liberty, then the liberty interest would crystallize into a substantive right. In the context of determining the extent of the right to abortion under section 1, the Supreme Court would need to consider whether the interests of the fetus at any point outweigh the liberty interests of the mother.[302]

A similar argument could be made for constitutionally prohibiting the state from limiting the practice of assisted suicide. In *Rodriguez,* the applicant maintained that the need to respect the human dignity of individuals constituted a principle of fundamental justice.[303] Although the Supreme Court reasonably refused to constitutionalize this principle, in *Carter* it found at the threshold stage of the section 7 analysis that the ability to choose the timing of one's death is fundamental to an individual's personal privacy and liberty.[304] It is therefore arguable that only reasonable procedural limits directed at ensuring that vulnerable persons are not encouraged to commit suicide in moments of weakness could be instituted to limit the substantive right to euthanasia.[305]

Turning to the remaining cases employing instrumental rationality principles, it is possible that the vagrancy offence in *Heywood* could have been struck down for violating a principle of criminal law theory: status offences are not crimes. Such offences are those that require neither an act nor an omission, instead punishing a person for her state of being. Use of criminal law in this context amounts to "punishing an individual for *who he or she is* rather than how he or she chose to act."[306] Quoting *R v Graf,*[307] the Supreme Court in *Heywood* agreed that the vagrancy prohibition placed the accused "in a permanent state of exile within his community who is, *because of his status*, absolutely prohibited from standing idly in vast areas of this country."[308] Leading commentators have suggested that a status offence would violate section 7 of the Charter.[309]

It is nevertheless questionable whether the vagrancy prohibition qualified as a status offence.[310] Such an offence prohibits one's state of being without reference to any act or omission.[311] The sex work laws in force in the 1970s are illustrative. Section 175(1)(c) of the *Criminal Code* prohibited "being a common prostitute or night walker ... in a public place."[312] Although sex work was legal, the provision effectively prohibited one from being a sex worker in public. The vagrancy prohibition differed in that it disallowed conduct because of a prior breach of the criminal law. If an accused was convicted for a sexual offence against children, then it was rational to prohibit that person from being in places where children were likely to be present.

It might nevertheless be argued that the vagrancy offence operated as a status offence to the extent that the impugned prohibition was disconnected from its objective. An offender convicted of sexual assault against an adult would receive the same prohibition as an offender convicted of child molestation. The former offender would be prohibited from being in public parks – where children are expected to be present – even though there is no rational connection between the offence and the prohibition. Convicting such a person for being in a place where children are likely to be present for the mere state of being a sex offender uses irrelevant criteria to sustain a conviction of vagrancy.

In *Demers*, the accused relied on the overbreadth principle to strike down a law requiring all individuals found permanently unfit to stand trial to undergo disposition hearings until they are fit to stand trial. Although it is difficult to conceive of an alternative, non-enumerated substantive principle to address this breach, it is contestable that the central issue with the impugned law in *Demers* is procedural in nature. The accused also argued that permanently unfit accused persons by definition could never be tried within a reasonable time, contrary to section 11(b) of the Charter.[313] As Justice LeBel observed in his dissenting reasons, "the violation results from the intersection of the legislation with an immutable personal characteristic of the accused."[314] If accused persons such as Demers cannot be tried within a reasonable time because of their permanent mental states, then legislation allowing for such prosecutions to continue indefinitely clearly violates section 11(b) of the Charter.[315]

The sex workers affected by the laws at issue in *Bedford* could have pleaded a constitutional principle that the Supreme Court had already constitutionalized under section 7: morally involuntary conduct is not criminal.[316] The court correctly recognized that many sex workers are involved in the trade for reasons other than personal choice. As the court observed, "whether because of financial desperation, drug addictions, mental illness, or compulsion from pimps, [sex workers] often have little choice but to sell their bodies for money."[317] As the court continued, "realistically, while they may retain some minimal power of choice ... these are not people who can be said to be truly 'choosing' a risky line of business."[318]

The Supreme Court's language in *Bedford* implicitly applies the conception of moral involuntariness constitutionalized in *R v Ruzic*.[319] It is arguable that sex workers, to protect themselves from the various dangers inherent in their work, will at times need to take basic precautions such as screening clients, working in indoor locations, and hiring people to protect them from abusive clients. When sex workers perform these illegal acts, some inevitably do so in a morally involuntary manner since they have no realistic choice but to be involved in the sex trade, and engaging in these illegal acts is necessary for self-preservation.

This reasoning would not apply to sex workers in the trade because of personal choice. The Supreme Court in *Bedford* nevertheless found that the impugned laws still violated the instrumental rationality principles in relation to voluntary sex workers. In the court's view, "the causal question is whether the impugned laws make this lawful activity more dangerous."[320] The court compared the sex work laws to a law prohibiting a cyclist from wearing a helmet. Although the cyclist chooses to ride her bike, this choice does not diminish the law's causal role in making the activity more dangerous.[321] Sex work, also legal at the time, was made similarly more dangerous for those who chose to work in a lawful field.

This analogy is unpersuasive. Unlike laws governing sex work, legislatures have no reason to prohibit a citizen from wearing a bike helmet. Parliament had a legitimate reason to prohibit sex work: it sought to deter it because of its dangers and the nuisance that arises in society more generally.[322] Although sex workers who act in a morally involuntary manner are improper objects of criminal sanction, those who choose to enter the trade might be deterred if restrictions on the activity make it materially more dangerous. Viewed in this way, the crown's argument that the impugned laws ought to be upheld because sex workers choose a risky vocation – and therefore might be deterred from making such a choice – becomes more palatable.[323] To the extent that the provisions catch those who act in a morally involuntary manner, the crown could have argued that their conduct would be subject to a constitutional defence based on the moral involuntariness principle.

As part of reading down the provision allowing for human smuggling convictions in *Appulonappa*, the Supreme Court crafted numerous "exceptions" that operate as defences to the charge. These exceptions were directed at the provision of humanitarian aid. The same result, however, could have been reached by focusing on the moral underpinnings of those who help people to settle in Canada for humanitarian purposes: their actions are rightful and worthy of praise, not criminal and deserving of punishment. The constitutional rationale for justification-based defences outlined in Chapter 2 therefore could have been applied to reach a similar result as that under the instrumental rationality principles.

The Supreme Court's use of the arbitrariness principle in *PHS* and *Smith* also could have been replaced with a justificatory defence. Although the general prohibition against consuming drugs is a legitimate use of criminal law,[324] the workers at issue in *PHS* could have pleaded that they were justified in disobeying the minister's order in their highly unusual circumstances given the clear good arising from use of their safe injection site. As the court concluded, "Insite has saved lives and improved health ... without increasing the incidence of drug use and crime in the surrounding area."[325] Similarly, the accused in *Smith* was able to show a medicinal purpose for selling edible forms of marijuana. He showed not only that they are more effective for some patients but also that ingesting marijuana avoids the clear harms that arise from smoking it.[326] Since any concern that the accused would exploit others was assuaged by the requirement that he be licensed to sell marijuana, he could have argued that he was justified in disobeying the law since a greater good comes from selling edible forms of marijuana to those with medical needs.

Finally, the defendant in *Safarzadeh-Markhali* employed the proportionality principle in sentencing as a principle of fundamental justice to attempt to strike down a law allowing for an increased jail term because a person was denied bail. Although this argument failed, I showed in Chapter 2 why the proportionality principle meets the criteria for qualifying as a principle of fundamental justice. The Supreme Court's preference for employing instrumental rationality resulted in its avoidance of any serious consideration of the proportionality principle in the constitutional status of sentencing even though the court previously recognized that the principle was fundamental to justice in its *obiter* reasons.[327]

Conclusion

The Supreme Court's development of the instrumental rationality principles has proceeded in a haphazard manner. Its initial jurisprudence illogically constitutionalized the proportionality test for justifying infringements of Charter rights. Individualizing the analysis brought the instrumental rationality principles more closely in line with the text of section 7 of the Charter and avoided imposing an unduly onerous burden of proof on accused persons. In so doing, however, the court neglected to ask a more basic question: Do the instrumental rationality principles still qualify as principles of fundamental justice? The court's preferred principle – overbreadth – does not meet this threshold. The other instrumental rationality principles nevertheless might qualify as principles of fundamental justice and can be developed in a manner that fairly distributes the burden of proof in Charter proceedings.

The Supreme Court's decision to stop constitutionalizing principles of criminal law theory and to rely on the principles of instrumental rationality derives from its concern about the legitimacy of constitutionalizing principles of substantive justice. Although criminal law theory principles create strict "no-go zones" for legislatures, the instrumental rationality principles facilitate dialogue between courts and legislatures on the legitimate scope of rights. Yet this "dialogue" often results in something more akin to a shouting match than calm and principled discussion. I am therefore skeptical of whether the court is correct to prefer using the instrumental rationality principles. Although these principles likely provide somewhat broader constitutional protections than the principles of criminal law theory, it is necessary to consider whether any gap in protection can be filled by other enumerated rights in the Charter. If so, then it is questionable whether there is any utility in preserving the instrumental rationality principles as a method of judicial review.

Acknowledgment: Parts of Chapter 3 first appeared in Colton Fehr, "Rethinking the Instrumental Rationality Principles of Fundamental Justice," *Alberta Law Review* 58 (2020): 133–52.

Enumerated Principles of Criminal Justice

4

In many of the cases that challenged the constitutionality of substantive criminal laws, the applicants maintained that the impugned laws violated multiple constitutional principles. These arguments often included principles of criminal law theory and instrumental rationality. However, litigants also maintained that many substantive criminal laws were inconsistent with enumerated constitutional rights. The most common were freedom of expression, the prohibition against cruel and unusual treatment or punishment, and the guarantee of equality before the law. Although lower courts frequently answered each constitutional question to facilitate appellate review, the Supreme Court of Canada typically chose from among competing arguments in finding that a law was inconsistent with the *Charter of Rights and Freedoms*. Rarely, however, did it choose to rely on enumerated rights over the principles of criminal law theory or instrumental rationality.

My aim in this chapter is to answer two questions. First, to what extent could the Supreme Court's decisions under section 7 of the Charter have been decided under an enumerated right? Second, to the extent that there was a choice between competing constitutional principles, what reasons can be inferred from the court's decisions and relevant commentaries for employing section 7 of the Charter over enumerated constitutional principles? The answers to these questions will be invaluable for devising a normative theory of how the Supreme Court and similarly situated apex courts should develop the relationship between criminal law and constitutional law.

Freedom of Expression
Section 2(b) of the Charter guarantees everyone "freedom of thought, belief, opinion and expression, including freedom of the press and other media of communication." The word *expression* has been interpreted broadly to include any activity that "attempts to convey meaning,"[1] with one exception: conduct causing or threatening to cause physical harm.[2] This conception of freedom of expression is meant to serve three purposes: increasing democratic discourse, truth finding, and self-fulfillment.[3] Given the court's broad interpretation of these objectives, nearly any restriction on non-violent criminal conduct will constitute a violation of section 2(b), raising the question of whether the impugned restriction is a justifiable infringement under section 1 of the Charter.[4]

Public Solicitation
In *Reference re ss 193 and 195.1(1)(c) of Criminal Code (Man)*,[5] the accused challenged the constitutionality of then sections 193 and 195.1(1)(c) of the *Criminal Code of Canada*. The latter provision prohibited communicating in public for the purpose of sex work. Since asking a person for money in exchange for sex clearly attempts to convey meaning, the provision violated section 2(b) of the Charter.[6] However, the majority also found that the provision was justified under section 1. In Chief Justice Dickson's view, the main objective of the provision was to rid society of the nuisances arising from public solicitation.[7] Since the economic underpinning of the speech was not anywhere near the core purposes of freedom of expression – democratic discourse, truth finding, and individual self-fulfillment[8] – Chief Justice Dickson found that the law struck a reasonable balance and it was upheld under section 1.[9]

Justice Lamer found that the objective of the law was significantly broader than the elimination of nuisance. In his view, the prohibition on public solicitation was also directed at deterring sex work and protecting the dignity interests of sex workers.[10] Given this more pressing objective, the law was upheld for reasons broadly similar to those of Chief Justice

Dickson.[11] Justice Wilson, however, adopted the narrower purpose of the law as avoiding the nuisance of street sex work.[12] Unlike Chief Justice Dickson, she found that the law was not minimally impairing of rights because it caught instances in which there is no reasonable prospect that solicitation would result in a nuisance.[13] In particular, the definition of "public place" was so broad as to include secluded areas where people are unlikely to be present.[14] Like the other judges, Justice Wilson focused on freedom of expression but glossed over the safety concerns raised twenty-three years later when the Supreme Court struck down the same provision in *Canada (Attorney General) v Bedford* for violating the instrumental rationality principles.[15]

Hate Speech

In *R v Keegstra*,[16] the accused was charged with wilful promotion of hatred under section 319(2) of the *Criminal Code*. That section criminalizes wilfully promoting hatred of any "identifiable group" unless the communication is private. Keegstra used his position as a high school teacher to publicly promote hatred of Jews.[17] He taught students that Jews were "treacherous," "subversive," "sadistic," "money-loving," "power hungry," and "child killers."[18] Keegstra further maintained that Jews "seek to destroy Christianity and are responsible for depressions, anarchy, chaos, wars and revolution."[19] He also taught students to deny the Holocaust since the Jews "created the Holocaust to gain sympathy."[20]

The trial judge found that the type of expression espoused by Keegstra did not constitute expression under the Charter. As Justice Quigley wrote, the impugned provision "cannot rationally be considered an infringement which limits 'freedom of expression,' but on the contrary it is a safeguard which promotes it."[21] This followed because the protections afforded in the Charter to equality and promotion of multiculturalism were used as interpretive guides for defining the scope of the right to freedom of expression.[22] As opposed to reconciling these conflicting values at the section 1 stage of the analysis, Justice Quigley placed them in a hierarchy as a means to limit the scope of the right to freedom of expression.

The Supreme Court was unanimous in its disapproval of this narrow application of the right to freedom of expression.[23] Two central arguments to delimit the scope of the right were rejected. First, the court considered the argument that hate speech itself is analogous to violence. As Chief Justice Dickson observed, "threats of violence can only be so classified by reference to the content of their meaning."[24] In other words, hate propaganda is prohibited because of the repugnancy of its meaning, not because it necessarily causes or threatens physical harm.[25] Second, the court rejected the contention that the right to freedom of expression must be consistent with other values protected in the Charter.[26] The governing approach to interpreting the Charter requires that courts give generous and liberal interpretations to rights in accordance with each right's purpose and the purpose of the Charter as a whole.[27] Unfortunately, Chief Justice Dickson failed to explain why a purposive approach to interpreting the Charter did not affect his understanding of freedom of expression. Both the right to equality in section 15 of the Charter and the requirement in section 27 that the Charter be interpreted in line with Canada's commitment to multiculturalism prima facie favoured a restrictive approach to freedom of expression.

Justice McLachlin, in her concurring reasons with respect to the scope of section 2(b) of the Charter,[28] contended that there was no conflict between the rights to equality and freedom of expression. In her view, the Charter does not compel but bars state action. Since there was no prohibition that engaged the right to equality in *Keegstra*, there was no conflict of rights, strictly speaking.[29] The requirement that the Charter be interpreted in accordance with Canada's commitment to multiculturalism presented a stronger challenge. However, as Sanjeev Anand later observed, "section 27 does not explicitly indicate which part of the *Charter* must be interpreted in accordance with the policy of multiculturalism."[30] As a result, Anand reasonably contended that "if section 27 influences the section 1 analysis of an impugned law – section 1 also being part of the *Charter* – the Court is using section 27 correctly."[31]

Despite the Supreme Court's broad approach to freedom of expression, a narrow majority upheld section 319(2) of the *Criminal Code* as a justifiable infringement on Charter rights.[32] Hate speech's tenuous furtherance of the purposes underlying freedom of expression paled in comparison to the pressing and substantial need to protect minority groups from discrimination.[33] In so concluding, the majority recognized that "freedom of expression is a crucial aspect of the democratic commitment" and that its restriction cannot "condemn a political view without to some extent harming the openness of Canadian democracy and its associated tenet of equality for all."[34] It nevertheless found that the restrictions on hate speech affect few people.[35] More importantly, such expression propagates "ideas anathemic to democratic values" since hate speech denies "respect and dignity [to many people] simply because of racial or religious characteristics."[36]

False News

The *Keegstra* decision was followed two years later by *R v Zundel*.[37] In that case, the Supreme Court considered the constitutionality of section 181 of the *Criminal Code*, which prohibited publishing any "statement, tale or news" that a person "knows is false and that causes or is likely to cause injury or mischief to a public interest." The accused published and distributed a pamphlet entitled *Did Six Million Really Die?*[38] This Holocaust denial was argued to fall outside the protection of free expression because false statements by definition cannot further the aims underlying the right: increasing democratic discourse, truth seeking, and self-fulfillment. In the view of the majority, however, even lies can have intrinsic value because of their ability to foster political participation or individual self-fulfillment.[39] A doctor in the context of a pandemic who exaggerates the extent of the danger in order to scare people into taking more precautions is illustrative.[40] Moreover, determining truth with respect to complex social and historical facts is often extremely difficult, making the prosecution of such statements constitutionally suspect in at least some cases.[41]

Given the breadth of the law, the majority found that it was unjustifiable under section 1 of the Charter. The objective of the law was indistinguishable from that of its precursor, the doctrine of *de scandalis magnatum*.[42] That doctrine required that "none be so hardy to tell or publish any false News or Tales, whereby discord, or occasion of discord or slander may grow between the King and his People, or the Great Men of the Realm."[43] The objective of the law, then, was to "preserve political harmony in the state by preventing people from making false allegations against the monarch and others in power."[44] Protecting those in power from slander was not deemed sufficiently pressing and substantial to warrant infringement of a Charter right.[45]

The majority also found that the prohibition against spreading false news, assuming that it had a legitimate purpose such as suppressing racial intolerance, would not satisfy the minimal impairment requirement under section 1 of the Charter. This followed because of the "undefined and virtually unlimited reach of the phrase 'injury or mischief to a public interest.'"[46] The term "public interest" allowed a wide interpretation that could catch conduct outside the scope of protecting minorities from racial intolerance.[47] As the majority queried, "should an activist be prevented from saying 'the rainforest of British Columbia is being destroyed' because she fears criminal prosecution for spreading 'false news' in the event that scientists conclude and a jury accepts that the statement is false and that it is likely to cause mischief to the British Columbia forest industry?"[48] The real possibility that such conduct could be prosecuted under the false news provisions suggested a mismatch between its objective and its effects.

Defamatory Libel

In *R v Lucas*,[49] the accused were convicted of defamatory libel for participating in a picket protest. They were protesting the negligence of a police officer who failed to take action against a foster child known to be sexually assaulting his sisters.[50] The officer explicitly stated that he thought it would make the children easier to treat psychologically if they were kept together.[51] The government authorities did not originally take action against the officer despite multiple complaints.[52] In response, the accused participated in a public protest with signs reading "did [the officer] just allow or help with the rape/sodomy of an [eight year old]?" and "if you admit it … you might get help with your touching problem."[53]

The accused's protest resulted in a charge of defamatory libel contrary to section 300 of the *Criminal Code*.[54] That section prohibits publishing a defamatory statement that the accused knows is false. Section 298 defines such a statement as a "matter published … that is likely to injure the reputation of any person by exposing him to hatred, contempt or ridicule, or that is designed to insult the person of or concerning whom it is published." Since the purpose of these provisions is to limit expression, the respondent rightly conceded that the provisions contravened the right to freedom of expression.[55] The aim of the impugned law – protecting reputation[56] – was nevertheless important enough to justify this infringement. The narrow scope of the provision, which required both knowledge that the statement was false and intent to defame,[57] was found to be minimally impairing and proportional to any infringement of the right to freedom of expression given the low social utility of defamatory statements.[58]

Obscenity

In *R v Butler*,[59] the accused was charged with various counts of selling and exposing obscene material to public view. The charges arose from the public sale of "hard-core" videotapes, magazines, and sexual paraphernalia.[60] Section 163(8) of the *Criminal Code* defined "obscene" as "any publication a dominant characteristic of which is the undue exploitation of sex, or of sex and any one or more of the following subjects, namely, crime, horror, cruelty and violence." The majority of the Manitoba Court of Appeal found that the sexually explicit materials at issue did not constitute expression because the acts were purely physical.[61] The Supreme Court had previously concluded that purely physical activities, such as parking a car, could not reasonably convey any meaning.[62] The court nevertheless disagreed with the appellate court's analogy and found that sexual activity – unlike parking a car – was clearly capable of conveying ideas, opinions, and feelings.[63]

In finding that this infringement was justified under section 1 of the Charter, the Supreme Court determined that the aim of the law was "the protection of society from harms caused by the exposure to obscene materials."[64] Harm, the court determined, was to be construed based on a community standard of tolerance. This test considered the impugned materials harmful or offensive if the community would not tolerate others being exposed to them.[65] The limited scope of the legislation – applying only to violent, degrading, or dehumanizing conduct without artistic merit[66] – constituted a minimal impairment of the right to freedom of expression. This followed given the likelihood that such material causes harm to society, especially given pornography's tendency to portray women as submissive and inferior to men.[67] The court's finding that such sexual expression "appeals only to the most base aspect of individual fulfilment" and that "it is primarily economically motivated" resulted in the effects on individual freedoms being outweighed by the law's objective of preventing harm to women in particular.[68]

Possession of Child Pornography

In *R v Sharpe*,[69] the accused was charged with possession of child pornography and possession of child pornography for the purpose of distribution or sale under sections 163.1(3) and 163.1(4) of the *Criminal Code*.[70] The application to strike down the possession (but not the distribution) offence for violating section 2(b) of the Charter was eventually heard by the Supreme Court.[71] The court concluded that the right to possess materials that express something about a person's preferences, including child pornography, "is integrally related to the development of thought, belief, opinion and expression."[72] As a result, the blanket ban on possession of child pornography was found to violate the accused person's right to freedom of expression.[73]

The accused further argued that the ban on child pornography was unjustifiable under section 1 of the Charter since it caught material that posed no reasonable risk of harm to children.[74] The provision was broad enough to include any visual representation explicitly showing minors engaging in sex or depicting the genitalia or anal region of a minor. This included "drawings, paintings, prints, computer graphics, and sculpture[s]" of both real and imagined persons.[75] Possession of child pornography further included nude auto-depictions made by minors for personal use.[76] Finally, the prohibitions included written material that advocated or counselled sexual activity with a minor.[77] Despite the availability of several defences,[78] those who possessed child pornography in these forms solely for private use were caught by the impugned provisions.[79]

Parliament's objective in prohibiting the possession of child pornography was to protect children from "reasoned risks of harm."[80] The Supreme Court accepted that possessing child pornography can endanger children in a variety of ways, including making those who otherwise would not pose a risk to sexually assault children more likely to engage in such activity.[81] This risk of harm is tenuous, however, with respect to drawings, written materials, and personal sexual recordings when these materials are retained for private use.[82] As the court observed, "to ban the possession of our own private musings ... falls perilously close to criminalizing the mere articulation of thought."[83] Although possessing child pornography does not engage a central freedom of expression value, viewing expressive materials in private is at the core of the right to freedom of expression.[84] Given the broad scope of the provision, the court concluded that the law failed to balance its salutary and deleterious effects and thus was unjustifiable under section 1 of the Charter.[85] As opposed to striking down the law, however, the court "read in" several exceptions related to private possession for personal use.[86]

The Limits of Expression
A significant number of offences commonly prohibited by criminal law include an element of violence and therefore fall out of the purview of section 2(b) of the Charter. It is notable, however, that every non-violent offence challenged at the Supreme Court for violating the right to freedom of expression was successful in proving an infringement. This was no doubt because of the court's broad interpretation of the right. Its jurisprudence is of interest for another reason. Other than the *Sex Work Reference* and *Bedford*, the cases at issue were not seriously challenged at the Supreme Court for violating section 7 of the Charter in addition to the right to freedom of expression.[87] The court therefore did not have the opportunity to employ section 7 over an enumerated right in any of the cases except those decided in the sex work context.

The trend of finding any non-violent expression to violate section 2(b) of the Charter is likely to continue. For instance, offences such as consensual incest or polygamy likely involve expression. In *Reference re Section 293 of the Criminal Code*,[88] however, the trial court tersely dismissed this argument with respect to the polygamy offence.[89] The court's reasons are difficult to square with the purpose underlying polygamy (as well as incest) for some individuals: expressing love or, at the least, mutual desire to have sexual intercourse. Even if these activities are typically aimed at an illegitimate purpose, such as exploiting other humans, the content-neutral approach to freedom of expression suggests that polygamous and incestual relationships can convey non-violent meanings.

The Supreme Court's approach to freedom of expression has been criticized for being overly expansive. As Patrick Monahan and his co-authors observe, this "catch-all approach to section 2(b) is arguably inconsistent with Dickson C.J.'s admonition ... that '[t]he meaning of a right or freedom guaranteed by the *Charter* [is] to be ascertained by an analysis of the purpose of such a guarantee' and is to be 'understood ... in the light of the interests it was meant to protect.'"[90] In other words, employing section 2(b) of the Charter to protect conduct only tenuously connected to the values underlying freedom of expression unduly subjects many clearly constitutional laws to scrutiny under section 1.

Yet, as the Supreme Court's decisions in *Zundel* and *Sharpe* revealed, legislatures can go too far in restricting expression broadly considered improper. Allowing this analysis to occur under section 1 of the Charter serves two main purposes. First, weighing competing values under section 1 allows a generous and liberal interpretation of the word *expression* to be adopted at the rights stage of the analysis. This is consistent with the court's "purposive" approach to Charter interpretation.[91] Second, it allocates the burden of proof in an equitable manner by requiring that the crown prove any harm arising from a particular form of expression. As the above review illustrates, the state often relies on the harm created by a form of expression to justify its law. Requiring litigants to disprove any link between their expression and harm places an onerous burden of proof on applicants similar to the one rejected by the court in the instrumental rationality context.[92]

Focusing a constitutional challenge on only the right to free expression might nevertheless be imprudent in some cases. In *Keegstra, Zundel, Lucas, Butler,* and *Sharpe*, each accused person's freedom of expression interests were the sole constitutional values at stake. In other cases, however, other important interests are implicated by a prohibition on freedom of expression. Failure to canvass these interests can result in a fundamentally unjust law being upheld under section 1 of the Charter simply because the freedom of expression and section 1 analyses are unlikely to raise any relevant collateral harms.

The *Sex Work Reference* is illustrative. The risks posed to sex workers by preventing them from screening customers did not factor into the section 1 analysis. Instead, the Supreme Court, including those writing in dissent, considered the extent to which the prohibited expression constituted a nuisance or forwarded some other goal, such as improving substantive equality. The gross disproportionality principle proved to be much more capable of capturing the actual effects of preventing sex workers from speaking to potential clients. An analysis of the law's potential to convict sex workers who act in a morally involuntary manner would also have revealed identical types of harm. Allowing sex workers to communicate in public for the purpose of sex work allows them to screen clients for sobriety or indications that the purchaser might become violent. In other words, the prohibition saved the public from a nuisance at the unacceptable cost of sex workers' security and safety interests. This clear disproportionality went unevaluated in the *Sex Work Reference* in large part because of the court's narrow focus on freedom of expression.

The Ontario Court of Justice's recent decision in *R v Anwar*,[93] considering the constitutionality of the new sex work laws, avoided making this mistake. Justice McKay found that the complete ban on advertising sexual services in section 286.4 of the *Criminal Code* violated section 2(b) of the Charter. In his reasoning, he was keenly aware of the potential consequences of restricting advertising of sexual services.[94] The constitutional challenge in *Anwar*, however, was multi-faceted. Although safety concerns were raised in the section 1 analysis, the trial judge was made aware of these concerns because of their relevance to the section 7 challenge that the law violated the instrumental rationality principles.[95] Although Justice McKay did not rule on whether the law violated section 7, it was likely that the section 1 analysis would have been conducted within a lacuna similar to the one in the *Sex Work Reference* without the multi-pronged Charter challenge.

The different analyses in *Anwar* and the *Sex Work Reference* suggest that, if a court is to decide an issue based on a narrow right, counsel should be diligent in requiring the state to disprove all potential effects on the litigant's constitutional interests during the section 1 analysis. It might be appropriate for the Supreme Court to facilitate this approach by deciding all rights claims pleaded in a case. As David Lepofsky suggests, "multiple rights violation[s] can be relevant to the section 1 balancing, the design of remedies and any offer of judicial guidance to a legislature on principles to weigh when designing a replacement law or policy."[96] This suggestion ignores, however, that courts are imperfect actors that make errors in judgment. Increasing the number of constitutional decisions that the Supreme Court makes – especially when applying its own principles of fundamental justice under section 7 of the Charter – risks judicial distortion of the underlying rights. An alternative proposal would simply require courts to consider all potential negative effects raised by the litigant at the section 1 stage of the analysis without explicitly deciding if these effects result in multiple Charter infringements.

Cruel and Unusual Punishment
For a law to violate the prohibition against cruel and unusual punishment found in section 12 of the Charter, state conduct must be more than disproportionate or excessive. Instead, "it must be 'so excessive as to outrage standards of decency' and 'abhorrent or intolerable' to society."[97] Put differently, the punishment must be "grossly disproportionate."[98] Although section 12 is typically employed to challenge mandatory minimum punishments,[99] the provision could have been employed as an alternative means of challenging many of the early Supreme Court cases constitutionalizing various aspects of criminal law.

Vagrancy
As the majority in *R v Heywood*[100] struck down the vagrancy prohibition for its overbreadth, they did not consider the accused person's alternative argument that the law violated section 12 of the Charter. The minority answered this question in the negative. Justice Gonthier found that "the lifetime prohibition of activities with a malevolent or ulterior purpose related to re-offending is both a minor and justifiable restraint of the affected persons' liberty."[101] This argument was notably inconsistent with the majority's interpretation of the term "loiter" in the vagrancy provision since the dissent required a malevolent intent to sustain a vagrancy conviction. Operating within the majority's plain understanding of the term, it is possible that the prohibition would constitute cruel and unusual punishment since the accused was prevented from visiting vast

areas of Canada regardless of the intent underlying the visit and without regard for whether the accused posed an actual danger to children.[102]

The dissenters further doubted whether the vagrancy prohibition constituted "punishment or treatment" under section 12 of the Charter.[103] The Supreme Court has subsequently determined that a punishment involves "a consequence of conviction that forms part of the arsenal of sanctions to which an accused may be liable ... and either is imposed in furtherance of the purpose and principles of sentencing, or ... has a significant impact on an offender's liberty or security interests."[104] The vagrancy prohibition flows directly from a conviction of one of several enumerated sexual offences, thereby satisfying the first branch of the test. Moreover, given its application to a broad range of places where children might be present, the vagrancy prohibition clearly had a significant impact on the offender's liberty interest. Since the effect on the offender might be incurred without any realistic chance that the punishment furthers the objective of the vagrancy provision,[105] it is reasonable to conclude that the provision imposes grossly disproportionate punishment on at least some offenders.

Proportionality in Sentencing

The restrictions on sentencing credit at issue in *R v Safarzadeh-Markhali*[106] were not constitutionally challenged based on section 12 of the Charter. Instead, the applicant relied exclusively on section 7, maintaining that the law violated the overbreadth and proportionality principles of fundamental justice.[107] The applicant nevertheless could have argued that denying enhanced credit to an accused if the judge stated on the record that her primary reason for denying bail was related to the accused person's criminal record would result in a grossly disproportionate punishment.[108] Take an accused who had served two years on remand and was given a sentence of three years. Denying this person 1.5:1 credit for the time served would result in a 150 percent increase in the sentence between her and an identical offender granted enhanced credit. Although it is difficult to draw the line quantitatively regarding when disparity between two identical offenders will qualify as grossly disproportionate punishment, the lack of penological purpose underlying the difference between the sentences favours such a finding.

Mandatory Minimum Sentences

In several of the cases analyzed in the previous chapters, the Supreme Court struck down a law under section 7 of the Charter but could have employed the prohibition against cruel and unusual punishment to partially address the harsh effects of the law. In the *Motor Vehicle Act Reference*,[109] the court struck down an absolute liability offence requiring a mandatory minimum punishment of seven days imprisonment for driving without a licence. The fact that an accused person could receive a suspended licence because of a missed payment resulting from a clerical error was one instance in which the impugned law caught entirely innocent conduct. Yet, as Jamie Cameron subsequently observed, the mandatory imprisonment of a morally innocent person would also violate the prohibition against cruel and unusual punishment.[110] Indeed, imprisoning the morally innocent is a paradigmatic instance of cruel and unusual punishment.

Similar alternative arguments could have been made in several other decisions invoking section 7 of the Charter. Felony murder resulted in the same mandatory minimum punishment as regular murder. Moreover, any act committed while in the state of being an automaton would not avoid the mandatory minimum punishment attached to the index offence. An accused who did not physically kill someone or intend that anyone die, or an accused who involuntarily committed an offence such as murder, would therefore receive a significant punishment: a life sentence with varying opportunities for parole depending on whether the murder was categorized as first or second degree.[111] A strong case can be made that such a result would constitute a grossly disproportionate punishment because of the lack of moral blameworthiness of each offender with respect to the cause of death.

It is much less likely that convicting and punishing an individual who acts involuntarily would constitute cruel and unusual punishment in instances in which sentencing judges are given discretion in tailoring the appropriate penalty. The offender in *R v Daviault*,[112] for instance, committed a sexual assault while extremely intoxicated. The sentencing judge may choose to ascribe minimal (if any) blame to the accused and thus justify imposing a discharge with minimal therapeutic conditions such as a requirement for the accused to take substance abuse counselling.[113]

If the judge decides to impose a higher penalty, then it need not be the limitations on pleading the intoxication defence that would be challenged as the suitability of the punishment imposed could be challenged under regular appellate review.

A similar conclusion follows from application of the Supreme Court's jurisprudence testing whether the restrictions on pleading intoxication to specific intent offences would violate section 12 of the Charter. In *R v Robinson*,[114] the court found that the common law requirement to prove incapacity to form intent as opposed to a reasonable doubt about intent to commit a specific intent offence violated the principle of fundamental justice requiring proportionality between *mens rea* and the moral blameworthiness of the act.[115] To conclude otherwise would allow for a conviction of murder despite a conviction of manslaughter being the appropriate verdict. The relevant punishment could readily count as cruel and unusual given that the murder offence contains a mandatory minimum punishment of life imprisonment and the manslaughter provisions typically do not impose a mandatory minimum sentence.[116]

It is nevertheless possible to commit some specific intent offences without being subjected to a mandatory minimum punishment. The offence of robbery qualifies as a specific intent offence,[117] but it does not impose a mandatory minimum punishment if the robbery is committed without the use of a firearm.[118] A conviction of robbery as opposed to the lesser included offence of assault would result in the same sentencing principles in determining the sentence and allow the sentencing court to avoid the imposition of a grossly disproportionate punishment. All applications of the intoxication defence to specific intent offences therefore need not result in a violation of section 12 of the Charter.

Allowing for an offender to be convicted of offences such as murder while acting under duress might also constitute cruel and unusual punishment. Appellate courts currently disagree about whether the exclusion of murder violates the moral involuntariness principle constitutionalized under section 7 of the Charter.[119] Assuming that it does not,[120] it can be argued that imposing the mandatory minimum punishment for murder violates section 12. A person who commits murder under compulsion – typically a "kill-or-be-killed" scenario – is surely not deserving of the harshest penalty known to Canadian criminal law.[121] The same cannot be said for an accused person who commits a less serious excluded offence such as assault causing bodily harm.[122] Denying the accused a duress defence can simply be taken into consideration at sentencing. Since the sentencing scheme allows a sentence with few or no consequences,[123] the restrictions on the duress defence are unlikely to violate section 12 of the Charter.

The difficulty with employing punishment principles over section 7 of the Charter is that it leaves some problematic laws intact. If section 12 were used in response to the *Motor Vehicle Act Reference*, then it is likely that the punishment portion of the provision would be struck down, whereas the absolute liability offence would remain in force. As such, the law would no longer engage the liberty interest and thus would not have to be consistent with the principles of fundamental justice. Such a result would arguably be problematic since innocent accused persons would still receive fines for their conduct. However, if one thinks that absolute liability offences serve legitimate policy ends (efficiency in prosecuting potentially dangerous conduct), then the mere existence of an absolute liability offence is not objectionable. Although this argument was presented to the Supreme Court in the *Motor Vehicle Act Reference*, the court explicitly preferred to determine the law's constitutionality under section 7.[124]

Relying solely on punishment to respond to the automatism rules would be much more problematic since accused persons could still be convicted of serious offences despite having acted in an involuntary manner. It is nevertheless likely that a different enumerated right could have been used to reform the automatism rules: the presumption of innocence protected under section 11(d) of the Charter. The common law prohibition against pleading intoxication to general intent offences allowed for a conviction despite neither of the statutorily required *actus reus* or *mens rea* of the offence having been proven beyond a reasonable doubt.[125] As for specific intent offences, the common law limitations on the intoxication defence violated the presumption of innocence because they allowed for a conviction even though there was a reasonable doubt about whether the accused actually possessed the statutorily required intent to commit the offence.[126] Given this alternative argument, the Supreme Court could have avoided employing section 7 or 12 and instead relied strictly on the presumption of innocence to reform the common law intoxication defence.

It is nevertheless unlikely that the presumption of innocence could substitute for the reasoning under section 7 of the Charter in the context of the felony murder rules. Although the Supreme Court found a violation of the presumption of innocence in these cases, it was not because the law allowed for conviction despite a statutorily required element of the offence failing to be proven beyond a reasonable doubt. As the court concluded in *R v Vaillancourt*,[127] the presumption of innocence was violated because the felony murder offences did not include an element required under section 7 of the Charter, namely subjective *mens rea* in relation to the death.[128] The violation of the presumption of innocence therefore relied entirely on a prior violation of section 7 of the Charter. Invoking only section 12 therefore would result in a modified punishment but still unfairly stigmatize the offender as a murderer.

The Limits of Punishment

The Supreme Court's jurisprudence striking down laws based on section 12 of the Charter has been relatively sparse. Although its first application of section 12 resulted in a mandatory minimum sentence being struck down,[129] it took nearly three decades before another law met the same fate.[130] This was particularly surprising given Parliament's increased use of mandatory minimum punishments during this period. Between the early 1980s and now, mandatory minimum sentences have increased from fifteen to over seventy-five.[131]

The Supreme Court's reluctance to employ section 12 over section 7 of the Charter where feasible is perplexing in one sense. Utilizing an enumerated right as opposed to constitutionalizing a principle of criminal law theory is more legitimate from a democratic standpoint because this approach involves applying, as opposed to imposing, a constitutional principle. Any court cognizant of the contentiousness of judicial review would act prudently in limiting its ruling to the least controversial means for resolving a constitutional question. The court's decision to utilize section 7 of the Charter in cases of overlap with an enumerated right might nevertheless be justifiable for a different reason. Employing section 7 review focuses on the fairness of using the criminal law in the first place. This in turn can *prevent* accused persons from being criminally charged and convicted pursuant to an unfair mode of liability. Section 12 concerns itself only with the fairness of the punishment imposed after a conviction is entered.

Equality
Section 15(1) of the Charter provides that "everyone has the right to the equal protection and equal benefit of the law without discrimination" based on several enumerated and analogous grounds. Section 15(2) further clarifies that section 15(1) must not be construed to prohibit action taken for the purpose of ameliorating a prior disadvantage. To violate the equality provision, then, it is necessary for the law to draw a distinction based on an enumerated or analogous ground and to do so for a discriminatory purpose.[132] Despite the ability of criminal law to profoundly affect the substantive equality of various groups, the Supreme Court has yet to strike down a federal criminal law on the basis that it violates the right to equality.[133]

Abortion
In *R v Morgentaler*,[134] the Supreme Court considered the constitutionality of various restrictions on access to abortion. Although the provisions were struck down under section 7 of the Charter, the two dissenting justices dismissed – in a single paragraph – the argument that the restrictions put in place to prevent women from receiving abortions violated their equality rights.[135] In so doing, the dissenting justices concerningly adopted the Ontario Court of Appeal's conclusion that "any inequality between the sexes in this area is not created by legislation but by nature."[136]

The majority abstained from commenting on the equality implications of Parliament's abortion restrictions. Justice Wilson's concurring reasons did strongly imply, however, that an equality challenge would be successful. As she wrote, "the right to reproduce ... is properly perceived as an integral part of modern woman's struggle to assert her dignity and worth as a human being."[137] The decision to terminate a pregnancy, Justice Wilson continued, "is one that will have profound psychological, economic and social consequences for the pregnant woman ... It is a decision that deeply reflects the way the woman thinks about herself and her relationship to others and to society at large."[138]

Building on Justice Wilson's reasoning in *Morgentaler,* most feminist scholars have expressed a decided preference for section 15 over section 7 review in the context of abortion.[139] In criticizing the Supreme Court's choice to the contrary,[140] these scholars maintain that equality and liberty interests express different underlying concerns about the political experience. Under section 7, the liberty interest employs a negative right or "freedom from" rationale.[141] Protection from state interference in an action shrouds the realities of any law regulating abortion. It not only limits what women can do with their bodies but also prevents them from achieving equality of opportunity to pursue their various conceptions of the good life. It is beyond contention, for instance, that requiring women to bear their children is linked to lower job security and increased poverty, among various other indices of substantive inequality.[142]

Sex Work
In the *Sex Work Reference,*[143] the Supreme Court did not hear any argument about how Canada's criminal regulation of sex workers affected their ability to be treated equally. Nor was any equality argument made at the lower courts. The Ontario Court of Appeal in *Canada (Attorney General) v Bedford*[144] did explicitly note that, "since gender, race, sexual orientation and disability are all enumerated or analogous grounds under s. 15 of the Charter, the s. 7 analysis must take into account that [sex workers] often hail from these very groups."[145] The underlying concerns about equality therefore became contextual factors within the section 7 analysis. There was not any recognition that section 15 of the Charter itself might serve as a means for striking down the various impugned provisions. Nor did the Supreme Court as much as mention that vulnerable sex workers tend to be disproportionately from minority backgrounds.[146]

Euthanasia
In *Rodriguez v British Columbia (Attorney General),*[147] the Supreme Court gave short shrift to the argument that limiting disabled people's ability to commit suicide gave rise to inequality. Justice McLachlin explicitly recognized that the effect of the distinction between allowing able-bodied

people to commit suicide and prohibiting non-able-bodied people from doing so "is to prevent people like Sue Rodriguez from exercising the autonomy over their bodies available to other people."[148] As opposed to explaining the disparate impacts of the prohibition against physician-assisted suicide on disabled people, the court "assumed" that the law breached section 15 of the Charter and then concluded that the breach was "clearly saved" under section 1.[149] Justice McLachlin justified this decision by suggesting that accepting the appellant's equality argument would "deflect the equality jurisprudence from the true focus of s. 15 – 'to remedy or prevent discrimination against groups subject to stereotyping, historical disadvantage and political and social prejudice in Canadian society.'"[150]

Justices Lamer and Cory, writing in dissent, found that the prohibition against assisted suicide prevented disabled citizens from relieving their suffering by committing suicide despite that option being available to other members of the public.[151] This distinction in turn undermined a decision of fundamental personal importance that infringed the dignity interests of disabled persons: the ability to choose the manner and timing of their death and thereby prevent unwanted suffering.[152] Their reasons provided the basis for the trial and appellate courts' decisions in *Carter v Canada (Attorney General)*[153] to strike down the ban on physician-assisted suicide under section 15 of the Charter. The latter reasons have subsequently been praised for enabling "a responsive and nuanced understanding of disability, the systemic disadvantages that people with disabilities experience, and the [various] disability rights responses to [physician-assisted dying]."[154]

Despite the detailed and thoughtful reasons provided by the lower courts, the Supreme Court in *Carter* declined to deal with the equality argument. Instead, it preferred to strike down the prohibition on physician-assisted death for violating the overbreadth principle.[155] Maneesha Deckha has criticized this choice since it prevents "the trial judgment's Section 15 analysis [from receiving] a broader airing and much needed juridical and social attention."[156] Similarly, David Lepofsky has commented that the "broad public discussion and debate about designing new legislation to address assisted dying would benefit from judicial recognition that disability equality is on the table."[157] It is probable that engaging with the equality right would have focused Parliament's response on the significant impacts that disability can pose to those seeking end-of-life treatment. As Lepofsky has persuasively contended, if the prohibition against assisted suicide violates section 15, then "the remedy of assisted dying should extend to persons with disabilities who are free from external coercion, and who cannot end their own life without assistance, due to their disability."[158] This is a more concrete remedy that Parliament would not be able to skirt by claiming to have "rebalanced" the relevant interests pursuant to an instrumental rationality analysis.

The "Spanking" Case
In *Canadian Foundation for Children, Youth and the Law v Canada (Attorney General)*,[159] the applicant challenged the constitutionality of section 43 of the *Criminal Code*. That provision allows parents and teachers to use "reasonable" corrective force against children. Since section 43 draws a distinction based on age, the question arose about whether the distinction is discriminatory.[160] This required determining "whether a reasonable person ... would conclude that the law marginalizes the claimant or treats her as less worthy on the basis of irrelevant characteristics."[161] In answering this question, the Supreme Court balanced four key factors: "1) pre-existing disadvantage; 2) correspondence between the distinction and the claimant's characteristics or circumstances; 3) the existence of ameliorative purposes or effects; and 4) the nature of the interest affected."[162]

The first factor was met since children clearly are a vulnerable group. Similarly, the fourth factor was engaged since the interest at stake – the physical integrity of children – is of the utmost importance.[163] Since the law did not seek to ameliorate any disadvantage, the Supreme Court had to balance the ability of the law to accommodate the actual needs and circumstances of children against the fact that the impugned law intruded on the physical integrity of a vulnerable group.[164] In conducting this balance, the court acknowledged that children must be protected from abusive treatment.[165] It nevertheless observed that "children also depend on parents and teachers for guidance and discipline, to protect them from harm and to promote their healthy development within society."[166] As a result, the court determined that Parliament's choice to exempt assaults against children from criminal sanction was not discriminatory as long as the force was aimed at educating the child and posed no more than a trifling degree of harm.[167]

Fitness to Stand Trial

In *R v Demers*,[168] the accused was declared unfit to stand trial because of an intellectual disability caused by his Down syndrome.[169] As a result, he was forced to undergo disposition hearings to determine if he would become fit to stand trial after the initial finding of unfitness. His mental disability, however, ensured that he would never become fit to stand trial. This resulted in his being permanently required to appear before disposition hearings, subject to the discretion of the prosecution. The Supreme Court found it "unnecessary" to determine whether the legislation violated section 15 of the Charter given its finding that the impugned scheme violated the overbreadth principle and was not justified under section 1 of the Charter.[170] The lower court had rejected the claim that the provision violated the right to equality.[171]

The appellant's challenge of the impugned provisions on equality grounds nevertheless had merit. In his concurring reasons, Justice LeBel recognized that persons with a mental disorder or disability constitute a historically disadvantaged group that continue to be subject to social prejudice.[172] In considering whether Parliament has jurisdiction to employ criminal law for permanently unfit accused persons, he used the language of section 15 of the Charter when he observed that "we should adopt an interpretation of s. 91(27) [of the *Constitution Act, 1867*] that does not perpetuate ... disadvantage and prejudice."[173] By subjecting permanently unfit accused persons such as Demers to perpetual criminal law hearings, they were treated as potential criminals as opposed to people in need of assistance in dealing with their disabilities. Although Justice LeBel used this reasoning to find the legislation *ultra vires*, his reasoning applies with equal force in the context of equality.[174]

Intermittent Sentences

Two other recent lower court cases also illustrate how the right to equality can help to shape the substantive criminal law. In *R v Turtle*,[175] several members of the Pikangikum First Nation applied for intermittent sentences under section 732 of the *Criminal Code*. This provision allows a sentencing judge who has imposed a sentence of ninety days or less to allow an accused person to serve a sentence at a time that is convenient to her. Typically, the sentence is served in a way that minimally disrupts employment, family care, and education. Although the crown did not oppose these applications, intermittent sentences were not practical because of the remote fly-in location of the First Nation, hundreds of kilometres from the nearest jail.[176] The option of each accused person driving or flying to the nearest jail to serve an intermittent sentence was agreed by all parties to be "logistically and financially prohibitive."[177]

The Ontario Court of Justice found that the intermittent sentencing provision, despite being a law of general application, was a clear instance of adverse effects discrimination because it deprived Indigenous people living in remote reserve communities of a benefit available to other criminal defendants.[178] As Justice Gibson observed, "counsel have been unable to identify a single case, anywhere, at any time, where an on-reserve resident of Treaty #5 has been granted an intermittent sentence."[179] In addition, the court concluded that deprivation of this benefit perpetuated a prejudice since requiring members of a First Nation to serve their sentences during a single time period would, among other things, break up families for unnecessarily lengthy periods of time that in turn would perpetuate many of the well-known effects of colonialism.[180] Although non-superior courts cannot strike down laws under the Charter,[181] Justice Gibson found that the current regime violated section 15 of the Charter based on its discriminatory impact on Indigenous people living on reserves.[182]

Conditional Sentence Orders

In *R v Sharma*,[183] the offender pleaded guilty to importing approximately a kilogram of cocaine contrary to section 6(1) of the *Controlled Drugs and Substances Act*.[184] The offence came with a mandatory minimum two-year punishment pursuant to section 6(3)(a.1) of the *CDSA*. In addition, the conditional sentencing order provision found in section 742.1 of the *Criminal Code* prohibited allowing for a conditional sentence in Sharma's case. Conditional sentences effectively allow offenders to serve jail sentences in their communities. Imposing a conditional sentence is nevertheless illegal if the offence contained a mandatory minimum punishment;[185] was prosecuted by indictment and contained a maximum possible penalty of fourteen years of prison;[186] or was prosecuted by way of indictment, had a maximum penalty of ten years, and was among a lengthy list of offences that included importing drugs.[187]

The trial judge struck down the mandatory minimum sentence for violating the prohibition against cruel and unusual punishment in section 12 of the Charter, a ruling that the crown did not appeal.[188] Since the offender was a prime candidate for a conditional sentence,[189] the question arose about whether the restrictions on imposing a conditional sentence for importing drugs were consistent with both sections 7 and 15 of the Charter. The section 7 argument, consistent with recent jurisprudence, focused on the applicability of the instrumental rationality principles. The section 15 argument, however, considered whether the impugned restrictions on conditional sentences indirectly discriminated against Indigenous people.

The legislative history of the conditional sentence regime was key to the applicant's section 15 argument. The conditional sentence order has become progressively stricter with each legislative amendment. Originally, it was only necessary to meet three conditions to qualify for a conditional sentence: "The offence did not carry a mandatory minimum sentence; the sentence imposed was less than two years; and serving the sentence in the community would not pose a danger to the community."[190] Alongside section 718.2(e) of the *Criminal Code*, which requires judges to consider all available sanctions other than imprisonment for "all offenders, with particular attention to the circumstances of aboriginal offenders," the conditional sentence regime was enacted in large part to reduce the gross overincarceration of Indigenous people in Canada.[191]

Successive amendments made a conditional sentence more difficult to receive. In 1997, Parliament clarified that conditional sentences are available only when they are consistent with the broader "fundamental purpose and principles of sentencing" found in sections 718–718.2 of the *Criminal Code*.[192] In a pair of amendments in 2007 and 2012, Parliament significantly narrowed the availability of conditional sentences by restricting their use with respect to numerous offences, including those applicable to the offender in *Sharma*.[193] In making these amendments, the Conservative Party did not publicly contemplate their impacts on Indigenous people and other minorities even though opposition parties raised this issue during debate.[194]

A narrow majority of the Ontario Court of Appeal found that Parliament's restrictions on conditional sentences violated section 15 of the Charter. Given the intricate connection between the conditional sentence regime and section 718.2(e) of the *Criminal Code*, the majority found that "conditional sentences take on a unique significance in the context of [Indigenous] offenders by conferring the added benefit of remedying systemic overincarceration."[195] By narrowing the availability of conditional sentences, the impact of the impugned provisions was to create a distinction between Indigenous and non-Indigenous offenders based on race.[196]

In so concluding, the majority rejected the crown's argument that the effect of the legislation existed independent of the challenged laws.[197] A similar argument was accepted by the Ontario Court of Appeal in *R v Nur*,[198] in which the court concluded that a mandatory minimum punishment did not violate the equality provisions simply because of its disparate impact on minority groups. The court distinguished the conditional sentence regime at issue in *Sharma* because it was passed alongside section 718.2(e) to reduce Indigenous incarceration. In the majority's view, it is only in circumstances in which a law retracts a specifically provided benefit that an otherwise facially neutral law can be found to draw a distinction based on an enumerated or analogous ground.[199]

The majority further found that the impugned law's impact reinforced, perpetuated, and exaggerated the disadvantage that Indigenous people face because of their identity.[200] The crown retorted that courts did not necessarily lose the ability to impose non-custodial sentences as a result of the limitations imposed on conditional sentences. This followed since suspended sentences could be imposed in place of conditional sentences.[201] This approach, however, not only contradicted the impugned legislation's purpose of ensuring that serious offences result in prison time[202] but also was inconsistent with the purpose of suspended and custodial sentences. Suspended sentences are used for rehabilitative purposes, whereas custodial sentences emphasize denunciation and deterrence.[203] Imposing a suspended sentence where a custodial sentence is justified is a legal error.[204] Suspended sentences are also typically much more difficult for Indigenous people to obtain. The factors in favour of imposing a suspended sentence over incarceration – including employment, education, post-offence rehabilitation, and familial and communal supports – can exclude "many, if not most, marginalized offenders."[205]

Since a suspended sentence was not available to the sentencing judge, the Ontario Court of Appeal found that narrowing the availability of conditional sentence orders would be discriminatory since more Indigenous people would inevitably be incarcerated. This was contrary to the intent of Parliament when originally enacting the conditional sentencing regime alongside section 718.2(e) of the *Criminal Code*. As the majority emphasized, however, their conclusion does not result in any criminal law that disproportionately affects Indigenous people violating section 15 of the Charter. It is only when amending remedial legislation that Parliament must ensure to do so in a non-discriminatory manner.[206]

Justice Miller's dissenting reasons rejected the majority's application of section 15 of the Charter. In his view, the majority's decision violated a basic principle of constitutionalism: one Parliament cannot bind successive Parliaments via the legislative process.[207] Any interpretation of section 15 of the Charter that prevents Parliament from amending ameliorative legislation effectively constitutionalizes the initial legislation.[208] Although Justice Miller agreed that the majority's interpretation of the equality provisions had some support in the Supreme Court's recent jurisprudence,[209] he queried whether the court took a misstep in its development of the right to equality. The court's prior conception of equality asked "whether it can fairly be said that the legislature – in accepting the unintended side-effects of the legislation on the claimant group – thereby failed to treat them as persons, 'equally capable and equally deserving of concern, respect and consideration.'"[210] The idea that all people are equally deserving of concern, however, cannot mean that all are entitled to have their interests prioritized.[211]

The Supreme Court diverged from this understanding of equality in *Kahkewistahaw First Nation v Taypotat*.[212] The previous emphasis on how a burden was imposed – not simply the fact that a burden or benefit for a group existed – was replaced by the broader category of "disadvantage."[213] As the court observed in *Taypotat*, discrimination turns on "whether the impugned law fails to respond to the actual capacities and needs of the members of the group and instead imposes burdens or denies a benefit in a manner that has the effect of reinforcing, perpetuating or exacerbating their disadvantage." This broader conception of equality is difficult to justify in light of its impact on the legislative process. It effectively constitutionalizes benefits provided by the legislative process without consideration of the broader public interest of the impugned law.[214] As Justice Miller concluded, "without considering the impact on the public good, it becomes impossible to determine whether the legislature was wrong to have accepted the side-effects imposed on the group members in pursuit of that good."[215]

The conditional sentence regime at issue illustrates the potentially problematic nature of the majority's approach. Consider a hypothetical scenario in which Parliament determined that the offences at issue in *Sharma* were precluded when the conditional sentence regime and section 718.2(e) of the *Criminal Code* were originally enacted. It is impossible to argue that such a law would violate the right to equality.[216] It should also be impossible, therefore, for the same restriction imposed at a later time to violate the right to equality. As Justice Miller put it, "these are two means to the same end."[217] He continues, "unless there is a constitutionally relevant distinction between enacting legislation and amending it ... treating these two means to the same end differently would be putting form over substance."[218]

It is nevertheless possible that the Supreme Court did not intend to develop section 15 in the manner suggested by the Ontario Court of Appeal. In *Quebec (Attorney General) v Alliance du personnel professionnel et technique de la santé et des services sociaux*,[219] Justice Abella explicitly ruled out this type of "form over substance" application of the equality provisions.[220] In that case, the Quebec government passed a pay equity law in 1996 to ensure equal pay for men and women.[221] Unimpressed by the results of the original legislation, the Quebec legislature amended it in 2009.²²² In so doing, the legislature supplemented the general obligation to maintain pay equity with a system requiring audits every five years.²²³ If an audit revealed discrimination in pay, then women had the right to have pay discrepancies rectified going forward.²²⁴ The employer, however, would not have to rectify past pay inequities as required under the previous act.²²⁵

Justice Abella held in *Alliance* that the legislation had "a discriminatory impact because, assessed on [its] own and regardless of the prior legislative scheme, the impugned provisions perpetuate the pre-existing disadvantage of women."²²⁶ Absent the original pay equity legislation, women still had a claim of discrimination pursuant to the Charter and/or human rights legislation because the amendment prevented them from receiving equitable retroactive pay. The analogy broke down when compared to the amendments to the conditional sentencing regime at issue in *Sharma* since these amendments did not constitute a violation of rights on their own. It was only when the amended conditional sentencing order provision was compared to the initially enacted provision that it was plausible to claim that a benefit was being denied. As a result, and for the reasons explained by Justice Miller, it is difficult to see why a future amendment instituting a rule that would not have infringed a right if initially enacted can somehow become a violation of constitutional rights absent clear evidence of legislative intent to discriminate. If correct, then it follows that the majority of the Ontario Court of Appeal's decision in *Sharma* misapplied the Supreme Court's recent equality jurisprudence.

"Missed Opportunities"

Analogy to the Supreme Court's section 7 jurisprudence nevertheless provides reason to think that the court might not be opposed to the broader conception of equality applied in *Sharma*. Consider the court's decision in *Canada (Attorney General) v PHS Community Services Society*.²²⁷ The joint decision of the federal and provincial governments to set up a safe injection site was meant to ameliorate the effects on the life, liberty, and security of the person faced by those addicted to drugs. The federal government's subsequent refusal to renew the exemption required to sustain Insite affected the users of its services in a manner that was arbitrary and grossly disproportionate to the decision's objective of upholding public health and safety. As in *Sharma*, it was the subsequent decision to retrench on a benefit that resulted in the breach of section 7.

A similar result would follow application of the conception of section 15 of the Charter utilized in *Sharma*. The Supreme Court in *PHS* recognized that, although those who use safe injection sites come from diverse backgrounds, "familiar themes emerge" since "many have histories of physical and sexual abuse as children, family histories of drug abuse, early exposure to serious drug use, and mental illness."[228] Moreover, as Jonathan Rudin observes in an article arguing that *PHS* is better framed as a violation of the right to equality, addicts are "made up disproportionately of the poor, Indigenous people, and those with mental health and addictions issues."[229] Thus, the state's refusal to renew Insite's exemption from the criminal law would disproportionately affect these minority groups in a manner that imposed a significant burden on their communities. Whether viewed through an equality or an instrumental rationality lens, the state's decision to retrench on a benefit provided can be the basis of a constitutional violation.

If the above conclusion is puzzling, then it is likely because the decisions in *Sharma* and *PHS* were wrongly decided. As Justice Miller observed in *Sharma*, it is a bedrock principle of constitutional law that current legislatures cannot bind future legislatures through ordinary legislation.[230] Constitutionally prohibiting the amendment of a law with an ameliorative purpose (*Sharma*) or requiring a minister to renew an exemption to avoid retrenching on a previously provided benefit (*PHS*) constitutionally entrenches the original policy decision. If such an approach is contrary to basic principles of constitutionalism, then *PHS* and *Sharma* were simply wrongly decided cases since neither the instrumental rationality principles nor the right to equality in section 15 (or any other enumerated right) could be interpreted broadly enough to support a violation of the Charter.[231]

It is also likely that some of the other cases discussed above would not result in a breach of the equality provision. The *Sex Work Reference* and *Bedford* cases are illustrative. Unlike the laws at issue in *Sharma* and *PHS*, the sex work laws were passed as laws of general application without any ameliorative purpose. Although the Supreme Court recognized that these laws affected minorities at a disproportionate rate,[232] it would be a significant broadening of the ambit of section 15 of the Charter to find that a law of general application violates the right to equality simply because it negatively affects certain groups of people more than others. Under this approach, every criminal law likely would be unconstitutional given the disproportionate impact of criminal law on various minorities.

Still other decisions might be reframed as equality cases despite an infringement of equality or any other enumerated right not considered at any level of court. Notably missing from the above review of the Supreme Court's substantive criminal law jurisprudence is *R v Smith*.[233] The court found that a criminal prohibition on non-dried forms of medical marijuana violated the arbitrariness principle since the law had no connection to its objective of protecting health and safety.[234] Requiring users of medical marijuana to smoke it rather than ingest it was proven not only to be detrimental to health but also less capable of relieving the medical condition for which marijuana was being used.[235] Forcing people with serious illnesses to take their medicine in a more dangerous and less effective manner arguably violates section 15 of the Charter by discriminating against a disadvantaged group in a manner that imposes a serious burden on their ability to live with their medical conditions.

A Preferred Method for Constitutionalizing Criminal Law?
The Supreme Court's jurisprudence implies several costs and benefits of using enumerated rights to constitutionalize criminal law. I have argued that employing enumerated rights increases the legitimacy of judicial rulings. It does so by ensuring that democratically enacted laws are struck down using the precise language enacted by the framers of the Charter, not a judicial interpretation of a vague term such as "fundamental justice." The latter term allows judges to choose from among various principles never contemplated by the drafters of the Charter to strike down a law. Although commentators dispute whether the court has given unduly broad or narrow meanings to various enumerated rights, the fact that the court used concrete language (as far as constitutional provisions go) in striking down a law brings a greater air of legitimacy to these decisions than those decided under section 7 of the Charter.[236]

Abandoning the substantive aspect of section 7 and relying only on enumerated rights nevertheless would come at a price. As the review above illustrates, it is likely that many decisions under section 7 could substitute enumerated rights reasoning for the principle of fundamental justice employed to strike down a law. However, there are several cases in which the language of enumerated rights would have to be stretched beyond recognition to find a breach of the Charter. It follows that some unjust laws – such as those allowing for convictions of felony murder or the law prohibiting the duress defence except for an unusually narrow set of claimants – would remain in the *Criminal Code* without the Supreme Court's substantive interpretation of the term "fundamental justice." Although the punishments for these offences might be mitigated by applying section 12 of the Charter, the fact that people would be convicted for a serious offence when they either did not intend to commit it or had no other realistic choice unjustly stigmatizes them.

Focusing on enumerated rights might nevertheless provide a further benefit. Jonathan Rudin argues that section 15 of the Charter in particular is more efficacious for challenging discriminatory legislation than section 7 for a simple reason: section 15 review "tells it like it is."[237] As Rudin puts it, the problem with relying on the means-ends rationality principles – and he could add the principles of criminal law theory – is that doing so "masks the reality of the disparate impact of criminal law on vulnerable groups."[238] Maneesh Deckha makes a similar point in the context of the jurisprudence on physician-assisted dying, noting that "an equality analysis can shine a much needed spotlight on systemic disadvantage against marginalized and non-normative bodies in invalidating traditional yet problematic legal norms."[239]

Rosemary Cairns Way identified criminal law's failure to engage with equality issues as "the most destabilizing competitive truth about criminal law which has emerged over the last 30 years."[240] Writing in 2012, she noted that "the dominant conception of the criminal law was, for the most part, devoid of equality awareness and binary in nature, with state power to name and punish criminal behaviour counterbalanced by the classical liberal (freedom from) rights afforded the individual accused."[241] Christine Boyle made a similar point over a quarter of a century ago when she observed that equality at no point had been at the forefront of our "thinking about the overall burdens and benefits of criminal prohibitions."[242] She argued that "it is a liberal illusion that equality concerns are effectively addressed by considerations of power imbalances as between the state and the accused," thereby necessitating that criminal law become more attuned to the broader role that it plays in maintaining (in)equality.[243]

This hesitancy to employ equality rights reasoning in the context of criminal law has practical implications. As Rudin observes, "the debates in Parliament regarding amendments to the laws on prostitution and assisted dying would have been very different if the proposed legislation was viewed through an equality lens rather than trying to ensure the law was somehow less arbitrary or overbroad."[244] Parliament's responses to these social issues claimed to have "rebalanced" the relevant individual and state interests in passing laws that either had substantively similar effects (sex work laws) or substantially narrowed the Supreme Court's decision (euthanasia laws). A violation of the equality provisions arguably would require Parliament to address the core problem underlying a provision: its ability to perpetuate substantive inequality for various vulnerable groups.

Focusing on equality considerations can in turn facilitate more open and honest debate about important social issues. Rudin's observations are again apt: "It matters that discrimination in the criminal justice system is identified as discrimination rather than as arbitrary or overbroad legislation ... because discussions regarding the nature of criminal law do not only take place in the courts and the law schools, they are part of the public discourse."[245] In other words, a legal determination that a law lacks "rationality" does not effectively communicate to the public the core problem with a piece of legislation. Rudin also notes that "there is nothing about criminal law that makes it less amenable to public scrutiny and discussion than foreign policy or economic theories. If we want a real public debate about criminal law reform then we have to situate these issues in a way that discussion can take place honestly."[246] To do otherwise "hides the truth of Indigenous over-representation but also the over-representation of other racialized minorities, the poor, and those with mental health issues."[247]

The multi-dimensionality of the interests inherent in criminal law nevertheless render the relationship between equality and criminal law extremely complex and arguably the most difficult to implement.[248] The Ontario Court of Appeal's decision in *Sharma* is illustrative. The equality interests of various minority groups are implicated by the fact that reducing general eligibility for conditional sentences will disproportionately affect these groups. However, general public safety is also furthered by more strictly denouncing and punishing serious crimes. Public perceptions of justice can also be furthered for those who think that serving "real" jail time is a more suitable punishment than house arrest. Moreover, Justice Miller's observation that requiring subsequent governments to uphold remedial legislation has a profound impact on the relationship between past and present governments and the democratic process as a whole. The difficulty in reconciling these competing interests within the confines of an equality-based analysis might explain, at least partially, why the Supreme Court has been prone to choose any right other than equality to strike down an unconstitutional criminal law.[249]

There are also structural reasons that might explain why courts choose rights other than equality to decide criminal law issues. Consider first the structure of the criminal trial. It focuses on the individual's actions and the effects of those actions on the public interest.[250] Although the state must represent the interests of all members of society, the accused person need not be concerned with broader public interests. Employing often meagre resources, the accused person's primary aim is to be acquitted via any means possible.[251] Providing evidence of the intrinsic rationality of a law is much more feasible than providing evidence of the systemic impact of criminal law on minority interests. The latter type of evidence often requires complex and expensive expert testimony to establish social science facts, although some instances of discrimination are so widely known that courts can take judicial notice. Discrimination against Indigenous people provides one example.[252]

An applicant's inability to provide an adequate record to raise equality issues can result in further problems at the appellate level. If a case that raises equality issues is appealed, then numerous intervenors typically seek leave to intervene to ensure adequate representation of under-argued viewpoints. The fact that litigants often do not leave an evidentiary record related to equality makes it difficult for concerned intervenors to make arguments on equality grounds since judges might be reluctant to admit fresh evidence on appeal to support these arguments. This in turn makes it easy – if not reasonable – for appellate justices to refuse to decide issues based on equality grounds when other Charter breaches are more readily proven.

It is also possible that the structure of the Charter discourages use of the equality provisions.[253] As Rudin observes, section 7, as well as section 12, fall under the "legal rights" heading. Based on the nature of the rights protected under that heading, these rights arguably are the ones applicable to criminal law.[254] This argument might nevertheless have limited staying power. The Supreme Court did not hesitate to use other relevant sections of the Charter outside the context of legal rights in cases in which they were obviously relevant. The jurisprudence discussing the limits of freedom of expression discussed earlier is illustrative. Yet those cases were decided long before employing the instrumental rationality principles became the constitutional norm in the criminal law context.[255] It is possible that the court would prefer employing section 7 if its freedom of expression cases were decided today.

The above review demonstrates that there are various obstacles to implementing the right to equality in the criminal law context. As opposed to focusing on ways to alter the section 15 analysis to fit the criminal law context, litigants might more fruitfully consider infusing equality considerations into other stages of the Charter analysis. For instance, equality considerations can be factored in at the rights stage of the analysis. As Sarah Chaster observes, it is possible to use reasonable hypothetical scenarios involving clear and common instances in which minority populations are disproportionately affected when invoking the instrumental rationality principles or the prohibition against cruel and unusual punishment. Chaster advocates a similar approach when considering whether a rights infringement is justified under section 1.[256]

The Supreme Court's decision in *R v Lloyd* is illustrative.[257] The court considered the constitutionality of section 5(3)(a)(i)(D) of the *Controlled Drugs and Substances Act*.[258] That provision stipulated a minimum sentence of one year of imprisonment for offenders convicted of a trafficking offence who had also been convicted within the past ten years of a "designated substance offence." The court recognized that the provision caught not only drug dealers but also drug addicts who share drugs with fellow users or traffic drugs only to support their own habits.[259] Recognizing the disproportionate impacts that these provisions are likely to have on addicts is a positive step forward since it ensures that section 12 analysis is infused with considerations relevant to the discriminatory impact of the law. Since sentencing is an individualized exercise, it is necessary to consider such a factor since it reduces the moral blameworthiness of the hypothetical offender used to assess the constitutionality of an impugned punishment.

Yet the Supreme Court could have gone much further and described other sadly common features of drug users. Recognizing that the mandatory minimum sentence at issue would disproportionately affect Indigenous people is particularly important. Mandatory minimum sentences prevent judges from considering the impact of section 718.2(e) of the *Criminal Code*, directly relevant to the compliance of a sentence with the fundamental principle of sentencing: proportionality. The proportionality principle requires not only proportionality between the punishment imposed and the gravity of the offence but also that the punishment be commensurate with the moral blameworthiness of the offender.[260] Many Indigenous people have become drug users and addicts in no small part because of the history of colonialism. They are considerably less blameworthy for their offences than those who do not have such social factors affecting their choices to use and deal drugs. Such a consideration, then, renders the hypothetical scenario at issue in *Lloyd* even more clearly in breach of section 12 of the Charter.

Courts can also infuse the section 1 analysis with equality considerations. In *Keegstra*, for instance, a law criminalizing hate speech was justified largely by a need to protect minority interests.[261] As the majority wrote, "the derision, hostility and abuse encouraged by hate propaganda [necessarily have] a severely negative impact on the individual's sense of self-worth and acceptance."[262] This finding provided an important context for the majority's conclusion that the impugned law was a minimally impairing and proportionate intrusion into constitutional rights.[263] In *Butler*, the Supreme Court's section 1 analysis considered the negative effects of "hard-core" pornography on women's equality interests. As the court determined, "materials portraying women as a class of objects for sexual exploitation and abuse have a negative impact on the 'individual's sense of self-worth and acceptance.'"[264] The court's section 1 analysis was again affected by the need to balance freedom of expression interests in obscene materials against furthering substantive equality for women.

Finally, it is notable that commentators have suggested that equality should be constitutionalized as a principle of fundamental justice under section 7 of the Charter.[265] The main motivation for constitutionalizing substantive equality under section 7 appears to be avoiding the doctrinal difficulties with applying equality rights in the context of criminal law. Writing in the context of abortion, Kerri Froc suggests that Justice Wilson's decision in *Morgentaler* to conduct her analysis under section 7 of the Charter "avoided the impossible: the direct comparison to men that would be required under section 15."[266] She continues,

> one can readily imagine judicial acceptance of an unhelpful mirror comparator in the constitutional challenge of the criminal prohibition of abortion: a person with a physical condition, other than an unwanted pregnancy, seeking treatment that the state has a significant interest in restricting to those legitimately entitled to obtain it on the basis of a threat to life and health.[267]

Given the strained nature of such a comparison, Froc concludes that section 7 analysis is more likely to imbue Charter analysis with substantive equality considerations than section 15 in at least some contexts.[268]

Without getting into the doctrinal details of her proposal,[269] I suggest that it strikes at the heart of the democratic objection to judicial review exacerbated when judges constitutionalize their own principles of justice. Unlike with principles of criminal law theory or instrumental rationality, the drafters explicitly chose the language in section 15 of the Charter. It is tantamount to a de facto redrafting of an enumerated right to constitutionalize the same principle without the restrictions applicable to the enumerated right. Justice Doherty made a similar point in *Philippines (Republic) v Pacificador*.[270] Unsurprisingly, though he found that "the equality rights created under s. 15 are principles of fundamental justice," he concluded that employing section 7 ought not "alter the required analysis or yield a different concept of equality."[271] It seems improper to skirt any issue with applying section 15 of the Charter by resorting to section 7. Either the wording of section 15 must be modified to fit the criminal law context better or, more plausibly, equality considerations should be fit into the analyses of other Charter provisions.

Conclusion

The Supreme Court's enumerated rights jurisprudence has been applied sparingly in the criminal law context. Although criminal prohibitions that directly implicate free speech values tend to be challenged under section 2(b) of the Charter, various prohibitions that are constitutionally suspect for violating section 12's prohibition against cruel and unusual punishment have been treated as section 7 cases. Cases that implicate equality are also rarely decided by employing section 15 of the Charter. The court's preference for section 7 review in the latter instance can be explained to some extent by the underdeveloped and complex nature of the court's equality jurisprudence, the evidentiary challenges of proving an infringement of equality rights, and the structure of the Charter encouraging litigants to use its "legal rights" provisions. The equality provision nevertheless could have been readily applied in several cases, including those dealing with criminal prohibitions on abortion and euthanasia.

The Supreme Court's preference for section 7 review is difficult to rationalize in light of the broader applicability of enumerated rights. Although it is possible that the court sought to centralize power in the judicial branch, this hypothesis seems to be overly cynical. In my view, the court's clear preference for using section 7 of the Charter can be explained by observing the limited substantive criminal law protections in the Charter. Without a substantive interpretation of section 7, the court would not have been able to adequately address various unjust criminal laws, including those that employ a harsh felony murder rule and an exceptionally narrow duress defence. The court's decision in the *Motor Vehicle Act Reference* foreshadowed these problematic cases and took early action to ensure that future litigants and courts would not be handcuffed by the strictures of enumerated rights. The court could have waited, however, two more years for a law to arise on its docket that could not be challenged under an enumerated right.[272] With the benefit of hindsight, perhaps the court would have chosen this more restrained option.

Although this reasoning provides a partial justification of the Supreme Court's decision in the *Motor Vehicle Act Reference*, it cannot count as a justification of its subsequent and persistent preference for employing section 7 rights. With forty years of jurisprudence to reflect on, the way forward must take into account the various costs and benefits of employing each of the court's three methods of constitutionalizing criminal law. That question – how to decide – engages the broader purpose(s) of each method of substantive review as well as each method's ability to achieve its laudable ends. In the remainder of the book, I will set out a clear path forward for the Supreme Court to constitutionalize criminal law in a manner that strikes an appropriate balance between these frequently competing interests. I will also provide guidance to similarly situated apex courts trying to devise a principled approach to developing the relationship between constitutional law and criminal law.

5

A Normative Approach to Constitutionalizing Criminal Law

In the preceding chapters, I have shown that the Supreme Court of Canada's three methods for constitutionalizing criminal law aspire to achieve laudable ends. Utilizing only a single approach nevertheless frustrates the objective underlying one or both of the other approaches. By exclusively applying enumerated rights, some unjust criminal laws will be shielded from constitutional challenges. Although applying criminal law theory principles can fill the void, I have suggested that the court reduces the legitimacy of judicial review by utilizing these principles since they impose, as opposed to apply, agreed-on constitutional rights. The instrumental rationality principles' greater potential to facilitate dialogue provides a response to the charge that section 7 review lacks democratic legitimacy. To date, however, the dialogue arising from the instrumental rationality jurisprudence has not been constructive since Parliament frequently passes response legislation that ignores the substance of judicial rulings.

How, then, should the Supreme Court approach constitutionalizing criminal law under the *Charter of Rights and Freedoms*? Fortunately, the court is not limited to adopting only one approach. In choosing from among the available options, the court should employ judicial review in a way that creates the most coherence and fairness in criminal law without unduly sacrificing democratic legitimacy. Although these aims are frequently in tension, a combination of methods would allow the court to strike an optimal balance among their objectives. As I contend below, the court can maximize each of these aims by employing enumerated rights whenever possible. The principles of criminal law theory should then be used to fill in clear gaps left by enumerated rights. In addition, the court can use both an enumerated right and a principle of criminal law theory in cases in which employing the principles of criminal law theory serves a clear communicative function. Put differently, the principles of criminal law theory should be used in addition to an enumerated right when they are capable of guiding Parliament and courts in resolving legal issues that inevitably will come before them for reform.

My proposal calls for a reversal of the Supreme Court's current approach to constitutionalizing criminal law. The court currently maintains a strong preference for employing the principles of instrumental rationality.[1] Although this approach is theoretically appealing, there is little evidence that these principles achieve their aim of fostering constructive dialogue between courts and legislatures. Moreover, there are significant doctrinal difficulties with the court's instrumental rationality principles. Most notably, the court's favoured principle – overbreadth – cannot reasonably be categorized as a principle of fundamental justice. For these reasons, instrumental rationality is a problematic method of substantive review. The argument for abandoning that method becomes even more persuasive if, as I contend below, employing enumerated rights and constitutionalizing limited principles of criminal law theory are capable of ridding criminal law of unjust doctrines of liability in a democratically acceptable manner.

Judicial Review
Before defending my proposed framework for constitutionalizing criminal law, it is necessary to explain more concretely the controversy underlying judicial review. The realization that majorities often unjustly affect minority interests originally provided a strong justification for judicial review.[2] Allowing judges to exercise judicial review in a well-functioning democracy nevertheless has received sustained criticism for allowing unelected and arguably ill-equipped judges to strike down democratically enacted laws.[3] By reviewing this literature, I do not mean

to take sides in this ongoing and complex debate. Rather, it is reasonable to find merit in many of the arguments for and against judicial review. This open-minded approach to the judicial review debate will allow me to devise a more flexible and principled approach to constitutionalizing criminal law under the Charter.

The Counter-Majoritarian Difficulty

Alexander Bickel identified a problem inherent in the institution of judicial review that he labelled the "counter-majoritarian difficulty."[4] As Bickel observed, the practice of judicial review "thwarts the will of representatives of the actual people of the here and now."[5] In other words, unelected judges who use the power of judicial review to strike down laws enacted by elected representatives run contrary to the principle of majority rule.[6] Since majority rule is thought by many to be a central political and democratic value, the very idea of judges striking down democratically enacted laws is problematic.

Building on Bickel's and other scholars' work, Jeremy Waldron identifies what he calls the "core of the case" against judicial review.[7] In referring to judicial review, he is careful to distinguish between "strong" and "weak" forms.[8] Polities with weak forms of judicial review can identify rights violations but cannot decline to apply the law.[9] Polities with strong forms of judicial review allow their courts to strike down laws or modify them to conform to constitutional rights.[10] Waldron is concerned only with the latter form of judicial review.[11] Notably, he explicitly counts Canada as a strong form model even though the legislature has the last word under the Charter if it invokes the notwithstanding clause.[12] Other scholars, such as Stephen Gardbaum, reluctantly classify Canada as an intermediary or "commonwealth" model of constitutionalism largely because of the notwithstanding clause.[13] Given the infrequent use of that clause, it is not unreasonable to categorize Canada prima facie as a strong form model of judicial review.[14]

Waldron also sets out four assumptions underlying his argument against the use of strong form models of judicial review. First, he assumes that there exist democratic institutions in reasonably good working order that include a representative legislature elected on the basis of universal adult suffrage.[15] This entity is also experienced in dealing with rights issues given its general law-making mandate and takes political equality considerations seriously when legislating.[16] The requirement that the legislature be in "reasonably good working order" does not mean that it will not make decisions on rights that some people believe to be unjust. Some of the decisions will be just, and others will be unjust, and people will reasonably disagree about which rights decisions fall into these categories.[17]

Second, Waldron assumes that there exists a set of judicial institutions set up to hear individual lawsuits, settle disputes, and uphold the rule of law.[18] The courts are further assumed (for the most part) to be non-elected.[19] These courts respond within a precedential system of rule making to particular claims brought by litigants in an adversarial form of presentation.[20] Lower courts respect the rulings of higher courts, and there exists an apex court to definitively resolve rights disputes.[21] The judges who render decisions are also either specifically trained for that task or selected based on merit from a body of eminent lawyers or jurists.[22] In both cases, the judges are insulated from political pressure by legislative bodies.[23] These judges, given their diverse educational backgrounds, will often disagree about the legitimate scope of rights and have devised systems of voting – normally majority rule – for settling disputes at the appellate level.[24]

Third, Waldron assumes that there is a general commitment by most members of society and its officials to the idea of individual and minority rights.[25] Although the polity pursues a general utilitarian conception of good, and believes that majority rule is an appropriate system of pursuing such ends, the polity also realizes that certain fundamental liberties should not be subject to the principle of majority rule.[26] This is possible because, as Waldron assumes, citizens "keep their own and others' views on rights under constant consideration and lively debate, and they are alert to issues of rights in regard to all the social decisions that are canvassed or discussed in their midst."[27] Given this concern with rights, citizens in his hypothetical state typically will enact a bill of rights to state these values concretely, though judges need not be able to strike down laws using this document.[28]

Fourth, Waldron assumes that there will be persistent, substantial, and good faith disagreements about rights.[29] People can reasonably disagree about whether certain rights ought to exist at all or how an agreed-on definition of a right applies in a tough case while still holding rights as central to their political morality.[30] Although a bill of rights is capable of assisting a polity in resolving difficult rights questions, it is incapable of resolving rights issues beyond a reasonable doubt given its broad language.[31] For Waldron, "the bland rhetoric of the Bill of Rights was designed simply to finesse the real and reasonable disagreements that are inevitable among people who take rights seriously for long enough to see such a Bill enacted."[32] He continues, "instead of encouraging us to confront these disagreements directly, judicial review is likely to lead to their being framed as questions of interpretation of those bland formulations."[33]

If these assumptions hold in a polity that exercises strong form judicial review, then the question arises about which reasons need to be taken into account when evaluating the relative merits of judicial and legislative decision making.[34] Waldron identifies both process- and outcome-related reasons for answering this question. The former "are reasons for insisting that some person make, or participate in making, a given decision that stand[s] independently of considerations about the appropriate outcome."[35] As Waldron observes, "the most familiar process-related reasons are those based on political equality and the democratic right to ... have one's voice counted even when others disagree with what one says."[36]

In contrast, outcome-related reasons design the decision-making process in a way that best ensures good, just, or right outcomes.[37] Since rights are important, it is crucial that disagreements about them be resolved correctly.[38] Given the unlikely nature of definitively resolving many rights disagreements based on substantive arguments, the only legitimate way to come to a conclusion about the "correct" decision on rights is to ensure that fair procedures are in place to resolve competing rights claims.[39] As Waldron puts it, as opposed to saying "that we should choose those political procedures that are most likely to yield a particular controversial set of rights, we might say instead that we should choose political procedures that are most likely to get at the truth about rights, whatever that truth turns out to be."[40]

For Waldron, process-related reasons clearly weigh in favour of preferring legislative determinations about rights. He comes to this conclusion by appealing to the response from a hypothetical litigant who loses a rights debate.[41] The litigant might ask "1) why should this [group of people in the legislature] be privileged to decide a question of rights affecting me and millions of others?; and 2) even if I accept the privileging of [these people], why wasn't greater weight given to the views of those legislators who agreed with me?"[42] For Waldron, the quality of the answers offered by the political and judicial arenas dictates which is more competent procedurally to decide rights issues.

Answering the first question in the legislative context is simple. Legislators receive their powers from free and fair elections.[43] The second question is answered by the process of majority decision making.[44] As Waldron observes, majority decision making "is neutral as between the contested outcomes, treats participants equally, and gives each expressed opinion the greatest weight possible compatible with giving equal weight to all opinions."[45] Although Waldron recognizes that political participation is not equal in the sense that one vote per person means *precisely* an equal voice, the fact that electoral systems or legislative procedures will not always provide perfect equality for participants is not sufficient to abandon the principle of majority rule. It is only a reason to compare majority rule to judicial procedures of decision making.[46]

The aggrieved litigant receives significantly more problematic answers when asking similar questions of judges. The litigant asks "1) why should these nine men and women determine the matter?; and 2) even if they do, why should they make their decision using the procedure that they use rather than a procedure that gives more weight to Justices with a view [similar to that of the hypothetical litigant]?"[47] Although courts might reply to the first question by observing that they were appointed by elected representatives, this response is wanting compared with the answer provided by legislatures. As Waldron observes, "legislators are regularly accountable to their constituents and they behave as though their electoral credentials were important in relation to the overall ethos of their participation in political decision-making."[48] To the contrary, courts are often criticized for using the vague language of bills of rights to instill their own values into the law.[49]

Any judicial response to the second question – why judges employ majority decision making – is even less convincing. The "fairness and equality" argument available to legislatures is not available to courts given their low numbers and lack of representation of the citizenry.[50] Majority voting, according to Condorcet's jury theorem, might mathematically enhance the overall competence of a group beyond that of the average member of the group.[51] Yet this argument is relevant to the *outcome* of a rights decision, not to the legitimacy of the decision-making process.[52] More importantly, Waldron maintains that any such argument in favour of judicial review would have to compete with the application of the same theory to legislatures that, given their higher numbers, serve to benefit to a far greater extent from group decision making.[53]

Waldron's latter argument ignores the realities of the legislative process. It is not intuitive that every legislator voting for or against a bill is acutely aware of the policy nuances of that bill. Given the breadth and complexity of government, individual legislators do not have time to become attuned to every issue before the legislature.[54] Although there is legislative debate, the vast majority of members do not participate in it, nor do they have any special training to qualify them to cast a vote on every nuanced issue.[55] In polities such as Canada where the leader of a political party whips votes, it is even more unlikely that the vast majority of legislators do anything more than raise their hands in support of a particular law. If true, then there are not necessarily more informed minds debating and providing reasons in support of a law. Instead, narrow groups (some of whom are elected, others of whom are bureaucrats) from a particular ministry develop and support individual policies, and the leader of the majority party in a parliamentary democracy requires others to follow suit. It is unclear that such a body would provide any greater insight than nine attuned justices absorbing lengthy written and oral arguments about a rights issue.

Waldron also questions whether judicial review is justified based on other outcome-related reasons. Although he admits that legislatures are more vulnerable to illegitimate external influences, the institutional features of courts can also make grappling with rights disagreements more difficult.[56] As Waldron suggests, it is likely that judges will be incapable of fully understanding the plight of classes to which they do not belong.[57] In his view, "legislatures are set up with structures of representation precisely in order to foster this sense of appreciation."[58] Presumably,

Waldron is referring to the need for politicians to campaign and take stock of rights issues to ensure that they are re-elected.

This argument again uncritically extols the virtues of legislators while tersely writing off the experiences of lawyers and judges. A lawyer goes through law school for several years with law professors who frequently discuss rights issues and facilitate understanding of diverse perspectives on these issues. Some lawyers then go on to represent those from diverse socio-economic backgrounds for many years, giving these lawyers, some of whom become judges, direct views of the experiences of marginalized classes. Moreover, those who become judges in the criminal courts would have to be oblivious not to develop an acute understanding of the structural inequality facing most criminal defendants. These judges, who often hear first instance constitutional arguments in criminal law cases, can set the factual record for deciding rights issues. It is not clear that legislators gain similar knowledge of criminal law by virtue of political campaigning or participating in the legislative process. At the least, such an argument cannot be accepted without detailed evidence.

Waldron further questions three other common outcome-related arguments used to bolster the case for judicial review. First, Waldron questions the value of the fact that rights claims are presented to courts by flesh-and-blood individuals.[59] This has the effect of "humanizing" the determination of whether the impugned law violates rights. In other words, since judges deal with these "on the ground, moral thought experiments" every day, one might assume that they are good at resolving them.[60] As Waldron retorts, however, "the particular idiosyncrasies of the individual litigants have usually dropped out of sight by the time the ... [apex court] addresses the issue."[61] To the contrary, he maintains that "the process of legislation is open to consideration of individual cases, through lobbying, in hearings, and in debate."[62] It follows that "legislatures are much better positioned to mount an assessment of the significance of an individual case in relation to a general issue of rights that affects millions and affects them in many different ways."[63] Although this is potentially true, one must also remember that the factual record in any given case underlying a rights issue is set by the trial court, which deals with flesh-and-blood individuals. This factual record is subject to significant deference on appellate review.[64]

Second, although the broad wording of a bill of rights can help to focus debate on the competing values inherent in rights disputes,[65] Waldron maintains that courts and their systems of precedents can become rigid and, as a result, stall discussion on rights.[66] Since judges are concerned about the legitimacy of judicial review, "they cling to their authorizing texts and debate [philosophies of] interpretation rather than ventur[e] out to discuss moral reasons directly."[67] Waldron suggests that legislatures can avoid the problem of being tied to a bill of rights by framing an issue not as a bill of rights issue but as an issue of political or moral philosophy.[68] This objection, although forceful, also falls a bit short in the Canadian context since judges are allowed to constitutionalize broad moral principles under the guise of concepts such as fundamental justice.

Third, Waldron responds to the argument that courts are better at deciding rights issues because they give more elaborate reasons for their decisions than legislatures.[69] In his view, proponents of this argument do not adequately assess the reasons given by legislatures, most notably found in the recorded pages of Hansard debates. As Waldron observes, this oversight occurs because "lawyers are trained to close study of the reasons that judges give; they are not trained to close study of legislative reasoning (though they will occasionally ransack it for interpretive purposes)."[70] Since both institutions give reasons for rights decisions, any argument about the superiority of one set of reasons over the other must be supported by something inherent in the quality of the reasons given.[71]

In Waldron's view, the reasons canvassed by courts are not the same as those of legislatures. Courts apply an often antiquated bill of rights, whereas legislatures are not restricted by the wording of a bill of rights and are therefore freer to debate the moral and political ramifications of a particular policy.[72] To the contrary, the reasons given by courts under bills of rights typically involve "an attempt to connect the decision the court is facing with some antique piece of ill-thought-through eighteenth- or nineteenth-century prose."[73] Laborious discussion of precedent also typically results in stretched analogies to previous decisions as opposed to principled reasoning about rights issues.[74] The result, Waldron asserts, is that judges often devote little text to the moral debate underlying a rights issue.

Waldron uses the US Supreme Court's seminal decision on abortion rights, *Roe v Wade*,[75] as an example. The fifty-page decision devotes only a page or two to the moral discussion of abortion rights.[76] In contrast, British legislators devoted significant time and energy to debating the same issue several years before *Roe* was decided. The British debate, Waldron observes, was well informed by both pro-choice and pro-life factions and came to well over one hundred Hansard pages of debate on the moral issues underlying abortion.[77] These issues included the ethical status of the fetus, the liberty and privacy interests at the core of many pro-choice arguments, as well as the proper role of the law with respect to deciding private moral questions.[78]

Although Waldron provides only one example, he generalizes that legislatures are more likely than courts to engage in meaningful debate about the nature of rights.[79] This raises an interesting empirical question about which institution more frequently engages in moral reasoning on rights issues.[80] I do not know of any relevant academic studies on point, let alone in the Canadian context. This lack of evidence makes it difficult to accept Waldron's argument outright. Moreover, it is notable that the example of principled legislative debate that Waldron provides is one in which legislators were "freed" from adhering to strict party discipline. Since this does not occur often in parliamentary systems of democracy, the example seems to be the exception to the rule that members of the governing party in a parliamentary democracy will be "whipped" to vote one way without explaining their views on a rights issue.[81]

Since Waldron maintains that the traditional outcome-based arguments do not bolster the case for employing judicial review in his hypothetical polity, he concludes that there is no reason to think that courts will come to more morally "correct" conclusions about rights than legislatures. Moreover, because the "process-based" reasons weigh in favour of legislatures deciding rights issues, the combination of both sets of reasons arguably weighs in favour of abandoning strong form judicial review in polities that meet Waldron's core assumptions. His analysis, although not the only one of its kind in the literature,[82] constitutes an oft-cited and powerful statement of the arguments against the institution of judicial review.

Justifications for Judicial Review

Shortly after Bickel raised the counter-majoritarian difficulty, constitutional law scholars became preoccupied with defending judicial review. One of the first notable responses maintained that judicial review was necessary to protect against malfunctions in the democratic process. Others later defended a broad moral reading of vaguely worded constitutional provisions as consistent with a constitutional conception of democracy. Still others defended judicial review to the extent that it facilitates democratic dialogue between courts and legislatures. A better understanding of each view will be invaluable in answering the question of which principles a court should rely on when striking down a criminal law under the Charter.

Procedural Justifications

In *United States v Carolene Products Co*,[83] the US Supreme Court considered whether a federal law prohibiting shipment of "filled milk" unconstitutionally affected interstate commerce. In determining the standard of review for economic issues, Justice Stone argued that a "rational" basis between the law's means and ends was all that was required to uphold the impugned law. However, this low standard for assessing constitutionality would not apply to all rights issues. Justice Stone suggested in a footnote to the decision that the court would undertake a much more searching level of scrutiny of statutes restricting "political processes" or embodying "prejudice against discrete and insular minorities."[84]

The rationale underlying the footnote inspired John Hart Ely's classic defence of judicial review.[85] Ely develops his theory by asking whether judges should confine judicial review to norms explicitly stated or clearly inferable from the text of the Constitution ("interpretivism") or enforce norms found outside the four corners of the constitution ("non-interpretivism").[86] Ely maintains that interpretivism is more easily reconciled with a majoritarian conception of democracy.[87] If the strict wording of the constitution and/or the intent of the framers is followed, then, as Ely puts it, "the judges do not check the people, the Constitution does, which means the people are ultimately checking themselves."[88]

Ely nevertheless maintains that the interpretivist approach to judicial review is impossible to implement because constitutions typically contain "several provisions whose invitation to look beyond their four corners ... cannot be construed away."[89] Scrutinizing the language of the American Constitution, Ely observes that many rights provide courts with a "sweeping mandate to judge ... the validity of governmental choices."[90] The fact that some constitutional rights are framed so broadly poses a dilemma for interpretivists: either they give these clauses some meaning, or they ignore these rights altogether. Since the latter approach is unprincipled, it is necessary either to employ non-interpretivist techniques to develop an understanding of such provisions or to develop interpretivist techniques consistent with democratic theory.[91]

Ely dismisses various non-interpretivist methodologies of judicial review as incompatible with democratic theory. Allowing judges to instill their own values in the constitution is quickly dismissed as undemocratic.[92] Employing "natural law" or "reason" is similarly found to be too subjective given the ease with which disagreeing factions can formulate arguments on either side of any rights issue.[93] Permitting judges to employ "neutral principles" is similarly implausible. As Ely observes, this methodology "does not by itself tell us anything useful about the appropriate content of those principles or how the Court should derive the values they embody."[94] Likening judges to "philosopher kings" is dismissed as elitist,[95] and relying on "tradition," Ely argues, is undemocratic since it allows yesterday's majority to govern today.[96] Requiring judicial "consensus" in determining the scope of constitutional principles is not only contrary to majority rule but also likely to narrow the scope of rights to only those most agreeable to the majority.[97] Finally, Ely maintains that "predicting progress" as a justification for judicial review is both outside the competence of a court and anti-democratic.[98]

Ely nevertheless maintains that a non-clause-based approach to interpretivism can be utilized in a manner consistent with democratic theory. Building on Justice Stone's footnote, Ely maintains that the broader focus of the footnote was to revive democracy where it is malfunctioning.[99] Such resuscitation is necessary in two circumstances. The first circumstance is when "the ins are choking off the channels of political change to ensure that they will stay in and the outs will stay out."[100] Using the

Constitution to ensure basic political participation is logically consistent with the broader aim of democratic government. Without rights such as freedom of speech and voting, citizens would be incapable of participating in the democratic process.[101]

The second circumstance is when "an effective majority [is] systematically disadvantaging some minority out of simple hostility or a prejudiced refusal to recognize commonalities of interest."[102] In such circumstances, the ability to vote and speak freely often will be insufficient to represent minority interests. As Ely observes, "no matter how open the process, those with most of the votes are in a position to vote themselves advantages at the expense of the others, or otherwise to refuse to take their interests into account."[103] Even those with common interests might ignore those interests because of prejudice against a particular minority. Racial prejudice is illustrative. Citing Frank Goodman, Ely observes that "race prejudice divides groups that have much in common (blacks and poor whites) and unites groups (whites, rich and poor) that have little else in common than their antagonism for the racial minority."[104]

Ely is nevertheless unclear about which groups will qualify as "discrete and insular minorities." The rights of women are not counted for numerical reasons. Since women were given the right to vote and constitute roughly half the population, Ely considers them no longer disadvantaged even though they still face substantial barriers to equality.[105] Similarly, it would be "cheating" to strike down bans on the sexual practices of LGBTQ2S+ people since doing so would involve upholding a substantive right based on the Supreme Court's conception of what is fundamental to privacy.[106] Ely's theory, then, faces problems of indeterminacy since Ely had no principled method to determine which groups of people qualify as "discrete and insular." His approach therefore risks significant underenforcement of important constitutional values.[107]

Ely nevertheless maintains that employing judicial review to ensure political participation and protect minorities would result in a "participation-oriented, representation-reinforcing approach to judicial review."[108] Given the need to appease the majority to preserve political power, elected legislatures cannot be trusted to identify either situation. Courts, however, are independent of the political process and therefore able to identify such malfunctions.[109] Importantly, Ely's support for a broader kind of interpretivism only allows for judges to clear the way for fair legislative rule making with respect to the application of rights. Judges therefore overstep their boundaries if they provide a broad, substantive interpretation of a constitutional right.[110]

The "Moral Reading"

Ely's procedural justification for judicial review can be contrasted with Ronald Dworkin's "moral reading" of the American Constitution.[111] Dworkin agrees with Ely that the wording of several provisions of the Constitution are too general to be narrowly construed.[112] Yet Dworkin would not limit a judge's ability to interpret the Constitution in a way that seeks only to uphold democratic process. Instead, he maintains that allowing judges to instill moral values into a bill of rights is "practically indispensable to democracy."[113] By this, Dworkin does not mean that states without judicial review cannot be democratic; instead, the fact that a state employs judicial review does not render that state undemocratic.[114]

The key to this argument is Dworkin's rejection of majoritarian rule as the foundational principle of democracy.[115] Although those who oppose judicial review recognize that majorities enact unjust legislation, they nevertheless suggest that a moral cost is incurred when society allows judges to strike down a rights-infringing law.[116] Dworkin rejects this conclusion, arguing that it stems from a failure to recognize what he calls the "constitutional conception" of democracy.[117] This conception takes the aim of democracy to be "that collective decisions be made by political institutions whose structure, composition, and practices treat all members of the community, as individuals, with equal concern and respect."[118] Departures from majority rule are therefore justified on special occasions when the state fails to treat a citizen with equal concern and respect.[119] Where the state does treat its citizens properly, the majoritarian principle provides a strong moral argument in favour of accepting collective decisions.[120]

Dworkin also views democratic action by the people in a communal as opposed to a statistical sense. In other words, democracy is more than tallying up what each individual does and attributing the result to the people. Instead, collective action is communal when it presupposes a collective agency.¹²¹ Two of the most powerful arguments for democracy – its ability to protect liberty and equality – presume a communal conception of democracy that, for Dworkin, counts against accepting majoritarianism as an unwavering democratic value. The majoritarian conception of democracy posits that one has these freedoms when majority rule is in place but not when a monarchy or aristocracy (to which the judiciary could be likened) makes decisions on behalf of the people.¹²² For Dworkin, however, it is unclear why someone is free when she must obey the rules of the majority even if she thinks that those rules are unjust. One can be made a slave, for instance, via a democratic process. Since such a person's liberty and equality interests would be violated, any conclusion that these citizens are "free" is incredulous.¹²³

This observation, Dworkin suggests, requires that citizens must qualify as "moral members" of the community before the polity can be described as democratic.¹²⁴ Before a citizen can count as a moral member, each person must be allowed to play a part and have a stake in any collective decision.¹²⁵ Thus, universal suffrage, effective elections, and political representation, as well as freedom of expression within political and informal life, are basic prerequisites of moral membership.¹²⁶ So is a bona fide acceptance of equal concern for the interests of all members in the community that, in turn, provides a basis for rejecting the authority of a society to discriminate against minority groups.¹²⁷ Finally, it is also necessary for society to allow its members to exercise moral independence. This requirement allows the government to decide issues of general importance to the polity but not per se issues central to the individual's control of her life and her self-respect.¹²⁸

Dworkin also responds to the assertion made by Waldron, among others, that the community loses out when moral issues are decided by courts.¹²⁹ If citizens are not forced to debate and come to conclusions about the legitimate scope of rights on their own – instead relying on an elite judiciary to decide rights issues for them – then arguably the polity loses the opportunity to learn from its mistakes. Dworkin maintains that this argument relies on a dubious assumption: public engagement with constitutional justice will be better if politicians as opposed to courts lead that discussion.¹³⁰ As he observes, "there is no necessary connection between a citizen's political impact of influence and the ethical benefit he secures through participating in public discussion or deliberations."[131] Assertions to the contrary rely on the idea that legislatures will give more thought to rights issues than judges, but this is unlikely given the impact of majoritarian bias on politicians.[132]

Despite his open-ended approach to interpreting a constitution, Dworkin should not be taken as suggesting that a constitution is open to whatever interpretation a judge wishes to adopt. The wording of constitutional provisions is often determinate and must be followed in such cases. In instances in which a constitution provides broad moral language, the requirement of "integrity" offers several further limits on the proper interpretation of constitutional rights.[133] First, it requires that judicial decisions be consistent with judicial precedents and the structural design of the constitution as a whole.[134] Second, judges must render decisions based on principles, not based on policies or political preferences.[135] Third, integrity requires that judges apply its principles neutrally to other cases in which those principles are fairly implicated.[136] Although judges, like other institutional actors, can abuse their power when interpreting the constitution, the moral reading is an approach to interpretation that assumes judges act in good faith.[137]

For Dworkin, then, "the best institutional structure is the one best calculated to produce the best answers to the essentially moral question of what the democratic conditions actually are, and to secure stable compliance with those conditions."[138] He thinks that the moral victories of judicial review will outweigh its moral losses since judges will approach questions about rights in a neutral manner and seek to find the best possible answers to those questions.[139] Even if courts make significant rights errors, however, Dworkin is confident that truly poor decisions will not be obeyed by the people and that better judges will eventually replace those who make poor decisions.[140]

Others have bolstered Dworkin's argument by suggesting that judicial decisions "over-constitutionalizing" rights are less morally serious than such decisions "under-constitutionalizing" rights. Richard Fallon, for instance, maintains that we should evaluate judicial review in a way similar to criminal law's standard of proof. The rationale behind requiring the state to prove a crime beyond a reasonable doubt is that convicting the morally innocent is a more serious moral wrong than acquitting accused persons who are probably guilty. The law therefore tolerates many wrongful acquittals to avoid convicting even a few morally innocent individuals. Similarly, under-constitutionalizing a right can result in continued rights violations that are more morally serious than constitutionalizing rights of questionable importance to justice.[141] If true, then it is substantially easier to prove that allowing judges to decide rights issues will lead to better "outcomes" than leaving such issues to majoritarian democracy.

Dworkin's moral reading of the American Constitution, although the most complete justification for judicial review, nevertheless runs into problems of indeterminacy. Reasonable people disagree about which rights derive from broad principles such as the right to "equal concern and respect."[142] Dworkin concedes this point, recognizing that his approach to interpreting the Constitution "inspired all the greatest constitutional decisions of the Supreme Court, and also some of the worst."[143] The fact that courts come to the "wrong" answers to at least some rights questions leads to two conclusions: either the empirical evidence in favour of or against judicial review must be more heavily relied on in debating the merits of such review, or polities should explore different paths to reconciling disagreements about rights between courts and legislatures.

Dialogue

The dialogical approach to judicial review is the most promising means for reconciling disagreements about rights between courts and legislatures. The term "dialogue" can, however, imply different institutional relationships. To some theorists, "genuine dialogue only exists when legislatures are recognized as legitimate interpreters of the constitution and have an effective means to assert that interpretation."[144] To conclude otherwise arguably ignores the fact that the Supreme Court's decisions under the Charter "are a monologue, with judges doing most of the talking and legislatures most of the listening."[145]

A similar critique arises from those on the left of the political spectrum. Judicial review arguably transfers power to a judicial elite, allowing citizens to be mere "eavesdroppers on the [judicial] doors of power."[146] These criticisms share the common premise that the Supreme Court's conception of dialogue as a reciprocal conversation about the legitimate scope of rights is a farce. There is some merit to these critiques of dialogue since scholars have provided empirical evidence to support the view that their respective understanding of what constitutes "true" dialogue rarely occurs under bills of rights such as the Charter.[147]

Skeptics of dialogue typically favour this coordinate interpretation approach. For others, however, this understanding of dialogue is "dangerous" because it "risks making a legislature a judge in its own majoritarian causes."[148] In other words, it ignores the majoritarian problem at the heart of rights protections. For people who are unpopular or from disadvantaged groups, it is unrealistic to expect their rights to receive any consideration by a majority that vilifies them. Politicians who want to run for office in the next term will be unlikely to oppose majority will even if they believe that the majority's demands are unjust.[149] Judges at least provide a forum in which these concerns can be heard and decided in a neutral manner.

Although coordinate interpretation runs up against the majoritarian problem, for those who prioritize majority rule as the central tenet of democracy, it provides a means for ensuring that such rule is respected. Theorists have devised other conceptions of dialogue, however, to soften the counter-majoritarian difficulty without ignoring problems related to majoritarianism. The first of these theorists was Bickel. As he wrote, "virtually all important decisions of the Supreme Court are the beginnings of conversations between the Court, the people and their representatives."[150] Bickel recognized that this conversation was not between equals because the Supreme Court, at least under the American Constitution, has the last word with respect to rights issues.[151] Regardless, he observed that the court still "interacts with other institutions, with whom it is engaged in an endlessly renewed educational conversation."[152]

Bickel recognized that dialogue will be problematic in a strong form model of judicial review because there is typically no mechanism for the legislature to respond meaningfully to judicial decisions. This problem is particularly acute under the American Constitution since there is no built-in means for legislatures to justify or override judicial decisions. Yet Bickel observed that dialogue often occurs when courts find ways *not* to decide constitutional cases.[153] The most common method is to interpret legislation in a manner consistent with constitutional rights. Only where the legislature expresses clear and unequivocal intent to breach a right is it necessary to invoke the Constitution. As Bickel observed, this common law approach allows the Supreme Court to engage "in a Socratic colloquy with the other institutions of government and with society as a whole concerning the necessity for this or that measure."[154] In other words, the common law dialogical approach allows for rights issues to remain in abeyance and ripen, in turn allowing the polity to (re)consider its position in light of the apex court's ruling.[155]

Bickel nevertheless recognized that the Supreme Court would have to decide constitutional cases based on legislative replies to its dialogical decisions. In rendering such decisions, Bickel maintained, the court should fulfill a function "which differs from the legislative and executive functions; which is peculiarly suited to the capabilities of the courts; [and] which will not likely be performed elsewhere if the courts do not assume it."[156] Although the Supreme Court is not competent to assess the will of the majority, courts are well situated to ensure that minority concerns are heard and adjudicated in a principled manner. The problem in the American context is that its Constitution does not promote dialogue once the Supreme Court renders its decision. This problem has led defenders of dialogue to devise "second look" doctrines that could justify increased deference to the legislature[157] or allow judicial supremacy and recognize as dialogue those "constitutional moments" when the people act affirmatively to overturn the court's rights decisions.[158]

This structural problem with facilitating dialogue is not present under every bill of rights. The Charter is exemplary in that it provides legislatures with two powers tailored to facilitating dialogue. First, it provides a means for legislatures to express their policy justifications for infringing rights under section 1. Second, legislatures may enact a rights-infringing law notwithstanding a violation of certain provisions (including all of the substantive criminal justice provisions) of the Charter under section 33.[159]

As Kent Roach explains, "proportionality analysis [under section 1] is inherently dialogic or interactional in nature [since it] allows legislatures to articulate their regulatory ambitions and explain the practical problems they face in achieving them."[160] Section 1 of the Charter also takes courts away from the text of constitutional rights and judicial precedents and instead asks them to engage with the evidence and justifications that the government offers in support of its law.[161] This should, and often does, lead to respectful conversations about rights by two parties with "different abilities, concerns, and perspectives."[162]

It has nevertheless been retorted that proportionality analysis under section 1 of the Charter merely camouflages the Supreme Court's desired policy judgments,[163] that such analysis does not qualify as "dialogue" since it refuses to include discussion about the meanings of rights,[164] and that courts do not have the institutional capacity to engage in section 1 analysis.[165] However, these retorts do little more than express doubts about the merits of judicial review, an immensely complex debate that shows no signs of ending any time soon. The benefit of a dialogical approach to constitutionalism is that it does not bear the burden of reaching "right answers" about difficult rights issues. Instead, it allows courts and legislatures to struggle together in coming to the best possible answers about rights issues.

Section 33 of the Charter also serves a useful dialogical function. Although initially it involves the legislature "shouting" at the Supreme Court to get its way, it also requires, after the override expires in five years, that cooler heads reconsider the rights question. The Canadian experience suggests that, after this cooling-off period, legislatures and courts tend to resolve their differences either by passing a new law compliant with the Charter or by accepting the original rights decision.[166]

The fact that invoking the notwithstanding clause requires legislatures to admit a rights violation nevertheless erects a political barrier to its use. As Andrew Petter suggests, "those who speak in the language of justice and rights have a huge rhetorical and political advantage over those who speak in the language of policy and interests."[167] The "new status quo" that arises from a judicial decision on rights likely makes it more difficult to respond to a rights violation.[168] Yet it is not intuitive that independent judicial minds should not have such sway in a polity when it comes to resolving rights issues. Since such issues often implicate a strong majoritarian bias against an unpopular or vulnerable minority group, the majority of the polity is unlikely to give much, if any, weight to rights-based reasons in contexts such as substantive criminal law.

Constitutionalizing Criminal Law

By taking stock of the various criticisms and defences of judicial review, it is possible to better understand the competing values at stake when courts determine that a criminal law is unconstitutional under the Charter. It would be imprudent, however, to proceed by assuming that one of the competing theories of judicial review is "correct."[169] The debate about the merits of judicial review has only intensified in recent years. It has also raised a variety of empirical questions about process- and outcome-related reasons for supporting or opposing judicial review. Despite this uncertainty, several general observations can be gleaned from the literature. These observations in turn can help to guide judges in determining which sets of rights to employ when striking down criminal laws under the Charter.

The first observation is that the consistent appeal to democratic norms in opposing judicial review suggests that there is something unsettling about allowing nine unelected, generalist judges to strike down laws passed by a majority of citizens.[170] Even Dworkin's strong defence of judicial review admits a significant degree of indeterminacy in deciding rights issues. Judges are therefore likely to render at least some constitutional decisions that are out of touch with conventional understandings of morality. Judges in Canada have been provided, however, with valuable guidance on rendering decisions: a bill of rights. Where the Charter provides specific guidance on the content of rights, I take the view that judges act with relatively more legitimacy since the polity at least agrees on the existence of the right. In other words, any sacrifice in legitimacy argued by Waldron and others to be inherent in judicial review is assuaged to a greater extent when judges employ the wording found in a particular bill of rights. The Supreme Court acts with less legitimacy when it decides to constitutionalize its own preferred principle of justice, especially when an enumerated right clearly applies. Choosing to apply the court's favoured principle in the latter circumstance flippantly ignores the rights that the polity democratically enacted.

Allowing a generalist apex court to constitutionalize its own principles of justice also risks creating incoherence in the law since it allows the court to develop the law with principles that it has less experience adjudicating.[171] Take the court's jurisprudence constitutionalizing fault.

Although the Supreme Court crafted several common law presumptions, the "presumptive" nature of these principles did not require it to think deeply about the core principle underlying *mens rea:* proportionality between fault and stigma. This principle needed to be developed under the Charter because it was evident to the vast majority of the court that the common law presumptions were too broad and admitted too many exceptions to qualify as principles of fundamental justice. The court was therefore left to pursue a more determinate path under the Charter. Its ensuing jurisprudence constitutionalizing a proportionality requirement between fault and stigma provided a principled general framework for developing the law. However, the court also took significant missteps in developing the law, and to this day it has not provided a concrete definition of its proportionality principle.

The Supreme Court's jurisprudence constitutionalizing criminal defences is also illustrative. Although the moral involuntariness principle was adopted under the common law, the court was able to avoid developing a broader relationship between moral involuntariness and criminal defences by maintaining that only the legislature had legitimate authority to develop justification-based defences.[172] However, after the Supreme Court constitutionalized the moral involuntariness principle, it logically followed that justifications should also be afforded constitutional status. To conclude otherwise would allow the Charter to mandate a defence for wrongful but excusable conduct but not rightful conduct. The court therefore again found itself in unsettled territory, for it could no longer defer to the legislature on the moral principles underlying justifications. Moreover, saying that a justification is a "rightful" act – as the court maintained under the common law – would not provide sufficient precision to qualify as a principle of fundamental justice. It is necessary to explain why an otherwise criminal act becomes rightful. In other words, the court was required to uncover principles that captured the moral underpinnings of justifications. Its refusal to do so and its choice to develop moral involuntariness as a catch-all constitutional principle for criminal defences provided an illogical and unworkable governing framework for criminal defences.

Both of these examples illustrate the different demands at common law and under the Charter when developing the general principles underlying criminal law. Common law principles are lower stakes since the legislature can be expected to respond with the ordinary legislative process. Courts can state general presumptions or decide to leave certain aspects of "policy" to the legislature without being leaned on to fill in the inevitable gaps. Under the Charter, stating principles too broadly fails to communicate a sufficiently precise principle to qualify as a principle of fundamental justice. As a result, the Supreme Court must provide more detail, which in turn makes the court prone to mistakes since it must enter what is often novel territory. However, understating the principles underlying an area of criminal law leaves litigants and legislatures guessing about what the Charter demands in terms of the principles underlying the law. These examples strongly suggest that courts – at least generalist courts – are institutionally ill equipped to develop a coherent constitutional theory of criminal law.

The second lesson to take from the judicial review debate is that there are legitimate concerns about the democratic process malfunctioning and allowing majorities to use their political power to cause injustice toward unpopular segments of the population and minority groups. One of Waldron's four assumptions – that citizens care about and consider the rights of others – ignores the majoritarian problem.[173] Even if people have regard in general for rights, it is doubtful that their consideration includes the criminal defendant's views on what can be legitimately criminalized. Waldron notably fails to engage with the majoritarian problem in the criminal law context despite the unusually high susceptibility of criminal defendants to majoritarian bias.[174] The neutrality and objectivity of the judiciary suggest that judges are more likely to render fair decisions in the criminal law context.

Unequal concern with substantive criminal justice is evident from a perusal of the basic rights in the Charter. Rights related to substantive criminal justice – those rights pertaining to the role of choice, proportionality, and innocence[175] – are not represented, whereas rights related to criminal investigations or the political process are dominant. Therefore, if there is a place where judges might be expected to "gap-fill" under a section 7–like provision, it would be in contexts in which majoritarian problems are particularly acute. The substantive criminal law is illustrative but by no means exclusive.[176] In playing this gap-filling role, the courts can increase the fairness of criminal law. This is a benefit that cannot be set aside lightly given the prevalence of majoritarian bias in the criminal justice system.

Such arguments, however, must also be viewed in light of what the Canadian experience reveals about judicial competence to constitutionalize its own principles of fundamental justice. Courts are imperfect institutions and can make mistakes. At the least, it is prudent to only allow courts to engage in the riskier exercise of constitutionalizing their own rights where there is some other policy reason weighing in favour of that approach. Allowing judges to exercise such powers in cases in which an unjust law may not be struck down by enumerated rights provides one such reason. Allowing the Supreme Court to constitutionalize principles of criminal law theory as a first resort, however, risks courts rendering poor rights decisions and allows them to glibly ignore the rights that the polity actually agreed on when enacting the Charter.

Finally, the idea that judges should listen to the policy reasons underlying a rights infringement has intuitive appeal given the ongoing debate between those who favour and oppose strong-form judicial review. The dialogue resulting from such engagement at least softens the counter-majoritarian critique since legislatures and courts at times do come to resolutions about the legitimate scope of rights. Unfortunately, the dialogue in Canada has been lacklustre in the substantive criminal law context. Parliament's increasing tendency to overrule the Supreme Court's decisions using the legislative process – more recently responding with a coordinate interpretation approach to violations of the instrumental rationality principles – ignores the court's reasoning on rights issues. This approach allows legislatures to claim that a law that has effects identical to those of a law previously found to be unconstitutional and does not substantially forward the law's new objectives is *consistent* with the Charter. The recent section 7 jurisprudence reviewed in Chapter 3 showed that Parliament is more likely to respond to a law where it can maintain that its new law is consistent with the Charter. The result, however, is complex, costly, and time-consuming relitigation of important rights issues.

Parliament's response to the instrumental rationality principles was predictable and provides a good reason to rid the law of these principles.

Not only do they encourage legislatures to utilize an illegitimate approach to interpreting rights, but also there are several doctrinal difficulties with implementing the principles. Moreover, there is no reason to think that enumerated rights and principles of criminal law theory together apply any more narrowly than the instrumental rationality principles.[177] As such, employing instrumental rationality is unnecessary to uphold a liberal and generous conception of rights, and preserving these principles risks watering down the dialogue available to courts and legislatures under the Charter.

The Supreme Court has also ignored dialogical principles in its jurisprudence under section 7 of the Charter. The court's initial reading of that section as being unjustifiable in almost all circumstances shut down dialogue under section 1. To fully utilize dialogue in the substantive criminal law context, it is therefore necessary to reconsider the court's approach to the relationship between these two Charter provisions. In essence, the court is saying that its favoured principles are more important (since justifications of section 7 rights are far less possible) than those rights specifically enumerated in the Charter. Although section 7 principles are "fundamental" to justice, so are enumerated rights. The court's disregard for the polity's explicitly enumerated rights therefore rightly gives rise to charges of institutional elitism.

The solution to the Supreme Court's approach to the relationship between sections 7 and 1, proposed by Roach, is for the court to approach section 1 justifications like it does for other rights provisions.[178] It can be countered, however, that section 7 rights ought to be *more* readily justifiable than enumerated rights. Since enumerated rights are specifically endorsed by the Charter, the court acts with relatively more legitimacy when it strikes down a democratically enacted law under those provisions. Since there was insufficient political agreement on what other substantive principles are fundamental to justice, judges are merely picking from among their favoured philosophers with few restrictions when using section 7 to strike down a law. Arguably, it follows that the court should show more deference to section 1 justifications for rights violations under section 7. Thus, when the Supreme Court finally decides the constitutionality of Parliament's response to cases such as *R v Daviault*,[179] it arguably ought to be more open to upholding the law under section 1, for the physical voluntariness principle's status as a constitutional principle is something less than an enumerated right.[180]

I do not find this argument persuasive. In my view, it ignores the second general lesson learned from the judicial review debate: majoritarian bias is present in well-functioning democracies, especially in the criminal law context. It is arguable that many substantive criminal laws are struck down under section 7 of the Charter because the types of rights that it affords – related to choice, proportionality, and innocence – rarely feature in any bill of rights because of their political unpopularity. In other words, it is likely the same majoritarian problem facing criminal defendants more generally that prevents a broader consideration of substantive criminal justice rights is also at play when a polity enacts a constitutional bill of rights. To apply section 1 in a different way for section 7 rights (at least those rights related to substantive criminal law) than for other enumerated rights would be to give with one hand and take with the other.

The problem of majoritarianism, however, does not necessarily imbue the Supreme Court's decision to employ section 7 with equal democratic credentials as when the court applies an enumerated right. This could follow if one agrees with Dworkin's critique of majority rule or if criminal defendants constitute a "discrete and insular minority" per Ely's defence of democracy. Since neither argument is obviously correct, the fact that the will of the majority is overturned by a small number of judicial elites remains democratically troublesome. If judicial review itself is problematic, then it follows for the reasons explained earlier that a judge who employs her favoured principles of justice is also more democratically troubling than a judge who employs an agreed-on constitutional right. Something more than an ability to increase the fairness and coherence of criminal law is therefore arguably required to respond adequately to the democratic objection to employing section 7 review.[181]

Fortunately, other structural features of the Charter also favour allowing limited resort to section 7. In addition to a section 1 justification, the notwithstanding clause found in section 33 of the Charter mitigates the risk that courts will be able to over-constitutionalize rights when engaging in section 7 review. As Roach maintains, the notwithstanding clause "does not mean that Canadian judges can abandon the search for constitutional theory or the right answers ... It does, however, lower the stakes of the quest for a foolproof theory of judicial review."[182] A similar logic applies to whether courts should be allowed to exercise the broader type of review available under section 7. Although courts can make mistakes when constitutionalizing their preferred principles of justice, the notwithstanding clause provides the legislature with a means to correct those mistakes if it sees fit to do so.

Legislative use of the notwithstanding clause has nevertheless been moribund in practice.[183] The federal government has yet to invoke the notwithstanding clause, and provincial legislatures have invoked it only on rare occasions.[184] This is likely because legislatures face a higher political obstacle in overturning a judicial decision if the Supreme Court determines that an impugned law violates rights.[185] Yet it is unprincipled for Parliament to maintain that the notwithstanding clause cannot serve its purposes when it has not seriously attempted to invoke it. Although using the clause might come with a political price, in other instances it might be viewed favourably by the polity. If there is one area of law where Parliament might reasonably expect to have public support when invoking the notwithstanding clause, surely it is the criminal law where majoritarian bias is most clearly present in the polity.[186]

The most obvious example in which the notwithstanding clause could have been implemented was in response to the Supreme Court's decision in *R v Daviault*.[187] The outcry in response to that decision to order a new trial was understandable. Recall that the court allowed Daviault to plead that he should be acquitted because he was extremely intoxicated when he sexually assaulted a disabled elderly woman. The media called the court's decision an "offence to reason"[188] and an "outrage."[189] Several authors subsequently observed that Parliament very likely would have had majority support to invoke the notwithstanding clause to overrule the court's decision.[190] Indeed, Parliament's response to *Daviault* – section 33.1 of the *Criminal Code* – expressly overruled the court's decision as it applied to violent offences. The enacting government was not worse off politically as a result. Although it is possible that invoking the notwithstanding clause – and therefore admitting a Charter violation – would have resulted in some political backlash, it likely would have paled in comparison to the political response that Parliament would have faced had it simply respected the court's decision.

Similarly, in response to *R v Sharpe*,[191] the Reform Party of Canada suggested utilizing the notwithstanding clause after lower courts struck down the child pornography prohibition. Parliament narrowly voted against the motion 143–129.[192] The reasons for this decision, however, are important. As Wayne McKay observes, the justice minister at the time, Anne MacLellan, "convinced her colleagues to vote against the motion because it was premature. If the motion were to arise again after the Supreme Court's decision, she strongly implied that she would have voted to invoke the notwithstanding clause."[193] Since the Supreme Court's remedies in *Sharpe* effectively repaired the constitutional defects in the child pornography laws, it was unnecessary for Parliament to respond. However, Parliament likely would have had public support for such a response given the general disdain expressed for the court's decision.[194]

A more recent example in which Parliament could have invoked the notwithstanding clause arose from the Supreme Court's decision in *R v Nur*.[195] The accused challenged the constitutionality of section 95(2)(a) of the *Criminal Code*,[196] which imposed a mandatory minimum punishment for the offence of possessing a prohibited or restricted firearm when the firearm is loaded or near ammunition. The offence was a hybrid offence, meaning that the crown could elect to proceed by summary conviction or indictment. Importantly, if the crown chose the former, then there was no mandatory minimum penalty. However, if the crown proceeded by indictment, then the minimum sentence was three years for a first offence and five years for a subsequent offence.[197] According to the crown, the fact that it could avoid imposition of a mandatory minimum sentence by proceeding by summary conviction ought to have resulted in the sentencing provision being upheld. Although the Supreme Court pointed to one case in which the crown imposed a harsh mandatory minimum proceeding by indictment,[198] the crown maintained that improper exercises of its discretion could be addressed under the abuse of process doctrine.[199]

A survey of several recent Supreme Court decisions found that more Canadians disagreed with the court's decision in *Nur* than agreed with it.[200] Notably, all of the other decisions surveyed – taken from between

2013 and 2015 – met with approval by the majority of Canadians. The mere fact that more people disagreed than agreed with the court's decision in *Nur* does not inevitably mean that Parliament was free to invoke the notwithstanding clause. Some citizens might reasonably disagree with the decision but respect the fact that the court's decisions are binding on the government. In other words, they might disagree with *Nur* but agree with the institution of judicial review. The fact that there was a powerful alternative argument to deal with injustices arising from the mandatory minimum punishment – utilizing the abuse of process doctrine to overturn improper decisions to proceed by indictment – nevertheless could have been used alongside substantial public disagreement with the court's decision to invoke the notwithstanding clause. It is unlikely, in my view, that the average Canadian understood the nuances of the crown's argument, and, if explained in plain language to the public, then more people likely would have agreed to reinstitute Parliament's mandatory minimum punishments for the impugned weapons offences.

Cases in which Parliament might have feasibly responded with the notwithstanding clause are likely rare overall.[201] It is impossible to say without more concrete empirical evidence testing Canadians' support for the Supreme Court's decisions in criminal law matters. Parliament is nevertheless capable of engaging in such study or judging the political climate based on the polity's reactions to various judicial decisions. In my view, there is no evidence that Parliament is seriously trying to engage the public on the merits of the court's decisions. If a decision is close in the vote count, or there is a particularly strong dissenting opinion, then there is no reason why Parliament cannot air its views with the polity and make a judgment call about whether it will pay a political price at the polls for invoking the notwithstanding clause.

Although Parliament might only infrequently be able to employ the notwithstanding clause, this is in large part because Canadians in general trust the Supreme Court of Canada to render rights decisions much more than Parliament. It is interesting that those opposed to judicial review rarely observe the significant trust that some polities have in their apex courts vis-à-vis their elected representatives. A poll conducted in Canada in 2015 is illustrative. Its central finding was that "there is a clear preference for the courts – especially the Supreme Court of Canada – over just about every other government institution in the country."[202] Indeed, 61 percent of Canadians expressed "a great deal" or "quite a lot" of confidence in the court, and 74 percent of Canadians held a "favourable" view of the court.[203] Comparable levels of confidence in other government institutions did not rise above 33 percent, with Parliament receiving an approval rating of only 28 percent.[204] The high esteem for the court derived largely from the public's approval of its Charter decisions, with 84 percent of Canadians agreeing that the Charter has been "good" for Canada.[205]

In subsequent studies, the Supreme Court's approval rating dropped to between 48 and 57 percent.[206] Importantly, however, these studies assessed the court's approval rating specifically in the criminal justice context. That context is one in which majoritarian bias predictably would lower levels of confidence in the court because it is the institution most responsible for blocking popular "tough on crime" measures. Typically, this is done via the court's interpretation and application of the Charter. The fact that there was still generally a majority in favour of the court even when it rules on the rights of one of the most unpopular groups of citizens suggests that Canadians, despite widespread biases against criminal defendants, are still highly likely to trust the court on questions of rights even if they do not like the results.

If Canadians are inclined to trust the Supreme Court more than Parliament, and this affects the latter's ability to invoke the notwithstanding clause, then the task of the legislature should be to work to change the current political and constitutional culture. Such a task is not easy, but there is an obvious starting point: good faith effort on behalf of those who do not favour judicial review to convince the majority of Canadians that it is an imperfect institution. Prime Minister Harper's government tried to effect such change by attempting to discredit the Supreme Court as an institution as opposed to convincing the public that a given decision was wrong. Harper's tactic was to repeatedly pass constitutionally suspect laws and then cry foul when the laws were inevitably struck down. The public was likely aware of his tactic since far more Canadians agreed than disagreed with the statement that "the Harper Conservative government has recently tried to provoke the courts for political gain."[207] If, instead, the government expressed a reasonable rights disagreement to the public and received majority support for its position – which could have occurred in the *Daviault, Sharpe,* and *Nur* cases – then Parliament might find the gap in support between it and the Supreme Court close.

Given these lessons from the judicial review debate, it is now possible to summarize how the Supreme Court should decide constitutional cases implicating substantive criminal law. If faced with a multi-pronged Charter challenge from counsel, then the court should first consider whether the impugned law violates an enumerated right. I focused on the three most common rights – freedom of expression, equality, and the prohibition against cruel and unusual punishment – but I do not exclude the possibility that a substantive criminal law could violate a different right. To facilitate appellate review, lower courts should decide all rights issues, including those raised under section 7. However, the Supreme Court typically should refrain from determining whether a law violates section 7 if an enumerated right applies. If a law violates an enumerated right, then the court can send the law back to Parliament to revise it in accordance with its ruling, and Parliament should respond in due course by accepting the court's decision, expressing its policy reasons for justifying a rights infringement under section 1, or invoking the notwithstanding clause.

If an enumerated right does not apply, then the Supreme Court should consider whether the impugned law is inconsistent with any principle of criminal law theory proposed by counsel. Although the court should be cautious about constitutionalizing principles of criminal law theory, it should not shy away from this task simply because such principles have less legitimacy than enumerated rights. The court in the *Motor Vehicle Act Reference*[208] offered a reasonable argument for why section 7 of the Charter protects substantive principles of justice. The mere fact that section 7 protects such principles is not sufficient, however, to justify the court's *preference* for resorting to that provision. By allowing section 7 to play a gap-filling role, the court will ensure that it strikes a reasonable balance between using the Charter in both a legitimate and a just manner.

There are limited circumstances, however, in which the court should consider applying both an enumerated right and a section 7 principle of criminal law theory as an enhanced form of dialogue. Imagine that

Parliament's removal of murder from the duress provisions was the first aspect of the duress defence to be challenged constitutionally. If the court found that the murder exclusion did not violate the moral involuntariness principle,[209] then it could still constitutionalize that principle because it has clear application to other aspects of the law of defences not challengeable under other enumerated rights. In other words, the decision to constitutionalize the moral involuntariness principle could be justified as a prudent form of dialogue aimed at helping future courts and lawmakers to rectify clear defects in the current law. The Supreme Court could then go on to find that a person who commits murder under duress receives a grossly disproportionate mandatory minimum punishment. This violation results from the fact that a person who kills in a "kill-or-be-killed" scenario is of significantly reduced moral blameworthiness compared with the average murderer.[210] Employing section 12 would therefore allow the court to do justice with respect to the punishment imposed, and employing section 7 would allow the court to ensure that justice would be done in future cases.

The Supreme Court's decision in the *Motor Vehicle Act Reference* would not call for a similar approach. The impugned law clearly imposed a grossly disproportionate punishment that would have been sufficient to strike down the unjust mandatory minimum punishment. Although the offence would have been upheld, that is not problematic since there is no constitutional barrier to absolute liability offences that do not engage the liberty interest. Legislatures might have legitimate reasons, based on the need for efficiency, for invoking absolute liability. As long as prison is not a possibility, this is arguably within a range of reasonable uses of regulatory law. Constitutionalizing the prohibition against convicting the morally innocent therefore added little to the section 7 jurisprudence. As Alan Young put it, this constitutional principle was "full of sound and fury signifying nothing."[211] In other words, there was no clear body of existing law that would take immediate guidance from the narrow application of the principle constitutionalized in the *Motor Vehicle Act Reference*.

Although subsequent case law built on the *Motor Vehicle Act Reference*'s holding that some element of fault is necessary where a law engages an individual's liberty interests, that body of case law developed an entirely separate principle: there must be proportionality between the *mens rea* and the stigma of an offence. This broader principle was in no way dependent on the particular principle constitutionalized in the *Motor Vehicle Act Reference*. The coherence of the criminal law was therefore only modestly increased by using section 7 of the Charter in the *Motor Vehicle Act Reference*.[212] Employing that section alongside an enumerated right, then, should occur only if there is a substantial likelihood that the principle of fundamental justice constitutionalized will further the purpose of increasing the coherence and fairness of criminal law. Where a principle of fundamental justice has no clear future application, the court sacrifices some degree of legitimacy in judicial review by employing section 7 without receiving much in return.

Conclusion

Constitutional scholars have yet to adequately apply the general principles arising from the debate on judicial review to the question of how courts ought to decide rights issues under the Charter. Given the inevitable overlap between various types of rights – principles of moral philosophy (enumerated or not) or instrumental rationality – litigants typically will plead all potential principles when challenging the constitutionality of a law. In my view, the broader lessons from the judicial review debate require that the Supreme Court decide constitutional issues based on enumerated rights where possible. Not only are these rights more legitimate, since they were explicitly chosen by the polity, but also courts are more likely to be familiar with them given their general acceptance by the polity. At the same time, failure to employ section 7 where no other enumerated right applies would result in profound injustice in the criminal law context. In determining which principles to constitutionalize, however, it is prudent to choose those that facilitate constructive dialogue between courts and legislatures. The instrumental rationality principles do not serve this end. The principles of criminal law theory can facilitate dialogue as long as the court stops insisting that its chosen principles of fundamental justice are somehow more fundamental (and therefore infringements less justifiable) than those rights enumerated in the Charter.

Lessons from the Canadian Experience   6

Section 7 of the *Charter of Rights and Freedoms* has affected how the Supreme Court of Canada shapes substantive criminal law more than any other rights provision. In its jurisprudence, the court has employed, without any explicit rationalization, two separate categories of "principles of fundamental justice." Each set of principles comes with unique issues. Allowing the court to constitutionalize principles of moral philosophy risks allowing it to engage in substantial judicial overreach and risks distorting the conceptual underpinnings of criminal law. The court's decision to constitutionalize its own principles of justice became relatively more questionable by its unprincipled decision to bar section 1 from justifying infringements of section 7 rights. This approach therefore resulted in powerful claims that the court was acting illegitimately when it struck down laws under section 7 of the Charter.

The Supreme Court's pivot toward the principles of instrumental rationality was designed to address this criticism. Pursuant to these principles, the court could credibly claim that its section 7 decisions facilitated legislative responses and therefore fostered dialogue between the two branches of the government. Yet the particular brand of dialogue promoted by the individualistic conception of the instrumental rationality principles was not constructive. Instead, it encouraged Parliament to engage in coordinate interpretation of constitutional rights. The instrumental rationality principles therefore ought to be abandoned since they risk reducing the strong mandate for judicial review under the Charter to a weak form of judicial review, incapable of checking legislative actions affecting Canada's most unpopular and vulnerable citizens.

The Supreme Court's prioritization of section 7 review had another important effect: it blinded the court to the applicability of the enumerated rights in the Charter.[1] As I have shown, enumerated rights were applicable in most circumstances in which a law was struck down under section 7 of the Charter. There are nevertheless several cases in which section 7 review was the only plausible means for striking down a clearly unjust criminal law. This poses a dilemma for the court moving forward: How can its constitutionalization of substantive criminal law ensure just results for criminal defendants while avoiding charges that it acts illegitimately?

It is not possible to satisfy both goals completely given the inherent tension between legitimacy and justice at the heart of judicial review. This is especially true in the criminal law context because majoritarian demands to be "tough on crime" typically have a negative impact on the rights of unpopular and vulnerable minorities. The Supreme Court therefore should seek to balance concerns about legitimacy and fairness by heeding the ability of each method for constitutionalizing criminal law to achieve its ends. Enumerated rights, reasonably interpreted, provide the most legitimate approach to striking down unconstitutional laws and in most cases achieve just results. As such, enumerated rights review ought to be prioritized.

Section 7 review invites criticism, with good reason, that the Supreme Court is engaging in judicial overreach since it is simply choosing from among its favoured principles of moral philosophy. This is especially unjustifiable when the court ignores applicable enumerated rights to facilitate the constitutionalization of its preferred moral philosophical principles. Yet sometimes justice will demand that the court engage in this broader form of judicial review. In these cases, the court can only respond by mitigating concerns about legitimacy. The most obvious path to achieving this end was blocked by the Supreme Court in the *Motor Vehicle Act Reference*[2] – using section 1 of the Charter to facilitate dialogue on the legitimate scope of Charter rights.[3] By opening the door to dialogue under section 1, and constitutionalizing principles of criminal law theory only as a last resort, the court would substantially increase the legitimacy of section 7 review without sacrificing the interests of justice.

Drawing Lessons

In closing, I want to address the last question posed in the introduction to this book: What might other jurisdictions learn from Canada's experience constitutionalizing principles of substantive criminal law? Although various polities have adopted section 7–like provisions, they interpret these provisions in different ways.[4] Singapore's and Malaysia's constitutions, for instance, offer a purely formal model of review that only requires the state to authorize a law before depriving a person of life or liberty.[5] The Indian Constitution includes a general right not to be deprived of life or liberty without due process of law.[6] Similar due process provisions have been interpreted more broadly in the United States to provide limited substantive protections against state interference with individual privacy or autonomy.[7] The American provisions have not included, however, substantive criminal law theory principles.[8] Finally, like Canada's Constitution, South Africa's Constitution applies a fully substantive approach to its section 7–like clause that allows courts to constitutionalize any principles of criminal law theory.[9]

These states frequently use the language in their respective constitutions to move along this interpretive continuum. Courts in Singapore and Malaysia have regressed from a due process model to a formal model of rights.[10] India has recently reinterpreted its procedural protections more broadly to incorporate similar American-style substantive due process.[11] On other occasions, India's apex court has flirted with constitutionalizing standards of fault.[12] Even though its Constitution seemingly allows for broad substantive review, South Africa's Constitutional Court has retrenched on this guarantee. As the court held in *S v Coetzee*,[13] it is "only when the Legislature has clearly abandoned any requirement of culpability, or when it has established a level of culpability manifestly inappropriate to the unlawful conduct or potential sentence in question, that a provision may be subject to successful constitutional challenge."[14]

Given this interpretive flexibility, which factors should be considered in determining the interpretive model that a court should adopt? Obviously, the wording of the governing provisions should be paramount, but experience suggests that the wording of section 7–like provisions is open ended. In my view, three aspects of the Canadian experience argue for or against allowing judges to constitutionalize limited principles of criminal law theory under section 7 of the Charter. First, the structure of the Charter mitigates the costs of "over-constitutionalization" of rights. Not only does section 1 allow for dialogue between courts and legislatures on the legitimate scope of rights, but also the Charter allows legislatures to pass laws notwithstanding a violation of rights pursuant to section 33. Although the latter provision is underused, I have argued that a legislature that acts responsibly should be able to convince the public that an unpopular rights decision in the criminal law context ought to be subject to legislative override.

Second, the lack of specialization of Canada's apex court militates against allowing it to constitutionalize principles of fundamental justice too aggressively. Importantly, the Supreme Court is not a specialized constitutional court that can be expected to bring substantial expertise in criminal law philosophy to its decision making. Instead, like its American counterpart, the Supreme Court of Canada is a generalist court. This fact casts significant doubt on the justices' ability to craft a coherent structure for criminal law. Although judges must apply broad principles under the common law, mistakes in this context can be readily corrected by the legislature. Constitutional decisions, for better or worse, are binding until a constitutional amendment occurs or the court decides to revisit its prior decisions. It is plausible, however, that specialized constitutional courts such as the one in South Africa or Germany are relatively better equipped to craft general theories of criminal law given their general focus on public law. Detailed comparative study of each apex court's jurisprudence would be necessary to confirm my suspicion, but I think that the hypothesis itself is reasonable.

Third, the degree of trust that citizens hold in their top court is also relevant to whether courts ought to be allowed to constitutionalize their own principles of justice. It is a strange fact of the judicial review debate that leading theorists pay no attention to the significant amount of trust that many polities have in their judiciaries. It seems to me that, where the legislature faces a significant gap in trust vis-à-vis its apex court, those in favour of majoritarian-style democracy ought to be more critical when evaluating whether elected representatives actually govern in accordance with majority will. If democracy is malfunctioning to the point where citizens display significantly more confidence in their apex court than in their elected leaders, then the majoritarian argument loses much of its potency. This fact in turn can be used to argue in favour of a more generous approach to allowing courts to constitutionalize their preferred principles of justice.

These are not the only factors that might be considered in determining whether an apex court should constitutionalize its own conception of criminal law. As George Fletcher suggests, it is also possible that the system of criminal law used by a state can influence whether it is prudent to allow an apex court to constitutionalize its own principles of justice. In his view, "Canada's unitary system of national criminal law sidesteps the problems faced in the United States in any effort to supervise a vast number of diverse state jurisdictions."[15] In other words, where there are multiple legislatures enacting criminal laws, allowing one apex court to dictate the structure of the law might aggravate regional beliefs that local governments are better able to govern local relations. In such circumstances, a doctrine that allows each jurisdiction to constitutionalize principles of substantive criminal justice might prove to be more workable.

Fletcher also raises the fact that a country's historical background can affect whether that country has an appetite for judicial reform of criminal law. Using Canada as his example, Fletcher notes that a failed attempt to provide a wholesale update of Canada's nineteenth-century *Criminal Code* the decade before the Charter was enacted provided courts with the impression that if they did not update the criminal law then no one would.[16] Although Parliament eventually did re-enact the *Criminal Code* with narrow updates in 1985, the statute remains woefully underdeveloped.[17] Fletcher's point is important since the history of any particular country might well provide the motivation necessary to undertake the gargantuan task of updating a largely out-of-date and ill-thought-through criminal law. In particular, perhaps states with sparser populations will have difficulty allocating resources to update criminal law. Moreover, states with more diverse populations might have greater difficulty coming to agreement on how to reform criminal law. If true, then an apex court might be relatively more justified in taking a more aggressive approach to constitutionalizing criminal law since other avenues to reform woefully outdated criminal laws are not tenable.

Even where the above factors favour providing courts with the discretion to constitutionalize their own principles of justice, I think that it would be better if legislatures considered explicitly constitutionalizing more substantive criminal law principles when enacting or amending a bill of rights. Legislatures, as opposed to courts, have sufficient time and resources to extol a coherent set of principles to guide judicial decision making, especially where the apex court is generalist in nature. If, however, a section 7–like provision is to be included in a bill of rights as a gap-filling provision, then the arguments in this book suggest that the enacting legislative body should make it clear that such a provision is applicable only where the constitution's enumerated rights are inapplicable.

Relying on the legislature to enact more robust substantive criminal justice rights might, however, be unrealistic. Such an approach operates on the assumption that those enacting a bill of rights are able to overcome majoritarian bias toward accused persons and convince the majority of citizens to pay attention to the substantive criminal justice rights of the accused. If this is not possible, then allowing for an apex court to constitutionalize substantive principles of justice under a section 7–like provision might provide the only reasonable alternative to ensuring that substantive criminal law is constitutionalized in a fair manner.

Notes

Chapter 1: Choosing among Rights

1 [1985] 2 SCR 486, 24 DLR (4th) 536 [*Motor Vehicle Act Reference*].
2 The *Motor Vehicle Act*, RSBC 1977, c 288, s 94(2), provided that "subsection (1) creates an absolute liability offence in which guilt is established by proof of driving, whether or not the defendant knew of the prohibition or suspension."
3 See *R v Sault Ste Marie*, [1978] 2 SCR 1299, 85 DLR (3rd) 161.
4 Part I of the *Constitution Act, 1982*, being schedule B to the *Canada Act 1982* (UK), 1982, c 11, s 7 [*Charter*].
5 See *Motor Vehicle Act*, supra note 2, 94(1)(c). I will discuss in later chapters the potential interpretation of section 7 providing for two rights, a right to life, liberty, and security of the person and a right "not to be deprived thereof except in accordance with the principles of fundamental justice."
6 *Canadian Bill of Rights*, SC 1960, c 44, s 2(e).
7 This was in fact the meaning given to the term used in the *Canadian Bill of Rights*, supra note 6. See, generally, *R v Duke*, [1972] SCR 917, 28 DLR (3rd) 129.
8 See *Motor Vehicle Act Reference*, supra note 1, 497–99. See also Wayne MacKay, "Fairness after the *Charter*: A Rose by Any Other Name?," *Queen's Law Journal* 10 (1985): 292–307.
9 See *Motor Vehicle Act Reference*, supra note 1, 497.
10 Ibid., 501–2.
11 For extensive reviews, see Michael Stephens, "Fidelity to Fundamental Justice: An Originalist Construction of Section 7 of the *Canadian Charter of Rights and Freedoms*," *National Journal of Constitutional Law* 13 (2002): 183–253; and Sujit Choudhry, "The Lochner Era and Comparative Constitutionalism," *International Journal of Constitutional Law* 2 (2004): 16–27.

12 Peter Hogg, *Canada Act 1982: Annotated* (Toronto: Carswell, 1982), 28. For similar commentary after the passing of the Charter, see John Whyte, "Fundamental Justice: The Scope and Application of Section 7 of the *Charter*," *Manitoba Law Journal* 13 (1983): 455–76; Martin Friedland, "Criminal Justice and the *Charter*," *Manitoba Law Journal* 13 (1983): 549–72; Eric Colvin, "Section Seven of the *Canadian Charter of Rights and Freedoms*," *Canadian Bar Review* 68 (1989): 560–85; and Paul Bender, "The *Canadian Charter of Rights and Freedoms* and the United States Bill of Rights: A Comparison," *McGill Law Journal* 28 (1983): 841–46.

13 See *Latham v Canada (Solicitor General)*, 9 DLR (4th) 393, 12 CCC (3rd) 9; *R v Mason*, 1 DLR (4th) 712, 7 CCC (3rd) 426; *R v Holman*, 28 CR (3rd) 378, 16 MVR 225, affirmed 143 DLR (3rd) 748, 2 CCC (3rd) 19; and *R v Potma*, [1983] OJ No 9 (ONCA).

14 See *Motor Vehicle Act Reference*, supra note 1, 508.

15 Ibid.

16 Ibid.

17 Ibid., 507–8, citing Joseph Magnet, "The Presumption of Constitutionality," *Osgoode Hall Law Journal* 18 (1980): 99–100. For other commentary in support of this broad interpretation of section 7, see Whyte, "Fundamental Justice," supra note 12, 469; Luc Tremblay, "Section 7: Substantive Due Process?," *University of British Columbia Law Review* 18 (1984): 250–51; Tom Cumming, "Fundamental Justice in the *Charter*," *Queen's Law Journal* 11 (1985): 153, 155, 157; Morris Manning, *Rights, Freedoms and the Courts* (Toronto: Emond Montgomery, 1983), 255–74; Timothy Christian, "Section 7 of the *Charter*," *Alberta Law Review* 22 (1984): 242; and Bender, "Canadian Charter," supra note 12, 845–46.

18 See *Motor Vehicle Act Reference*, supra note 1, 503.

19 Ibid.

20 Ibid., 513–15. The text is open, of course, to a "two right" interpretation. See *Gosselin v Québec (Attorney General)*, 2002 SCC 84, [2002] 4 SCR 429 (reasons of Justice Arbour). This reading, however, has yet to be adopted. For an argument against this interpretation, see Eric Colvin, "Section 7 of the *Canadian Charter of Rights and Freedoms*," *Canadian Bar Review* 68 (1989): 563 ("a free-standing right to life, liberty and security would cover any ground on which guarantees of due process and fundamental justice might work. The latter guarantees would be [unnecessary]. The conjunctive reading of the provision enables this result to be avoided.")

21 See *Motor Vehicle Act Reference*, supra note 1, 492.

22 See George Fletcher, *The Grammar of Criminal Law: American, Comparative, and International* (Oxford: Oxford University Press, 2007), 101. The various limitations on what principles qualify as principles of fundamental justice will be canvassed in Chapter 2.

23 See *Gosselin*, supra note 20, para 77, citing *New Brunswick (Minister of Health and Community Services) v G(J)*, [1999] 3 SCR 46 at 79, 177 DLR (4th) 124 ("the

dominant strand of jurisprudence on s. 7 sees its purpose as guarding against certain kinds of deprivation of life, liberty and security of the person, namely, those 'that occur as a result of an individual's interaction with the justice system and its administration'").

24 See, generally, *Motor Vehicle Act Reference*, supra note 1. In my other work, I argue that the moral innocence principle also applies to justificatory versions of the defences of duress, necessity, and self-defence. See Colton Fehr, "(Re-)Constitutionalizing Duress and Necessity," *Queen's Law Journal* 42 (2017): 99–134; and Colton Fehr, "Self-Defence and the Constitution," *Queen's Law Journal* 43 (2017): 85–122.

25 See *R v Vaillancourt*, [1987] 2 SCR 636, 47 DLR (4th) 399; and *R v Martineau*, [1990] 2 SCR 633, 58 CCC (3rd) 353.

26 See *R v Parks*, [1995] 2 SCR 836, 99 CCC (3rd) 1; and *R v Daviault*, [1994] 3 SCR 63, 118 DLR (4th) 469.

27 See *R v Ruzic*, 2001 SCC 24, [2001] 1 SCR 687.

28 See *Canada (Attorney General) v Bedford*, 2013 SCC 72 at para 107, [2013] 3 SCR 1101, citing Hamish Stewart, *Fundamental Justice: Section 7 of the Canadian Charter of Rights and Freedoms* (Toronto: Irwin Law, 2012), 151; and Peter Hogg, "The Brilliant Career of Section 7 of the *Charter*," *Supreme Court Law Review* 58 (2nd) (2012): 209.

29 See *Bedford*, supra note 28, paras 110–23.

30 Ibid. For more detailed explanations and attempts to render these principles coherent, see Hamish Stewart, "*Bedford* and the Structure of Section 7," *McGill Law Journal* 60 (2015): 575–94; Colton Fehr, "The 'Individualistic' Approach to Arbitrariness, Overbreadth, and Gross Disproportionality," *University of British Columbia Law Review* 51 (2018): 55–74; Colton Fehr, "Instrumental Rationality and General Deterrence," *Alberta Law Review* 57 (2019): 53–68; and Colton Fehr, "Re-Thinking the Instrumental Rationality Principles of Fundamental Justice," *Alberta Law Review* 58 (2020): 133–52.

31 See *Bedford*, supra note 28, para 111.

32 Ibid., para 112.

33 Ibid., para 120.

34 See *Carter v Canada (Attorney General)*, 2015 SCC 5 at para 72, [2015] 1 SCR 331.

35 See, for example, Jamie Cameron, "Fault and Punishment under Sections 7 and 12 of the *Charter*," *Supreme Court Law Review* 40 (2nd) (2008): 553–92; and Jonathan Rudin, "Tell It Like It Is – An Argument for the Use of Section 15 over Section 7 to Challenge Discriminatory Criminal Legislation," *Criminal Law Quarterly* 64 (2017): 317–33.

36 See *Charter*, supra note 4, s 2(b).

37 Ibid., s 12.

38 Ibid., s 15.

39 For a review, see Victor Ramraj, "Four Models of Due Process," *International Journal of Constitutional Law* 2 (2004): 492–524.

40 See Fletcher, *Grammar of Criminal Law*, supra note 22, 101 (identifying Canada as "one of the leading jurisdictions in the world in applying constitutional provisions to the general part of criminal law"). See also Kent Roach, "Mind the Gap: Canada's Different Criminal and Constitutional Standards of Fault," *University of Toronto Law Journal* 61 (2011): 546.

41 See Ramraj, "Four Models," supra note 39, 516 ("the only way to achieve coherence, consistency, and predictability in the criminal law is through a constitutionally rooted theory of criminal fault"). See also Benjamin Berger, "Constitutional Principles in Substantive Criminal Law," in *The Oxford Handbook of Criminal Law*, ed. Markus Dubber and Tatjana Hörnle (Oxford: Oxford University Press, 2014), 424 (the interaction between substantive criminal law and the Charter "has proved as likely to limit change and entrench the old as to offer a lever for enlightened reform").

42 See, for example, *Canada (Attorney General) v PHS Community Services Society*, 2011 SCC 44, [2011] 3 SCR 134 (safe injection sites); *Bedford*, supra note 28 (sex work laws); *Carter*, supra note 34 (euthanasia laws); *R v Appulonappa*, 2015 SCC 59, [2015] 3 SCR 754 (human smuggling); and *British Columbia Civil Liberties Association v Canada (Attorney General)*, 2019 BCCA 228, 377 CCC (3rd) 420 (solitary confinement).

43 See Peter Hogg and Allison Bushell, "The *Charter* Dialogue between Courts and Legislatures (Or Perhaps the *Charter of Rights* Isn't Such a Bad Thing after All)," *Osgoode Hall Law Journal* 35 (1997): 75–124.

44 This has been suggested elsewhere but without empirical support. See Andrew Menchynski and Jill Presser, "A Withering Instrumentality: The Negative Implications of *R. v. Safarzadeh-Markhali* and Other Recent Section 7 Jurisprudence," *Supreme Court Law Review* 81 (2nd) (2017): 86.

45 See Chapter 2. I use the felony murder laws and the statutory duress defence as my primary examples.

46 I will provide examples in Chapter 4.

47 Although section 1 justifications of section 7 rights infringements are infrequent in Canadian law (see *Motor Vehicle Act Reference*, supra note 1, 518), there is reason to believe that the Supreme Court has changed its position and will allow for greater dialogue on the substantive scope of criminal justice. See *Bedford*, supra note 28, para 129.

48 See *Bedford*, supra note 28, para 129.

49 See, for example, Angus Reid Institute, "Canadians Have a More Favourable View of Their Supreme Court Than Americans Have of Their Own," 17 August 2015, http://angusreid.org/supreme-court/.

Chapter 2: Principles of Criminal Law Theory

Acknowledgment: Parts of Chapter 2 first appeared in Colton Fehr, "(Re-)Constitutionalizing Duress and Necessity," *Queen's Law Journal* 42 (2017): 99–134.

1 See George Fletcher, *The Grammar of Criminal Law: American, Comparative, and International* (Oxford: Oxford University Press, 2007), 101. See also Kent Roach,

"Mind the Gap: Canada's Different Criminal and Constitutional Standards of Fault," *University of Toronto Law Journal* 61 (2011): 546.

2   See Benjamin Berger, "Constitutional Principles in Substantive Criminal Law," in *The Oxford Handbook of Criminal Law*, ed. Markus Dubber and Tatjana Hörnle (Oxford: Oxford University Press, 2014), 424. See also Jamie Cameron, "Fault and Punishment under Sections 7 and 12 of the *Charter*," *Supreme Court Law Review* 40 (2nd) (2008): 569 (calling the court's constitutionalization of criminal law theory "no more than a modest success").

3   See *R v Ruzic*, 2001 SCC 24 at para 45, [2001] 1 SCR 687.

4   Intoxication is often referred to as a "defence" in the lay sense of the term since it results in an acquittal. As I explain below, the result of a successful intoxication plea is that the state is unable to prove the *actus reus* (general intent offences) or *mens rea* (general and specific intent offences) of the offence. Criminal defences (at least those commonly referred to as "justification" or "excuse") assume that the *actus reus* and *mens rea* of the offence have been committed and instead ask whether the reasons underlying the accused person's offence are justified or excused. In legal terms, intoxication is therefore not a "defence." See John Gardner, *Offences and Defences* (Oxford: Oxford University Press, 2007), 141–53.

5   Since the *mens rea* for general intent offences is inferred from the commission of the *actus reus* (see *R v Théroux*, [1993] 2 SCR 5 at 17, 100 DLR (4th) 624), it is sensible to organize the application of the intoxication defence for general intent offences as a predominantly *actus reus* issue. However, whether the intoxication defence for specific intent offences is made out solely concerns whether intent is present. As such, it will be analyzed under the *mens rea* heading.

6   See *R v Tatton*, 2015 SCC 33 at paras 30–45, [2015] 2 SCR 574.

7   I say "typically" because not all instances of murder require intent. See *Criminal Code of Canada*, RSC 1985, c C-46, s 229(c). It is also notable that an accused person can be convicted of first-degree murder in the absence of planning and deliberation in narrow circumstances. See ibid., ss 231(4) and (5).

8   See *Tatton*, supra note 6, paras 30–45.

9   Ibid.

10 [1978] 1 SCR 29, 74 DLR (3rd) 103.

11 Ibid. The Supreme Court followed the reasoning of the House of Lords decision in *Director of Public Prosecutions v Majewski*, [1977] AC 443.

12 [1994] 3 SCR 63, 118 DLR (4th) 469. For the law on involuntary intoxication, see *R v King*, [1962] SCR 746, 133 CCC 1.

13 For a review of the facts, see *Daviault*, supra note 12, 104–6.

14 See, generally, the reasons of Justice Cory as well as the reasons of Chief Justice Lamer and Justice LaForest. The conclusion that extreme intoxication is better framed as a failure to prove the *actus reus* of the offence was affirmed in *Ruzic*, supra note 3, para 43. See also *R v Daley*, 2007 SCC 53, [2007] 3 SCR 523.

15 See *Daviault*, supra note 12, 87.

16 See *Ruzic*, supra note 3, paras 43–45, summarizing the physical voluntariness principle of fundamental justice. There is one notable exception to this rule: impaired driving. See *R v Penno*, [1990] 2 SCR 865, 59 CCC (3rd) 344.
17 See *R v Parks*, [1992] 2 SCR 871, 95 DLR (4th) 27.
18 See *Rabey v The Queen*, [1980] 2 SCR 513, 114 DLR (3rd) 193; and *R v Stone*, [1999] 2 SCR 290, 173 DLR (4th) 66. The latter case, however, has made these defences difficult to plead successfully. See David Paciocco, "Death by *Stone*-ing: The Demise of the Defence of Simple Automatism," *Criminal Reports* 26 (5th) (1999): 273–85.
19 See the public reaction as reviewed in Don Stuart, *Canadian Criminal Law: A Treatise*, 6th ed. (Toronto: Thomson Carswell, 2011), 469–70; Isabelle Grant, "Second Chances: Bill C-72 and the *Charter*," *Osgoode Hall Law Journal* 33 (1995): 383n12; and Gerry Ferguson, "The Intoxication Defence: Constitutionally Impaired and in Need of Rehabilitation," *Supreme Court Law Review* 57 (2nd) (2012): 125n60.
20 See *Criminal Code*, supra note 7, s 33.1(1).
21 Ibid., s 33.1(2–3).
22 See *R v Sullivan*, 2020 ONCA 333, 151 OR (3rd) 353.
23 See *R v McCaw*, 2018 ONSC 3464, 48 CR (7th) 359 (struck down); *R v Dunn* (1999), 28 CR (5th) 295, 44 WCB (2nd) 47 (ONCJ) (struck down); *R v Brenton*, 180 DLR (4th) 314, [2000] 2 WWR 269 (NTSC) (struck down); *R v Vickberg* (1998), 16 CR (5th) 164, 18 CPC (4th) 357 (BCSC) (upheld); *R v TBJ*, 2000 SKQB 572, 200 Sask R 42 (upheld); *R v Fleming*, 2010 ONSC 8022, 94 WCB (2nd) 252 (struck down); and *R v SN*, 2012 NUCJ 2, 99 WCB (2nd) 841 (upheld). For academic works, see Michelle Lawrence, "Voluntary Intoxication and the *Charter*: Revisiting the Constitutionality of Section 33.1 of the *Criminal Code*," *Manitoba Law Journal* 40 (2017): 391–424; Grant, "Second Chances," supra note 19; Martin Shain, "The *Charter* and Intoxication: Some Observations on Possible *Charter* Challenges to an Act to Amend the *Criminal Code* (Self-Induced Intoxication) 1995, C-72," *Contemporary Drug Problems* 23 (1996): 731–34; and Heather MacMillan-Brown, "No Longer 'Leary' about Intoxication: In the Aftermath of *R v Daviault*," *Saskatchewan Law Review* 59 (1995): 311–34.
24 See *Reference re Section 94(2) of the Motor Vehicle Act*, [1985] 2 SCR 486 at 518, 512, 24 DLR (4th) 536 [*Motor Vehicle Act Reference*]. The Supreme Court has subsequently relaxed this strict standard.
25 [1993] 3 SCR 519, 107 DLR (4th) 342.
26 Ibid., 588–89.
27 Ibid.
28 Ibid.
29 Ibid., 592.
30 Ibid.
31 Ibid., 592–93.
32 Ibid.

33 See, for example, Article 1 of German Basic Law (1949) ("human dignity is inviolable"). For a discussion on how human dignity as a constitutional principle can influence criminal law, see George Fletcher, "Human Dignity as a Constitutional Value," *University of Western Ontario Law Review* 22 (1984): 171–82.
34 Such an originalist understanding of human dignity has been eschewed in other contexts. German Basic Law is again illustrative. See Lorraine Weinrib, "Human Dignity as a Rights-Protecting Principle," *National Journal of Constitutional Law* 17 (2004): 342–43.
35 2003 SCC 74, [2003] 3 SCR 571.
36 Ibid., para 90, citing John Stuart Mill, *On Liberty and Considerations on Representative Government* (Oxford: Basil Blackwell, 1946).
37 *Malmo-Levine*, supra note 35, para 238, citing Patrick Devlin, *The Enforcement of Morals* (Oxford: Oxford University Press, 1965).
38 See Devlin, *Enforcement of Morals*, supra note 37; and H.L.A. Hart, *Law, Liberty, and Morality* (Stanford, CA: Stanford University Press, 1977). The authors debated the Wolfenden Report's recommendation to decriminalize homosexuality. See United Kingdom, House of Commons, "Report of the Committee on Homosexual Offences and Prostitution," Cmnd 247 in *Sessional Papers* 14 (1956–57): 85.
39 For a review and critique of the literature, see Bernard Harcourt, "The Collapse of the Harm Principle," *Journal of Criminal Law and Criminology* 90 (1999): 120–38.
40 See *R v Malmo-Levine*, 2000 BCCA 335, 145 CCC (3rd) 225; *R v Clay* (2000), 49 OR (3rd) 577, 188 DLR (4th) 468 (ONCA); and *R v Murdock* (2003), 173 OAC 171, 176 CCC (3rd) 232 (ONCA).
41 The Supreme Court also asserts that the harm principle did not pass a third, less-employed factor: that the principle be a "legal principle." Since the court did not explain its reasoning on this point, I will not discuss it further. See *Malmo-Levine*, supra note 35, para 114.
42 See *Rodriguez*, supra note 25, 591.
43 See Devlin, *Enforcement of Morals*, supra note 37. For a concise review, see Harcourt, "Collapse," supra note 39, 124–29.
44 See, for example, Catharine MacKinnon, *Only Words* (Cambridge, MA: Harvard University Press, 1993); and Catharine MacKinnon, *Toward a Feminist Theory of the State* (Cambridge, MA: Harvard University Press, 1989).
45 See George Kelling and James Wilson, "Broken Windows: The Police and Neighbourhood Safety," *Atlantic*, March 1982, https:// www.theatlantic.com/magazine/archive/1982/03/broken-windows/304465/. For one of many critiques of these theories, see Bernard Harcourt and Jens Ludwig, "Broken Windows: New Evidence from New York City and a Five-City Social Experiment," *University of Chicago Law Review* 73 (2006): 271–320.
46 See *Malmo-Levine*, supra note 35, para 127, citing Harcourt, "Collapse," supra note 37, 113.

47 Ibid.
48 *Canadian Foundation for Children, Youth and the Law v Canada (Attorney General)*, 2004 SCC 4 at para 8, [2004] 1 SCR 76.
49 Ibid.
50 See *Motor Vehicle Act Reference*, supra note 24, 503.
51 See *Malmo-Levine*, supra note 35, para 115.
52 Ibid., paras 116–22.
53 Ibid., para 117, citing *Criminal Code*, supra note 7, s 182.
54 Ibid., citing *Criminal Code*, supra note 7, s 160.
55 Ibid., para 118, citing *Criminal Code*, supra note 7, s 71. It is notable that consent does not negate the fact that harm does occur from a duel.
56 Ibid., citing *Criminal Code*, supra note 7, s 155. For an argument outlining why instances of consensual incest do not result in any provable harm in many instances, see Colton Fehr, "Consent and the Constitution," *Manitoba Law Journal* 42 (2019): 243–47.
57 This point was made in *Malmo-Levine (BCCA)*, supra note 40, paras 33–36. See also Paul Burstein, "What's the Harm in Having a 'Harm Principle' Enshrined in Section 7 of the *Charter*?," *Supreme Court Law Review* 24 (2nd) (2004): 188.
58 See Harcourt, "Collapse," supra note 39, 163–67.
59 See Hart, *Law, Liberty, and Morality*, supra note 38, 50.
60 The fact that this narrow understanding of the harm principle is unlikely to be invoked also cannot impede the harm principle's recognition as a principle of fundamental justice. Kent Roach makes a similar argument in his article "The Changed Nature of the Harm Debate," *Criminal Law Quarterly* 60 (2014): 321–23. It is not difficult to find narrow and rarely used principles of fundamental justice. The vagueness doctrine is exemplary since only one provision has been invalidated using this principle. See *R v Morales*, [1992] 3 SCR 711, 77 CCC (3rd) 91 (denial of bail in the "public interest").
61 See Joel Feinberg, *The Moral Limits of the Criminal Law* (Oxford: Oxford University Press, 1984), vol. 1, *Harm to Others*, 12; vol. 4, *Harmless Wrongdoing*, 323.
62 See ibid., vol. 4, 323.
63 *Constitution Act, 1867* (UK), 30 & 31 Vict, c 3, reprinted in RSC 1985, Appendix II, No 5.
64 See *Malmo-Levine*, supra note 35, para 74, citing *Reference re Firearms Act (Can.)*, 2000 SCC 31, [2000] 1 SCR 783; *RJR-MacDonald Inc v Canada (Attorney General)*, [1995] 3 SCR 199, 127 DLR (4th) 1; and *Labatt Breweries of Canada Ltd v Attorney General of Canada*, [1980] 1 SCR 914, 110 DLR (3rd) 594.
65 See *Malmo-Levine*, supra note 35, para 77. ("The protection of vulnerable groups from self-inflicted harms does not ... amount to no more than 'legal moralism.' Morality has traditionally been identified as a legitimate concern of the criminal law although today this does not include mere 'conventional standards of propriety' but must be understood as referring to societal values beyond the simply prurient or prudish.")

66 Ibid., para 67, citing *R v Hauser*, [1979] 1 SCR 984 at 1000, 98 DLR (3rd) 193.
67 Ibid.
68 Ibid., paras 67–72.
69 See Roach, "Mind the Gap," supra note 1, 546.
70 [1957] SCR 531, 118 CCC 129.
71 RSC 1952, c 201 [*ONDA*].
72 See *Beaver*, supra note 70, 534.
73 Ibid., 537, quoting *Attorney General v Bradlaugh* (1885), 14 QBD 667 at 689–90. It is notable that the common law in England was still binding in Canada when *Beaver* was decided.
74 Ibid., 542. The Supreme Court later affirmed this rule in *R v Pappajohn*, [1980] 2 SCR 120 at 139, 111 DLR (3rd) 1.
75 Ibid., 541–42.
76 [1978] 2 SCR 1299, 85 DLR (3rd) 161.
77 Ibid., 1310.
78 Ibid., 1326.
79 Supra note 24.
80 Ibid., 492.
81 Ibid.
82 The Supreme Court has affirmed that absolute liability offences are permissible to the extent that they do not engage section 7. See, generally, *Lévis (City) v Tétreault; Lévis (City) v 2629–4470 Québec Inc*, 2006 SCC 12, [2006] 1 SCR 420.
83 It is particularly notable that even high fines do not engage the life, liberty, and security of the person interests. See *R v 1260448 Ontario Inc* (2003), 68 OR (3rd) 51 (ONCA); and *R v Polewsky* (2005), 202 CCC (3rd) 257 (ONCA). If the failure to pay the fines might result in imprisonment, then the law will engage the liberty interest.
84 This was affirmed in *R v Wholesale Travel Group Inc*, [1991] 3 SCR 154 at 183, 84 DLR (4th) 161.
85 [1987] 2 SCR 636, 47 DLR (4th) 399.
86 Ibid., 643.
87 Ibid., 653–54.
88 Ibid.
89 [1990] 2 SCR 633, 58 CCC (3rd) 353.
90 Ibid., 641.
91 Ibid., 644.
92 [1990] 2 SCR 731, 73 DLR (4th) 40.
93 Ibid., 743.
94 See Roach, "Mind the Gap," supra note 1, 557, citing the *mens rea* standard developed under the common law in *R v Ancio*, [1984] 1 SCR 225, 6 DLR (4th) 577.
95 See *Logan*, supra note 92, 743.
96 See *R v Finta*, [1994] 1 SCR 701, 112 DLR (4th) 513.
97 See *Logan*, supra note 92, 744, citing *Vaillancourt*, supra note 85, 653.

98 See *R v Khawaja*, 2012 SCC 69, [2012] 3 SCR 555. It is likely, however, that subjective principles of fault were implemented to avoid a section 7 challenge of this sort. See Kent Roach, *The 9/11 Effect* (Cambridge: Cambridge University Press, 2011), 379–82; and Stanley Cohen, "Safeguards in and Justifications for Canada's New Anti-Terrorism Act," *National Journal of Constitutional Law* 14 (2002–03): 99–123. For critical commentary on the lower court's decision not to apply constitutional principles of subjective fault, see Kent Roach, "Terrorism Offences and the *Charter*: A Comment on *R v Khawaja*," *Canadian Criminal Law Review* 11 (2007): 271–300.
99 See *Vaillancourt*, supra note 85, 653.
100 Ibid., 661 (Justices Beetz and Le Dain concurring).
101 Supra note 84.
102 RSC 1970, c C-23.
103 Ibid., s 36(5).
104 Ibid., s 37.3(2).
105 See *Wholesale Group*, supra note 84, 252–53.
106 Ibid., 235–41.
107 For a review of the multiple decisions forming this view, see James Stribopoulos, "The Constitutionalization of 'Fault' in Canada: A Normative Critique," *Criminal Law Quarterly* 42 (1999): 272–73.
108 [1992] 2 SCR 606, 74 CCC (3rd) 209.
109 Ibid., 659.
110 [1992] 2 SCR 944, 95 DLR (4th) 595.
111 See *Criminal Code*, supra note 7, s 269.
112 See *DeSousa*, supra note 110, 967. For jurisprudence suggesting the contrary, see 963.
113 [1993] 3 SCR 3, 105 DLR (4th) 632.
114 See *Criminal Code*, supra note 7, s 222(5)(a).
115 See *Creighton*, supra note 113, 40–41.
116 Ibid., 46–49. Justice LaForest, 37–40, cast the deciding vote in favour of this view. For the opposing view, see 17–23.
117 Ibid., 50–52. For similar reasoning in the context of the offence of failing to provide the necessaries of life, see *R v Naglik*, [1993] 3 SCR 122 at 143–44, 105 DLR (4th) 712. It is also notable that the Ontario Court of Appeal subsequently found the thin skull principle to be consistent with section 7 of the Charter based on the reasoning in *Creighton*. See *R v Cribbin* (1994), 18 CCC (3rd) 67, 28 CR (4th) 137. For a competing view, see Gerry Ferguson, "Causation and the *Mens Rea* for Manslaughter: A Lethal Combination," *Criminal Reports* 99 (6th) (2013): 351.
118 [1993] 1 SCR 867, 79 CCC (3rd) 97.
119 Ibid., 886.
120 Ibid., 884.
121 Ibid., 884–85.

122 Ibid., 885.
123 Ibid., 888. The modified objective standard has since been described more fully in *R v Roy*, 2012 SCC 26, [2012] 2 SCR 60.
124 (1992), 76 CCC (3rd) 219, 10 OR (3rd) 596.
125 Ibid.
126 [1993] 3 SCR 103, 105 DLR (4th) 699.
127 Ibid., 117–19. This interpretation was confirmed in *R v Beatty*, 2008 SCC 5 at paras 7, 36, [2008] 1 SCR 149.
128 [1956] SCR 640, 4 DLR (2nd) 406.
129 Ibid., 647.
130 Ibid., 645–46 (Justice Taschereau), 648 (Justice Rand, Justice Locke concurring), and 652 (Justice Cartwright, Justice Nolan concurring).
131 Supra note 74, 139 (the majority agreed with Justice Dickson's dissenting comments on this point).
132 See *DeSousa*, supra note 110, 967.
133 Ibid., 966.
134 Ibid., 967.
135 See *Creighton*, supra note 113, 53.
136 Ibid.
137 Ibid.
138 Ibid., citing *R c Lippé*, [1991] 2 SCR 114 at 142, 61 CCC (3rd) 127; *Wholesale Travel Group*, supra note 82, 186; *Finlay*, supra note 125, 330.
139 [1920] AC 479.
140 Ibid.
141 Ibid.
142 [1996] 1 SCR 683, 133 DLR (4th) 42.
143 Ibid., 708.
144 Ibid. See also *Daley*, supra note 14. For my explanation of why intoxication is not a "defence," see note 4.
145 See Roach, "Mind the Gap," supra note 1, 546–47; Berger, "Constitutional Principles," supra note 2, 16–19; Alan Brudner, "Guilt under the *Charter:* The Lure of Parliamentary Supremacy," *Criminal Law Quarterly* 40 (1998): 308; and Sarah-jane Nussbaum, "Diminishing Protection of Subjective Fault? A Case Comment on R. v. A.D.H.," *Saskatchewan Law Review* 77 (2014): 279–300.
146 See Roach, "Mind the Gap," supra note 1, 555–59.
147 Ibid., 547, 549, 568, citing George Fletcher, *Rethinking Criminal Law* (Oxford: Oxford University Press, 2000), 6.8; Victor Tadros, *Criminal Responsibility* (Oxford: Oxford University Press, 2005). For Canadian support of objective fault around the time that the Supreme Court constitutionalized fault standards, see Don Stuart, "Criminal Negligence: Deadlock and Confusion in the Supreme Court," *Criminal Reports* 69 (3rd) (1989): 331–36; Marc Rosenberg, "The *Mens Rea* Requirements of Criminal Negligence: *R. v. Waite* and *R. v. Tutton*," *Journal of Motor Vehicle Law* 2

(1990): 248; and Anne Stalker, "The Fault Element in Recodifying Criminal Law: A Critique," *Queen's Law Journal* 14 (1989): 127.
148 See Roach, "Mind the Gap," supra note 1, 547, citing Ulrich Beck, *Risk Society: Toward a New Modernity* (London: Sage, 1992); David Garland, *The Culture of Control* (Chicago: University of Chicago Press, 2001).
149 Ibid.
150 See Roach, "Mind the Gap," supra note 1, 550–51.
151 Ibid.
152 See *Canada (Attorney General) v Bedford*, 2013 SCC 72 at para 129, [2013] 3 SCR 1101.
153 Ibid. As explained earlier, the previous standard derived from the *Motor Vehicle Act Reference*, supra note 24, 518 ("exceptional conditions, such as natural disasters, the outbreak of war, epidemics, and the like").
154 Only a breach of the overbreadth principle has been justified. See *R v Michaud*, 2015 ONCA 585, 127 OR (3rd) 81.
155 See Hamish Stewart, "*Bedford* and the Structure of Section 7," *McGill Law Journal* 60 (2015): 593n73 (responding specifically to Roach's article and calling his position "unwise").
156 Roach provides some reasons, but none strikes me as compelling. See Roach, "Mind the Gap," supra note 1, 564–67. For literature supporting the use of objective standards of fault, see Stribopoulos, "The Constitutionalization of Fault," supra note 107, 267–72, building on the work of others, such as George Fletcher, "The Theory of Criminal Negligence: A Comparative Analysis," *University of Pennsylvania Law Review* 119 (1971): 401–38; and R.A. Duff, *Intention, Agency and Criminal Liability: Philosophy of Action and the Criminal Law* (Oxford: Basil Blackwell, 1990).
157 This argument is especially forceful given the Supreme Court's reasons for rejecting the harm principle in *Malmo-Levine*, supra note 35, discussed above. Because the principles of fundamental justice must not admit many (if any) exceptions, a rule that relies on section 1 to compensate for the many exceptions to a general rule seems to be ill suited to qualify as a principle of fundamental justice.
158 See Berger, "Constitutional Principles," supra note 2, 9–10, 18. Berger asserts this to be true but does not unpack the jurisprudence applying fault review only to "high stigma" offences, which leaves out a broader conception of proportionality.
159 See *Martineau*, supra note 89, 645, citing H.L.A. Hart, *Punishment and Responsibility* (New York: Oxford University Press, 1968), 162.
160 Ibid.
161 See Brudner, "Guilt under the *Charter*," supra note 145, 319. See also Alan Brudner, "Proportionality, Stigma and Discretion," *Criminal Law Quarterly* 38 (1996): 302–21.
162 See Brudner, "Guilt under the *Charter*," supra note 145, 323.
163 Ibid., 318.

164 Ibid., 323.
165 See Terry Skolnik, "Objective *Mens Rea* Revisited," *Canadian Criminal Law Review* 22 (2017): 319–20. See also Don Stuart, *Canadian Criminal Law*, 7th ed. (Toronto: Carswell, 2014), 291. ("Is the majority [in *Creighton*] really serious that a jury must be instructed to ignore the age of the accused and to apply the standard of the average, experienced driver? This would defy common sense and the jury would likely ignore it.")
166 See Skolnik, "Objective *Mens Rea*," supra note 165, 319–20.
167 Hypothetical scenarios such as the one proposed by Skolnik, "Objective *Mens Rea*," supra note 165, 320–21, are, with respect, far-fetched. Even if a person were to receive a licence because he had a surprisingly competent driver's test despite typically being an incompetent driver, it is not unreasonable for the law to demand that such a person reflect on his actual capabilities before driving.
168 For a review of this argument, see ibid., 324–26.
169 For a review of the disorder and its implications for the criminal justice system, see Kent Roach and Andrea Bailey, "The Relevance of Fetal Alcohol Spectrum Disorder and the Criminal Law from Investigation to Sentencing," *University of British Columbia Law Review* 42 (2009): 1–68; and Suzanne Tough and Monica Jack, "Frequency of FASD in Canada, and What This Means for Prevention Efforts," in *Fetal Alcohol Spectrum Disorder: Management and Policy Perspectives of FASD*, ed. Edward Riley et al. (Weinheim: Wiley-Blackwell, 2011), 29.
170 See Maria Catterick and Liam Curran, *Understanding Fetal Alcohol Spectrum Disorder: A Guide for Parents, Carers, and Professionals* (London: Jessica Kingsley, 2014), 19–20.
171 Gideon Koren et al., "Fetal Alcohol Spectrum Disorder," *Canadian Medical Association Journal* 169 (2003): 1181.
172 2002 SKPC 37, 53 WCB (2nd) 441.
173 Ibid., para 46.
174 Ibid.
175 See, for example, *R v Ramsay*, 2012 ABCA 257, 536 AR 174; *R v Charlie*, 2015 YKCA 3, 366 BCAC 254; *R v Friesen*, 2016 MBCA 50, 330 Man R (2nd) 32; and *R v JP*, 2020 SKCA 52, 62 CR (7th) 328.
176 See *Ruzic*, supra note 3, paras 32–41.
177 See Fletcher, *Rethinking Criminal Law*, supra note 147, Chapter 10.
178 See *R v Paquette*, [1977] 2 SCR 189, 70 DLR (4th) 129.
179 See *R v Ryan*, 2013 SCC 3, [2013] 1 SCR 14.
180 Section 17 of the *Criminal Code* excludes a variety of offences from the duress defence, including robbery, assault with a weapon, and arson. For a review of the constitutionality of these exclusions, see *R v Allen*, 2014 SKQB 402, 318 CCC (3rd) 335; and *R v Willis*, 2016 MBCA 113, 344 CCC (3rd) 443. For a discussion of the constitutionality of excluding any offences (including murder) from the common law defence, see *R v Aravena*, 2015 ONCA 250, 323 CCC (3rd) 54.
181 See *Perka v The Queen*, [1984] 2 SCR 232, 13 DLR (4th) 1.

182 The moral involuntariness principle was originally applied to the defences of duress and necessity. See ibid. Also see *R v Hibbert*, [1995] 2 SCR 973, 99 CCC (3rd) 193; and *R v Latimer*, 2001 SCC 1, [2001] 1 SCR 3. The Supreme Court extended the reach of the moral involuntariness principle to mental disorder in *R v Bouchard-Lebrun*, 2011 SCC 58 at para 51, [2011] 3 SCR 575.
183 See *Perka*, supra note 181, 249–50, citing Fletcher, *Rethinking Criminal Law*, supra note 147, 804–5.
184 Supra note 181.
185 Ibid., 251.
186 Supra note 3.
187 Ibid., para 16.
188 Ibid., para 20.
189 See *Perka*, supra note 181, 248.
190 Ibid., 245–46.
191 See *Ruzic*, supra note 3, para 25.
192 Ibid., para 47.
193 The same rationale was later used to strike down a variety of offences excluded under section 17 from being eligible for the duress defence. For a review of the constitutionality of these exclusions, see *Allen*, supra note 180; *Aravena*, supra note 180; and *Willis*, supra note 180.
194 See *Ruzic*, supra note 3, para 101.
195 Ibid., paras 32–41.
196 See the earlier discussion in this chapter on absolute liability offences and the Charter.
197 See *Ruzic*, supra note 3, para 39.
198 Ibid.
199 Ibid.
200 (New York: Avon Books, 1974).
201 See Stephen Coughlan, "Duress, Necessity, Self-Defence, and Provocation: Implications of Radical Change," *Canadian Criminal Law Review* 7 (2002): 188; Benjamin Berger, "Emotions and the Veil of Voluntarism: The Loss of Judgment in Canadian Criminal Defences," *McGill Law Journal* 51 (2006): 118; and Colton Fehr, "(Re-)Constitutionalizing Duress and Necessity," *Queen's Law Journal* 42 (2017): 116.
202 See *Perka*, supra note 181, 248.
203 In a series of articles, I develop a principle of fundamental justice that prohibits convicting people for "morally permissible" conduct. See Fehr, "(Re-)Constitutionalizing Duress and Necessity," supra note 201; Colton Fehr, "Self-Defence and the Constitution," *Queen's Law Journal* 43 (2017): 85–122; and Fehr, "Consent," supra note 56.
204 See *Ruzic*, supra note 3, para 41. The Supreme Court's refusal to recognize justification-based defences under the Charter echoes the common law position in *Perka*, supra note 181, 248, that the legislature is to determine when an act is justified.

205 See *Perka*, supra note 181, 246; and *Ryan*, supra note 179, para 31.
206 See Coughlan, "Implications of Radical Change," supra note 201, 188; Berger, "Veil of Voluntarism," supra note 201, 118; and Fehr, "(Re-)Constitutionalizing Duress and Necessity," supra note 201, 116.
207 It is notable that the *Criminal Code*, supra note 7, s 8(3), gives courts the explicit authority to preserve common law justifications. Thus, the Supreme Court's decision in *Perka*, supra note 181, not to use the common law to preserve justification-based defences is not persuasive.
208 See Fehr, "(Re-)Constitutionalizing Duress and Necessity," supra note 201, 101.
209 See Coughlan, "Implications of Radical Change," supra note 201, 157–58; Bruce Archibald, "The General Part of Canadian Criminal Law and Criminal Law Reform" (unpublished paper, n.d.), 93; Don Stuart, *Canadian Criminal Law*, 3rd ed. (Toronto: Carswell, 1995), 475; Jeremy Horder, "Self-Defence, Necessity and Duress: Understanding the Relationship," *Canadian Journal of Law and Jurisprudence* 11 (1998): 160; Zoë Sinel, "The Duress Dilemma: Potential Solutions in the Theory of Right," *Appeal: Review of Current Law and Legal Reform* 10 (2005): 64; Hamish Stewart, "The Constitution and the Right of Self-Defence," *University of Toronto Law Journal* 61 (2011): 899–919; Alan Brudner, "Constitutionalizing Self-Defence," *University of Toronto Law Journal* 61 (2011): 867–97; Fehr, "(Re-)Constitutionalizing Duress and Necessity," supra note 201; and Fehr, "Self-Defence," supra note 203.
210 See Berger, "Veil of Voluntarism," supra note 201, 103, 109.
211 Ibid., 111.
212 Ibid.
213 Ibid., 112–13, relying on the provocation case of *R v Fraser* (1980), 26 AR 33, 15 Alta LR (2nd) 25 (ABCA).
214 See Stanley Yeo, "Revisiting Necessity," *Criminal Law Quarterly* 56 (2010): 20; and Fehr, "(Re-)Constitutionalizing Duress and Necessity," supra note 201, 115.
215 Ibid.
216 See Fehr, "(Re-)Constitutionalizing Duress and Necessity," supra note 201, 115–16.
217 Ibid., 106, citing *Ryan*, supra note 179, para 73.
218 See *Ruzic*, supra note 3, para 47.
219 See *Ryan*, supra note 179, para 71; emphasis added.
220 See Fehr, "(Re-)Constitutionalizing Duress and Necessity," supra note 201, 109.
221 Ibid., citing Coughlan, "Implications of Radical Change," supra note 201, 157–58.
222 For a more detailed review of this criticism, see Fehr, "(Re-)Constitutionalizing Duress and Necessity," supra note 201, 119–20.
223 See Coughlan, "Implications of Radical Change," supra note 201, 198–99.
224 See *Perka*, supra note 181, 246.
225 See *Ruzic*, supra note 3, para 25.
226 In Canada, this provision is found in section 12 of the Charter.

227 See, for example, *R v Smith (Edward Dewey)*, [1987] 1 SCR 1045, 40 DLR (4th) 435; *R v Nur*, 2015 SCC 15, [2015] 1 SCR 773; *R v Morrisey*, 2000 SCC 39, [2000] 2 SCR 90; and *R v Ferguson*, 2008 SCC 6, [2008] 1 SCR 96.
228 2008 SCC 25, [2008] 2 SCR 3.
229 SC 2002, c 1.
230 See *DB*, supra note 228, para 41.
231 Ibid.
232 See Nicholas Bala, "Changing Professional Culture and Reducing Use of Courts and Custody for Youth: *The Youth Criminal Justice Act* and Bill C-10," *Saskatchewan Law Review* 78 (2015): 127–80.
233 See *R v Ipeelee*, 2012 SCC 13 at para 36, [2012] 1 SCR 433.
234 Ibid., citing *R v Wilmott*, [1966] 2 OR 654, 58 DLR (2nd) 33 (ONCA); *R v Solowan*, 2008 SCC 62 at para 12, [2008] 3 SCR 309; *R v Nasogaluak*, 2010 SCC 6 at paras 40–42, [2010] 1 SCR 206.
235 See *Ipeelee*, supra note 233, para 37.
236 Supra note 233.
237 Ibid., para 36.
238 2014 SCC 41 at para 21, [2014] 2 SCR 167.
239 See Kent Roach, Benjamin Berger, Emma Cunliffe, and James Stribopoulos, *Criminal Law and Procedure: Cases and Materials*, 11th ed. (Toronto: Emond Montgomery, 2015), 1032.
240 2016 SCC 14, [2016] 1 SCR 180. See also *R v Lloyd*, 2016 SCC 13 at paras 39–47, [2016] 1 SCR 130.
241 These restrictions were adopted by the *Truth in Sentencing Act*, SC 2009, c 29.
242 See *Safarzadeh-Markhali*, supra note 240, para 8, citing *R v Summers*, 2014 SCC 26 at para 28, [2014] 1 SCR 575. ("Remand detention centres tend not to provide the educational, retraining or rehabilitation programs that are generally available when serving a sentence in corrections facilities ... [O]vercrowding, inmate turnover, labour disputes and other factors also tend to make pre-sentence detention more onerous.")
243 Ibid.
244 See *Criminal Code*, supra note 7, ss 515(9.1), 719(3.1).
245 See *Safarzadeh-Markhali*, supra note 240, paras 14–17.
246 Ibid., para 17.
247 Ibid., paras 67–73.
248 See *R v Safarzadeh-Markhali*, 2014 ONCA 627 at paras 82, 85, 122 OR (3rd) 97.
249 See *Safarzadeh-Markhali*, supra note 240, paras 67–73.
250 See Andrew Menchynski and Jill Presser, "A Withering Instrumentality: The Negative Implications of *R. v. Safarzadeh-Markhali* and Other Recent Section 7 Jurisprudence," *Supreme Court Law Review* 81 (2nd) (2017): 92.
251 Ibid.
252 Ibid., 91.

253 Ibid.
254 Ibid.
255 Ibid.
256 Ibid.
257 2015 SCC 5, [2015] 1 SCR 331.
258 Ibid., paras 91–92.
259 Ibid., para 91.
260 Ibid.
261 Ibid., para 92; emphasis added.
262 See *Malmo-Levine*, supra note 35, paras 138–39.
263 See Hamish Stewart, *Fundamental Justice: Section 7 of the Canadian Charter of Rights and Freedoms* (Toronto: Irwin Law, 2019), 145.
264 Supra note 238.
265 Ibid., para 1.
266 See former *Criminal Code*, supra note 7, s 255. The identical scheme now exists under s 320.19(1).
267 See *Anderson*, supra note 238, para 2.
268 Ibid., para 4. For a review of the abuse of process doctrine, see para 41. "The jurisprudence pertaining to the review of prosecutorial discretion has employed a range of terminology to describe the type of prosecutorial conduct that constitutes abuse of process. In *Krieger v Law Society of Alberta*, 2002 SCC 65, [2002] 3 SCR 372, this Court used the term 'flagrant impropriety' (para. 49). In *R v Nixon*, 2011 SCC 34, [2011] 2 SCR 566, the Court held that the abuse of process doctrine is available where there is evidence that the Crown's decision 'undermines the integrity of the judicial process' or 'results in trial unfairness' (para. 64). The Court also referred to 'improper motive[s]' and 'bad faith' in its discussion (para. 68)."
269 See *R v Anderson*, 2013 NLCA 2, 331 Nfld & PEIR 308.
270 See, generally, *R v Gladue*, [1999] 1 SCR 433, 171 DLR (4th) 385; and *Ipeelee*, supra note 233.
271 See *Anderson*, supra note 238, para 1.
272 Ibid., para 20.
273 Ibid., para 30.
274 Ibid., para 32, citing *R v Power*, [1994] 1 SCR 601 at 627, 89 CCC (3rd) 1.
275 See Marie Manikis, "Towards Accountability and Fairness for Aboriginal People: The Recognition of *Gladue* as a Principle of Fundamental Justice That Applies to Prosecutors," *Canadian Criminal Law Review* 21 (2016): 183–84.
276 Ibid., 183.
277 Ibid., 183–84, citing Peter Hogg, "The Brilliant Career of Section 7 of the *Charter*," *Supreme Court Law Review* 58 (2nd) (2012): 200–1.
278 See Stewart, *Fundamental Justice*, supra note 263, 124–27.
279 See Colton Fehr, "Infusing Reconciliation into the Sentencing Process," *Constitutional Forum constitutionnel* 28 (2019): 25.

280 It is notable that Berger, "Constitutional Principles," supra note 2, 7–10, identifies the former two as themes arising from the Supreme Court's jurisprudence.
281 See *Ruzic*, supra note 3, paras 42–47.
282 See Berger, "Constitutional Principles," supra note 2, 8–10, citing Paul Kahn, "Comparative Constitutionalism in a New Key," *Michigan Law Review* 101 (2003): 2677–2705; Alec Stone Sweet and Jud Mathews, "Proportionality Balancing and Global Constitutionalism," *Columbia Journal of Transnational Law* 47 (2008): 72–164; and Benjamin Berger, "The Abiding Presence of Conscience: Criminal Justice against the Law and the Modern Constitutional Imagination," *University of Toronto Law Journal* 61 (2011): 579–616.
283 See the discussion on *mens rea* earlier in this chapter.
284 Stribopoulos, "The Constitutionalization of Fault," supra note 107; Rosemary Cairns Way, "Constitutionalizing Subjectivism: Another View," *Criminal Reports* 79 (3rd) (1990): 262–63; Don Stuart, "Progress on the Constitutional Requirement of Fault," *Criminal Reports* 64 (3rd) (1988): 352.
285 See Skolnik, "Objective *Mens Rea* Revisited," supra note 165, 334.
286 Ibid., 323.
287 See Guyora Binder, "The Culpability of Felony Murder," *Notre Dame Law Review* 83 (2008): 966 (stating that commentators are "almost unanimous in condemning felony murder"). For a defence of the felony murder rule in limited contexts, see David Crump, "Reconsidering the Felony Murder Rule in Light of Modern Criticisms: Doesn't the Conclusion Depend upon the Particular Rule at Issue?," *Harvard Journal of Law and Public Policy* 32 (2009): 1155–86.
288 See *Texas Penal Code*, s 19.02(b)(3) (2008). "A person commits an offense if he: (3) commits or attempts to commit a felony, other than manslaughter, and in the course of and in furtherance of the commission or attempt, or in immediate flight from the commission or attempt, he commits or attempts to commit an act clearly dangerous to human life that causes the death of an individual."
289 See Bruce Archibald, "The Constitutionalization of the General Part of Criminal Law," *Canadian Bar Review* 67 (1988): 420.
290 For a review, see *Allen*, supra note 180.
291 For competing views, see *Aravena*, supra note 180; and *Willis*, supra note 180.
292 For academic scholarship condemning these provisions, see Martha Shaffer, "Scrutinizing Duress: The Constitutional Validity of Section 17 of the *Criminal Code*," *Criminal Law Quarterly* 40 (1998): 444–75; Fehr, "(Re-)Constitutionalizing Duress and Necessity," supra note 201; Colton Fehr, "The (Near) Death of Duress," *Criminal Law Quarterly* 62 (2015): 123–49; and Colton Fehr, "The Constitutionality of Excluding Duress as a Defence to Murder," *Manitoba Law Journal* 44 (2021): 109–33.
293 See *DB*, supra note 228, para 41.
294 See *Anderson*, supra note 238, para 40.
295 Ibid., paras 30–32.

296 See Chapter 1.
297 See Roach, "Mind the Gap," supra note 1, 547.
298 See *Logan*, supra note 92, 741.
299 See *Creighton*, supra note 113, 55–57.
300 See *DeSousa*, supra note 110, 966.
301 See *Vaillancourt*, supra note 85, 653.
302 See *Ruzic*, supra note 3. The Supreme Court's refusal to develop justifications under the common law in *Perka*, supra note 181, influenced its decision to limit the concept of moral blamelessness in *Ruzic*.
303 For a similar observation, see Roach, "Mind the Gap," supra note 1, 558.
304 For a review of this commonly accepted rationale, see Donald Dripps, "Criminal Procedure, Footnote Four, and the Theory of Public Choice; or, Why Don't Legislatures Give a Damn about the Rights of the Accused?," *Syracuse Law Review* 44 (1993): 1079–1102.

Chapter 3: Principles of Instrumental Rationality

1 The Supreme Court has constitutionalized only two principles of fundamental justice related to criminal law theory this century. See *R v Ruzic*, 2001 SCC 24, [2001] 1 SCR 687 (moral involuntariness); and *R v DB*, 2008 SCC 25, [2008] 2 SCR 3 (presumption of reduced moral blameworthiness for youth).
2 See *Canada (Attorney General) v Bedford*, 2013 SCC 72 at para 107, [2013] 3 SCR 1101, citing Hamish Stewart, *Fundamental Justice: Section 7 of the Canadian Charter of Rights and Freedoms* (Toronto: Irwin Law, 2012), 151. This preference was directly expressed in *Carter v Canada (Attorney General)*, 2015 SCC 5 at para 72, [2015] 1 SCR 331.
3 See *Bedford*, supra note 2, para 111.
4 Ibid., para 112.
5 Ibid., para 120.
6 See, generally, Colton Fehr, "The 'Individualistic' Approach to Arbitrariness, Overbreadth, and Gross Disproportionality," *University of British Columbia Law Review* 51 (2018): 55–74.
7 See, for example, Lisa Dufraimont, "*Canada (Attorney General) v. Bedford* and the Limits on Substantive Criminal Law under Section 7," *Supreme Court Law Review* 67 (2014): 496–98.
8 See *R v Oakes*, [1986] 1 SCR 103 at 135–42, 26 DLR (4th) 200.
9 Ibid.
10 See Dufraimont, "Limits on Substantive Criminal Law," supra note 7, 496–98; Hamish Stewart, "*R. v. Khawaja*: At the Limits of Fundamental Justice," *Supreme Court Law Review* 63 (2nd) (2013): 411; and Alana Klein, "The Arbitrariness in 'Arbitrariness' (and Overbreadth and Gross Disproportionality): Principle and Democracy in Section 7 of the *Charter*," *Supreme Court Law Review* 63 (2nd) (2013): 392.

11 See *Bedford*, supra note 2, paras 15, 127.
12 Supra note 2.
13 Ibid., para 123.
14 Ibid., para 125.
15 Ibid., para 126.
16 Ibid., para 127.
17 See *R v Michaud*, 2015 ONCA 585, 127 OR (3rd) 81, leave to appeal to the SCC refused, 36706 (5 May 2016).
18 For a review, see Stewart, *Fundamental Justice*, supra note 2, 168–69.
19 Ibid., 169.
20 Ibid. Several laws have been challenged for being arbitrary, but the challenges have been dismissed readily. These cases do not require full elaboration here. See *R v Beare*, [1988] 2 SCR 387, 55 DLR (4th) 481 (taking fingerprints incident to arrest); *R v Arkell*, [1990] 2 SCR 695, 59 CCC (3rd) 65 (rationale for classifying murders as first degree); *Chiarelli v Canada (Minister of Employment and Immigration)*, [1992] 1 SCR 711, 90 DLR (4th) 289 (deporting permanent residents scheme); *R v Skalbania*, [1997] 3 SCR 995, 120 CCC (3rd) 217 (power of courts of appeal to substitute guilty verdict); and *R v Conception*, 2014 SCC 60, [2014] 3 SCR 82 (fitness to stand trial).
21 [1988] 1 SCR 30, 44 DLR (4th) 385.
22 *Criminal Code of Canada*, RSC 1985, c C-46.
23 See *Morgentaler*, supra note 21, 64.
24 Ibid., 70, 72.
25 Ibid., 65–66.
26 Ibid., 66.
27 Ibid., 66–67.
28 Ibid., 67, citing *Public Hospitals Act*, RSO 1960, c 322 (allowing abortion committees to be established only where there were ten or more active medical staff).
29 For instance, the choice of some doctors to exclude psychological health significantly narrowed the number of women eligible for an abortion.
30 See *Morgentaler*, supra note 21, 109–10. See also 114–22. At 114–15, however, the Supreme Court discusses the requirement for performing abortions in hospitals. This requirement is necessary in some cases in which medical complications are likely; however, in the vast majority of cases, it is not required given the relatively simple and non-dangerous nature of the procedure. This explanation suggests that there is a rational connection between the law and its objective but that in many cases the law does not achieve its objective. This is the modern-day language of overbreadth, not arbitrariness. At 120–22, the court nevertheless suggests that the "manifest unfairness" of the combined restrictions makes the law more akin to arbitrariness as understood in section 7.
31 Ibid., 174–80.
32 Ibid., 174.
33 See Stewart, *Fundamental Justice*, supra note 18, 173–74.
34 [1993] 3 SCR 519, 107 DLR (4th) 342.

35 Ibid., 595.
36 Ibid.
37 Ibid., 620–21 (Justice McLachlin summarizing the majority's argument).
38 Ibid., 620, reasons of Justice McLachlin (Justice L'Heureux-Dubé concurring). Justice Cory concurred with Justice McLachlin.
39 Ibid.
40 As Hamish Stewart observes, this reasoning would now support an overbreadth contention since the law clearly is connected to its objectives in circumstances in which a person is vulnerable and might agree to euthanasia as a result. See Stewart, *Fundamental Justice*, supra note 18, 171n104.
41 See *Rodriguez*, supra note 34, 621.
42 Ibid., 627. It is unclear which prong of the proportionality test was violated under section 1. The fact that Justice McLachlin appealed to potential procedures to protect the vulnerable implies that the law was not minimally impairing.
43 2003 SCC 74, [2003] 3 SCR 571.
44 Ibid., para 1.
45 Ibid., paras 41, 135.
46 Ibid., paras 40–61, 135.
47 Ibid., para 136.
48 Ibid., para 138.
49 Ibid., para 139.
50 Ibid., paras 135–36.
51 SC 1996, c 19, s 55. Parliament created regulations entitled the *Marihuana for Medical Purposes Regulations*, SOR/2013–119.
52 See *Malmo-Levine*, supra note 43, para 117, citing *Suresh v Canada (Minister of Citizenship and Immigration)*, 2002 SCC 1, [2002] 1 SCR 3.
53 2011 SCC 44, [2011] 3 SCR 134.
54 Ibid., para 129.
55 Ibid., para 131.
56 2015 SCC 34, [2015] 2 SCR 602.
57 Ibid., para 1.
58 Ibid., para 5.
59 Ibid., para 6.
60 Ibid., para 24.
61 Ibid., para 25.
62 Ibid.
63 Ibid.
64 Ibid.
65 See Hamish Stewart, "*Bedford* and the Structure of Section 7," *McGill Law Journal* 60 (2015): 587.
66 See Stewart, *Fundamental Justice*, supra note 18, 167, noting that prior to *Bedford*, supra note 2, overbreadth claims rarely succeeded.
67 [1994] 3 SCR 761, 120 DLR (4th) 348.

68 Ibid., 772.
69 Ibid., 773–74.
70 Ibid., 792–93. This interpretation of pre-*Bedford* overbreadth was affirmed in *R v Khawaja*, 2012 SCC 69, [2012] 3 SCR 555.
71 Ibid., 794.
72 Ibid., 794–95.
73 Ibid., 796–97.
74 Ibid., 798–99.
75 2004 SCC 46, [2004] 2 SCR 489.
76 Ibid., para 3.
77 See *Criminal Code*, supra note 22, ss 672.45 (court) and 672.47 (review board).
78 Ibid., s 672.33.
79 See *Demers*, supra note 75, para 41.
80 Ibid., para 53.
81 Ibid., paras 42–43, 55.
82 Supra note 70.
83 Ibid., para 41.
84 Ibid., para 42.
85 See Kent Roach, "The New Terrorism Offences and the Criminal Law," in *The Security of Freedom: Essays on Canada's Anti-Terrorism Bill*, ed. Ronald Daniels, Patrick Macklem, and Kent Roach (Toronto: University of Toronto Press, 2001), 161.
86 Ibid.
87 See *Khawaja*, supra note 70, para 45.
88 Ibid., paras 46–47.
89 Ibid., para 49.
90 Ibid.
91 Ibid., para 51.
92 Ibid.
93 See Stewart, "At the Limits," supra note 10, 407–8.
94 Ibid., 403.
95 Supra note 2.
96 See *Reference re ss. 193 and 195.1(1)(c) of the Criminal Code (Man)*, [1990] 1 SCR 1123, 56 CCC (3rd) 65 [*Sex Work Reference*].
97 The trial judge identified four differences, but the two identified above drove the Supreme Court's reasoning. See *Bedford*, supra note 2, para 17.
98 See ibid., para 15.
99 These principles were not developed by the Supreme Court in 1990 when the *Sex Work Reference*, supra note 96, was decided.
100 See ibid. The prohibition that a law must not be vague is an infrequently employed principle of fundamental justice considered moribund by some. See, for example, Don Stuart, *Charter Justice in Canadian Criminal Law*, 3rd ed. (Scarborough,

ON: Carswell, 2001), 104; and Alan Young, "Fundamental Justice and Political Power: A Personal Reflection on Twenty Years in the Trenches," *Supreme Court Law Review* 16 (2002): 143. As such, it does not receive significant comment in this book.
101 See *Bedford*, supra note 2, paras 130–59.
102 Ibid., para 137.
103 Ibid., para 141, citing *Shaw v Director of Public Prosecutions*, [1962] AC 220 (HL).
104 Ibid., para 142.
105 Ibid., para 145.
106 Supra note 2.
107 Ibid., para 11.
108 Ibid., para 13.
109 Ibid., paras 74–75.
110 Ibid., para 84. To the contrary, see the minority's reasoning described earlier in this chapter.
111 Ibid., para 86.
112 Ibid., paras 87–88.
113 Ibid., paras 102–21.
114 2015 SCC 59, [2015] 3 SCR 754.
115 SC 2002, c 27 [*IRPA*].
116 See *Appulonappa*, supra note 114, para 70.
117 Ibid.
118 Ibid., para 72.
119 See, for example, *R v Nur*, 2015 SCC 15, [2015] 1 SCR 773. The accused maintained that a particular mandatory minimum violated the prohibition against cruel and unusual punishment. The state maintained that the provision was constitutional since it allowed the prosecutor to elect whether to proceed by way of summary conviction or indictment, only the latter of which required the judge to impose the mandatory minimum sentence. The Supreme Court nevertheless struck down the mandatory minimum because allowing crown discretion to be exercised does not guarantee that abuses will not occur.
120 See *Appulonappa*, supra note 114, para 72.
121 Ibid., para 74; emphasis added.
122 Ibid., paras 73–77.
123 Ibid., para 85.
124 2016 SCC 14, [2016] 1 SCR 180.
125 These restrictions were adopted by the *Truth in Sentencing Act*, SC 2009, c 29.
126 See *Criminal Code*, supra note 22, ss 515(9.1), 719(3.1).
127 For a more detailed review, see Chapter 2.
128 See *Safarzadeh-Markhali*, supra note 124, para 47.
129 Ibid., para 53.
130 Ibid., para 50; emphasis added.

131 This inconsistency was first raised by Stewart, *Fundamental Justice*, supra note 18, 162n56, citing *Bedford*, supra note 2, para 101; emphasis added.
132 In addition to the above-mentioned cases, other litigants have pleaded that a substantive criminal law is inconsistent with the individualistic conception of the overbreadth principle but failed. See, for example, *Nur*, supra note 121; *R v Boutilier*, 2017 SCC 64, [2017] 2 SCR 936; and *R v Moriarity*, 2015 SCC 55, [2015] 3 SCR 485. Overbreadth was also pleaded in *R v Boudreault*, 2018 SCC 58, [2018] 3 SCR 599, but the impugned law was struck down for violating section 12 of the Charter.
133 See Stewart, "Structure," supra note 65, 589–91; Fehr, "Individualistic Approach," supra note 6, 61, 65–66; and *Michaud*, supra note 17, paras 146–53.
134 See, generally, *Bedford*, supra note 2.
135 See Michael Coenen, "Rules against Rulification," *Yale Law Journal* 124 (2014): 646, citing Louis Kaplow, "Rules versus Standards: An Economic Analysis," *Duke Law Journal* 42 (1992): 557; Duncan Kennedy, "Form and Substance in Private Law Adjudication," *Harvard Law Review* 89 (1976): 1685–1778; Antonin Scalia, "The Rule of Law as a Law of Rules," *University of Chicago Law Review* 56 (1989): 1175–88; Pierre Schlag, "Rules and Standards," *UCLA Law Review* 33 (1985): 379–430; Kathleen Sullivan, "The Supreme Court, 1991 Term – Foreword: The Justices of Rules and Standards," *Harvard Law Review* 106 (1992): 22–123; and Cass Sunstein, "Problems with Rules," *California Law Review* 83 (1995): 953–1026.
136 Ibid.
137 Supra note 17. Leave to appeal to SCC refused, 36706 (5 May 2016).
138 RSO 1990, c H8 [*HTA*].
139 RRO 1990, Reg 587.
140 See *HTA*, supra note 138, s 68.1(1).
141 See *Michaud*, supra note 17, paras 72–73.
142 Ibid., para 147.
143 Ibid., para 148.
144 Ibid., para 149.
145 Ibid., para 151.
146 See Stewart, "Structure," supra note 65, 589 ("whenever a law is conceived of as an instrument to achieve purposes that are defined independently of the law itself ... there is likely to be some degree of overbreadth").
147 See *Reference re Section 94(2) of the Motor Vehicle Act*, [1985] 2 SCR 486 at 515, 24 DLR (4th) 536.
148 I borrow this example from Stewart, "Structure," supra note 65, 589–90.
149 See *Criminal Code*, supra note 22, s 151.1(2–6).
150 See Stewart, "Structure," supra note 65, 589–90. For a subsequent case ruling to the contrary, see *R v AB*, 2015 ONCA 803, 342 OAC 346. Stewart has subsequently provided a persuasive rebuttal to this case. See Stewart, *Fundamental Justice*, supra note 18, 161–62.

151 See *Suresh*, supra note 52, para 47.
152 See *Malmo-Levine*, supra note 43, para 169.
153 See Kent Roach, "The Changed Nature of the Harm Debate," *Criminal Law Quarterly* 60 (2014): 321–23.
154 See *Malmo-Levine*, supra note 43, para 172.
155 Ibid.
156 Ibid.
157 Ibid., para 176.
158 Ibid., para 177.
159 Ibid., para 178.
160 Ibid.
161 See *Boudreault*, supra note 132.
162 See *Cannabis Act*, SC 2018, c 16.
163 See *PHS*, supra note 53, para 133.
164 Ibid., para 131.
165 Ibid., para 133.
166 See the earlier discussion in this chapter on the sex work laws.
167 See *Bedford*, supra note 2, paras 69, 154.
168 Ibid.
169 Ibid., para 155.
170 Ibid., para 159.
171 Ibid., para 64. Pickton was a serial killer who targeted sex workers.
172 Ibid., para 134.
173 Ibid.
174 See *Khawaja*, supra note 70, para 39.
175 Ibid., para 40.
176 See *Bedford*, supra note 2, para 107.
177 2003 SCC 75, [2003] 3 SCR 735.
178 Ibid., para 38. It is notable, however, that the court has also suggested that overbreadth subsumes gross disproportionality. See *Heywood*, supra note 67, 793 ("the effect of overbreadth is that in some applications the law is arbitrary or disproportionate"). See also Fehr, "Individualistic Approach," supra note 6.
179 See *Canada (Attorney General) v Bedford*, 2012 ONCA 186 at paras 253–54, 109 OR (3rd) 1.
180 See *Carter v Canada (Attorney General)*, 2013 BCCA 435 at paras 165–66, 51 BCLR (5th) 213.
181 Ibid., para 166.
182 See *Malmo-Levine*, supra note 43, para 159, citing generally *Motor Vehicle Act Reference*, supra note 147. Although it might be thought that the word *treatment* could be interpreted broadly enough to include legal prohibition of conduct, the Supreme Court rejected this interpretation in *Rodriguez*, supra note 34, 611–12.
183 See *Bedford*, supra note 2, para 125.

184 See the review of the two conceptions of the instrumental rationality principles earlier in this chapter.
185 See Fehr, "Individualistic Conception," supra note 6, 64, citing *R v Preston* (1990), 47 BCLR (2nd) 273 at 15, 79 CR (3rd) 61 (BCCA).
186 I make a similar point with respect to an arbitrariness challenge to the general deterrence principle. See Colton Fehr, "Instrumental Rationality and General Deterrence," *Alberta Law Review* 57 (2019): 53–68.
187 See *Michaud*, supra note 17, para 142.
188 The prohibition against unreasonable searches and seizures in section 8 of the Charter is illustrative. The "reasonableness" standard applied by the provision makes it difficult, if not impossible, to "justify" an unreasonable law. No case to date has done so.
189 See *Carter*, supra note 2, para 72. In *Safarzadeh-Markhali*, supra note 124, crown counsel went even further, suggesting that the Supreme Court has now limited the principles of fundamental justice under section 7 to arbitrariness, overbreadth, and gross disproportionality. See Andrew Menchynski and Jill Presser, "A Withering Instrumentality: The Negative Implications of *R. v. Safarzadeh-Markhali* and Other Recent Section 7 Jurisprudence," *Supreme Court Law Review* 81 (2nd) (2019): 85.
190 See Stewart, "At the Limits," supra note 10, 403–4.
191 I will elaborate this point in Chapter 5.
192 Contrast *Motor Vehicle Act Reference*, supra note 147, 518, with *Bedford*, supra note 2, para 129.
193 See *Motor Vehicle Act Reference*, supra note 147, 518.
194 See, for example, *Safarzadeh-Markhali*, supra note 124, para 57 ("it is difficult, but not impossible, to justify a s. 7 violation under s. 1").
195 It is notable that no appellate court to date has justified a breach of a section 7 moral philosophical principle under section 1 of the Charter.
196 A similar suggestion has been made by Menchynski and Presser, "Withering Instrumentality," supra note 189, 86:

> It may be tempting for the Court to step away from even creating the impression of over-activism by re-imagining section 7 as simply dealing with the flawed rationality of bad laws – and not as a method of interfering with the substance of Parliament's laws. In this way, the judicial branch can be seen to be merely policing Parliament's good legislative drafting practices, while in fact utilizing the doctrines of arbitrariness and overbreadth [and gross disproportionality] to achieve its desired substantive results.

197 When legislatures have not responded to a judicial ruling to strike down a law based on a principle of criminal law theory, the impugned laws tend to stay on the books until eventually they are repealed. See, generally, *An Act to Amend the Criminal Code, the Youth Criminal Justice Act and Other Acts and to Make Consequential Amendments to Other Acts*, SC 2019, c 25, s (i).
198 [1994] 3 SCR 63, 118 DLR (4th) 469.

199 See Michelle Lawrence, "Voluntary Intoxication and the *Charter:* Revisiting the Constitutionality of Section 33.1 of the *Criminal Code*," *Manitoba Law Journal* 40 (2017): 400, citing Isabel Grant, "Second Chances: Bill C-72 and the *Charter*," *Osgoode Hall Law Journal* 33 (1995): 383; Elizabeth Sheehy, "The Intoxication Defense in Canada: Why Women Should Care," *Contemporary Drug Problems* 23 (1996): 595–630; Robin Room, "Drinking, Violence, Gender and Causal Attribution: A Canadian Case Study in Science, Law and Policy," *Contemporary Drug Problems* 23 (1996): 649–86; Susan Bondy, "Self-Induced Intoxication as a Defence in the *Criminal Code of Canada*: Issues and Discussion around *Daviault v. R.*," *Contemporary Drug Problems* 23 (1996): 573–74; and Don Stuart, *Canadian Criminal Law: A Treatise*, 7th ed. (Toronto: Carswell, 2014).
200 For a recent review of the case law and underlying principles, see Lawrence, "Voluntary Intoxication," supra note 199.
201 [1991] 3 SCR 154, 84 DLR (4th) 161.
202 See *Competition Act*, RSC 1985, c C-34, s 52(1); 1999, c 2, s 12; 2009, c 2, s 414.
203 For an overview of public choice theory, see Philip Frickey and Daniel Farber, *Law and Public Choice: A Critical Introduction* (Chicago: University of Chicago Press, 1992); and Denis Mueller, *Public Choice III* (Cambridge: Cambridge University Press, 2003).
204 Supra note 147.
205 See, for example, British Columbia's *Motor Vehicle Act*, RSBC 1996, c 318, s 95.
206 See, for example, Alberta's *Traffic Safety Act*, RSA 2000, c T-6, s 160(3).
207 Parliament did not respond to the Supreme Court's arbitrariness decisions in *Morgentaler*, supra note 21, or *Smith*, supra note 56. Parliament also did not respond to the court's decision in *Heywood*, supra note 67. Section 179(1)(b) of the *Criminal Code* was eventually repealed. See s 60. Parliament adopted the proposed changes in *Demers*, supra note 76. See *An Act to Amend the Criminal Code (Mental Disorder) and to Make Consequential Amendments to Other Acts*, SC 2005, c 22, s 20.
208 See *Respect for Communities Act*, SC 2015, c 22.
209 See Bill C-36, *Protection of Communities and Exploited Persons Act*, SC 2014, c 25.
210 See *An Act to Amend the Criminal Code and to Make Related Amendments to Other Acts (Medical Assistance in Dying)*, SC 2016, c 3.
211 See *Truchon c Procureur général du Canada*, 2019 QCCS 3792, 158 WCB (2nd) 246.
212 The Liberal government, however, has had to seek two extensions given the COVID-19 pandemic. The law appears to repeal the "reasonable foreseeability of death" requirement, among other changes.
213 See *An Act to Amend the Criminal Code and the Department of Justice Act and to Make Consequential Amendments to Another Act*, SC 2018, c 29, s 66.
214 Supra note 115.
215 See *Protecting Canada's Immigration System Act*, SC 2012, c 17, ss 41(1) and 41(4).
216 SC 1992, c 20, ss 31–37.

217 See Bill C-83, *An Act to Amend the Corrections and Conditional Release Act and Another Act*, SC 2019, c 27 [*CCRA*], in response to *British Columbia Civil Liberties Association v Canada (Attorney General)*, 2019 BCCA 228, 377 CCC (3rd) 420; and *Canadian Civil Liberties Association v Canada (Attorney General)*, 2019 ONCA 243, 144 OR (3rd) 641.
218 Each case was granted leave on 13 February 2020.
219 See Peter Hogg and Allison Bushell, "The *Charter* Dialogue between Courts and Legislatures (Or Perhaps the *Charter of Rights* Isn't Such a Bad Thing after All)," *Osgoode Hall Law Journal* 35 (1997): 80.
220 See Kent Roach, *The Supreme Court on Trial: Judicial Activism or Democratic Dialogue?* (Toronto: Irwin Law, 2016), 308.
221 Ibid.
222 See ibid., Chapter 13, for a more general review.
223 Ibid.
224 See Mark Tushnet, *Taking the Constitution Away from the Courts* (Princeton, NJ: Princeton University Press, 1999), 33, 175, 186. In Canada, see Christopher Manfredi and James Kelly, "Six Degrees of Dialogue: A Response to Hogg and Bushell," *Osgoode Hall Law Journal* 37 (1999): 520; and Christopher Manfredi, "The Day the Dialogue Died: A Comment on *Sauvé v Canada*," *Osgoode Hall Law Journal* 45 (2007): 105–24.
225 See Roach, *Supreme Court*, supra note 220, 272–73, 311.
226 Ibid., 273.
227 SC 2015, c 22.
228 See Kent Roach, "Dialogue between the Court and Parliament: A Recent *Charter* Trilogy," *Criminal Law Quarterly* 63 (2016): 251–54. Despite Parliament's opposition to safe injection sites, even the Vancouver police urged addicts to use Insite. See Ian Bailey, "Vancouver Police Urge Drug Addicts to Use Insite following Deaths," *Globe and Mail*, 16 September 2013, S2.
229 See Andrea Woo, "Bill C-2 Could Impede Harm-Reduction Sites," *Globe and Mail*, 24 March 2015, https://www.theglobeandmail.com; and Carol Strike et al., "Increasing Public Support for Supervised Injection Facilities in Ontario, Canada," *Addiction* 109 (2014): 946–53.
230 It is notable that these restrictions were significantly relaxed after the Liberal government came into power. See *An Act to Amend the Controlled Drugs and Substances Act and to Make Related Amendments to Other Acts*, SC 2017, c 7.
231 See Hamish Stewart, "The Constitutionality of the New Sex Work Law," *Alberta Law Review* 54 (2016): 69–88; and Angela Campbell, "Sex Work's Governance: Stuff and Nuisance," *Feminist Legal Studies* 23 (2015): 27–45.
232 See Bill C-36, *Protection of Communities and Exploited Persons Act*, SC 2014, c 25, Preamble.
233 Sex work is illegal per section 286.1, but prosecution of the offence is not allowed against sex workers per section 286.5(2). This allows Parliament to express moral condemnation of sex work but to forgo prosecuting it.

234 See Bill C-36, supra note 232, Preamble.
235 See *Criminal Code*, supra note 22, s 286.2(1).
236 Ibid, s 286.1.
237 For a more detailed explanation of these provisions, see Stewart, "Sex Work Law," supra note 231.
238 See *Criminal Code*, supra note 22, s 286.2(5)(e).
239 See Stewart, "Sex Work Law," supra note 231, 78–79.
240 See *Bedford*, supra note 2, para 86:

> Street [sex] workers, with some exceptions, are a particularly marginalized population. Whether because of financial desperation, drug addictions, mental illness, or compulsion from pimps, they often have little choice but to sell their bodies for money. Realistically, while they may retain some minimal power of choice – what the Attorney General of Canada called "constrained choice" – these are not people who can be said to be truly "choosing" a risky line of business [citations omitted].

241 I provide a more detailed description of this argument in Colton Fehr, "Re-Thinking the Instrumental Rationality Principles of Fundamental Justice," *Alberta Law Review* 58 (2020): 133–52. For an alternative instrumental rationality challenge to the new sex work schemes based on the "arbitrariness of inconsistent policies," see Stewart, "Sex Work Law," supra note 231, 86–88.
242 2018 ONSC 7205, 51 CR (7th) 207.
243 Ibid., paras 38–45.
244 See *R v Anwar*, 2020 ONCJ 103 at para 126, 62 CR (7th) 402.
245 Ibid., paras 126–27.
246 Ibid., paras 166–74, 200–1.
247 The court's decision only briefly mentions and provides little analysis of whether each impugned offence violates the gross disproportionality principle. See paras 173 and 209.
248 There are other arguments that the legislation is unconstitutional because it excludes psychiatric and mental illnesses and youth from applying for assisted dying. See, for example, Constance MacIntosh, "*Carter*, Medical Aid in Dying, and Mature Minors," *McGill Journal of Law and Health* 10 (2016): S1–S34.
249 See *Criminal Code*, supra note 22, s 241.2(2)(d).
250 See *Carter*, supra note 2, para 147.
251 For a more detailed recitation of this argument, see Thomas McMorrow, "MAID in Canada? Debating the Constitutionality of Canada's New Medical Assistance in Dying Law," *Queen's Law Journal* 44 (2018): 86–90.
252 See Peter Hogg, "Legal and Constitutional Affairs: June 6, 2016," 6 June 2016, 00h:58m:17s, 01h:59m:51s, www.cpac.ca/en/programs/in-committee-from-the-senate-of-canada/episodes/47941576; and Standing Senate Committee on Legal and Constitutional Affairs, "Bill C-14, *An Act to Amend the Criminal Code and to Make Related Amendments to Other Acts (Medical Assistance in Dying)*," in *Proceedings*

of the Standing Senate Committee on Legal and Constitutional Affairs 42–1, no. 10 (6 June 2016): 10:75 ("I think it's incredible to think that what was intended by the court, when it said to pass legislation consistent with the constitutional parameters of the case, was to exclude a whole category of people who had won the right through three stages of litigation up to the Supreme Court of Canada").

253 See *Truchon*, supra note 211. This case left open, however, the issues of whether minors should be allowed to access assisted dying and whether advanced directives ought to be allowed as evidence in assisted dying applications. See para 16. It is unclear whether Parliament's legislation will respond to all of these controversial aspects of the euthanasia laws.

254 See Emmett Macfarlane, "Dialogue, Remedies, and Positive Rights: *Carter v Canada* as a Microcosm for Past and Future Issues under the *Charter of Rights and Freedoms*," *Ottawa Law Review* 49 (2017): 115.

255 See Sean Fine and Laura Stone, "In Absence of Federal Law, Assisted Dying Enters Era of Uncertainty," *Globe and Mail*, 6 June 2016, https://www.theglobeandmail.com/news/national/leading-constitutional-expert-says-assisted-dying-law-unconstitutional/article30283048/.

256 See Eleni Nicolaides and Matthew Hennigar, "*Carter* Conflicts: The Supreme Court of Canada's Impact on Medical Assistance in Dying Policy," in *Policy Change, Courts, and the Canadian Constitution*, ed. Emmett Macfarlane (Toronto: University of Toronto Press, 2018), 313–35.

257 See *CCRA*, supra note 217, ss 31–37, 44. See also *BCCLA*, supra note 217, paras 158–59.

258 See *United Nations Standard Minimum Rules for the Treatment of Prisoners (the Nelson Mandela Rules)*, 70/175 (8 January 2016), Rule 44.

259 Ibid. The rules define "prolonged solitary confinement" as anything more than fifteen days in a row.

260 See *BCCLA*, supra note 217, paras 165–72 (overbroad and grossly disproportionate); *CCLA*, supra note 217 (cruel and unusual punishment).

261 Ibid.

262 Supra note 218.

263 See Adelina Iftene, Kim Pate, and Debra Parkes, "Solitary Confinement and the Supreme Court," *Vancouver Sun*, 10 May 2020, https://vancouversun.com/opinion/adelina-iftene-kim-pate-debra-parkes-solitary-confinement-and-the-supreme-court-missed-opportunities/wcm/.

264 Ibid.

265 Ibid.

266 See Roach, *Supreme Court*, supra note 220; Hogg and Bushell, "Dialogue," supra note 219.

267 As Kent Roach observes, albeit in the section 1 context and in response to Grégoire Webber, *The Negotiable Constitution* (Cambridge: Cambridge University Press, 2009), "my concern with seeing all aspects of *Charter* interpretation as based on duelling legislative and judicial interpretations of rights is that it can transform dialogue into a zero-sum contest. In such a contest, legislative interpretations or

even implicit rejections of the rights of unpopular groups are likely to dominate judicial ones." See Roach, *Supreme Court*, supra note 220, 395.
268 See, for example, Hart Schwartz, "Circularity, Tautology and Gamesmanship: 'Purpose' Based Proportionality-Correspondence Analysis in Sections 15 and 7 of the *Charter*," *National Journal of Constitutional Law* 35 (2016): 105–29; Klein, "Arbitrariness," supra note 10, 384–87; David Lepofsky, "*Carter v. Canada (Attorney General)*, the Constitutional Attack on Canada's Ban on Assisted Dying: Missing an Obvious Chance to Rule on the *Charter*'s Disability Equality Guarantee," *Supreme Court Law Review* 76 (2nd) (2016): 99–107; Menchynski and Presser, "A Withering Instrumentality," supra note 189, 76.
269 See Schwartz, "Circularity," supra note 268, 108.
270 Ibid., 108–9.
271 See *M v H*, [1999] 2 SCR 3 at 70, 171 DLR (4th) 577.
272 See *PHS*, supra note 53, para 129.
273 See *CDSA*, supra note 51, s 56.
274 See Schwartz, "Circularity," supra note 268, 122.
275 See *Bedford*, supra note 2, paras 131, 147.
276 Ibid., paras 130, 137, 146.
277 See Schwartz, "Circularity," supra note 268, 124.
278 See *Carter*, supra note 2, para 75.
279 Ibid., paras 76–78.
280 See Marcus Moore, "*R. v. Safarzadeh-Markhali*: Elements and Implications of the Supreme Court's New Rigorous Approach to Construction of Statutory Purpose," (2nd) *Supreme Court Law Review* 77 (2017): 238–42, citing *Moriarity*, supra note 132; *Safarzadeh-Markhali*, supra note 124; and *Appulonappa*, supra note 114.
281 See *Safarzadeh-Markhali*, supra note 124, para 26; and *Moriarity*, supra note 132, para 27.
282 See *Safarzadeh-Markhali*, supra note 124, para 27; and *Moriarity*, supra note 132, para 28.
283 See *Safarzadeh-Markhali*, supra note 124, paras 26, 28; and *Moriarity*, supra note 132, para 29.
284 See *Safarzadeh-Markhali*, supra note 124, para 29; and *Moriarity*, supra note 132, para 30.
285 For a summary, see *Safarzadeh-Markhali*, supra note 124, para 31.
286 See *Moriarity*, supra note 132, para 32.
287 See Moore, "Construction of Statutory Purpose," supra note 280, 242–43 ("because [of its] more thorough analysis and justification, greater transparency and consistency, improved communications and diminished conflict between legislatures as democratic organs and courts as guardians of the Constitution, [the 'rigorous approach'] consequently contributes to enhancing public confidence in the integrity of the justice system").
288 Ibid., 250.

289 Ibid.
290 Ibid.
291 See Schwartz, "Circularity," supra note 280, 109; and Menchynski and Presser, "Withering Instrumentality," supra note 189, 87–88.
292 See *Moriarity*, supra note 132, para 28.
293 See *Morgentaler*, supra note 21, 174–80. Although Justice Wilson wrote for herself, it would be surprising if any court came to a different conclusion today.
294 410 US 113 (1973).
295 See *Blencoe v British Columbia (Human Rights Commission)*, 2000 SCC 44 at para 54, [2000] 2 SCR 307.
296 See *Morgentaler*, supra note 21, 174–80. I will explain in Chapter 4 why the enumerated right to equality was the more logical path for striking down the abortion laws.
297 I will discuss in Chapter 4 in detail the available principles.
298 2002 SCC 84, [2002] 4 SCR 429.
299 Ibid., para 338. For criticism of this approach, see Eric Colvin, "Section Seven of the *Canadian Charter of Rights and Freedoms*," *Canadian Bar Review* 68 (1989): 563 ("a free-standing right to life, liberty and security would cover any ground on which guarantees of due process and fundamental justice might work. The latter guarantees would be otiose. The conjunctive reading of the provision enables this result to be avoided. The cost, of course, is grammatical distortion. There is, however, no easy resolution to the problems presented by these provisions").
300 Ibid., paras 81–82.
301 For a review of the court's limited jurisprudence finding a liberty to be "fundamental," see Stewart, *Fundamental Justice*, supra note 18, 83–88.
302 This is how the Supreme Court of the United States circumscribed the right to abortion. See, generally, *Roe*, supra note 294. I do not wish to be taken as supporting the American approach. It is possible in the Canadian context that the interests of the fetus would not outweigh the liberty interests of the mother at any point.
303 See *Rodriguez*, supra note 34, 592.
304 See *Carter*, supra note 2, paras 64–69.
305 This argument ultimately failed in *Washington v Glucksberg*, 521 US 702 (1997).
306 See Kent Roach et al., *Criminal Law and Procedure: Cases and Materials*, 11th ed. (Toronto: Emond Montgomery, 2015), 355.
307 (1988) 42 CRR 146, 5 WCB (2nd) 167.
308 See *Heywood*, supra note 67, 795, citing *Graff*, supra note 307, 150; emphasis added.
309 See Roach et al., *Criminal Law*, supra note 306, 355.
310 Ibid. The authors imply that the vagrancy prohibition would not qualify as a status offence, though it is "perhaps the closest that the modern law has to a status offence."
311 Ibid.
312 See *Criminal Code of Canada*, RSC 1970, c C-34.

313 See *Demers*, supra note 75, para 94 (dissenting reasons of Justice LeBel).
314 Ibid.
315 See, generally, *R v Jordan*, 2016 SCC 27, [2016] 1 SCR 631.
316 See, generally, *Ruzic*, supra note 1.
317 See *Bedford*, supra note 2, para 86.
318 Ibid.
319 Supra note 1.
320 Ibid., para 87.
321 Ibid.
322 Notably, the objectives of the law were not challenged as falling outside the legitimate scope of what may be criminalized.
323 See *Bedford*, supra note 2, para 80.
324 See, generally, *Malmo-Levine*, supra note 43.
325 See *PHS*, supra note 53, para 19.
326 See *Smith*, supra note 56, para 25.
327 See Chapter 2, citing *R v Ipeelee*, 2012 SCC 13, [2012] 1 SCR 433; and *R v Anderson*, 2014 SCC 41, [2014] 2 SCR 167.

Chapter 4: Enumerated Principles of Criminal Justice

1 See *Reference re ss 193 and 195.1(1)(c) of Criminal Code (Man)*, [1990] 1 SCR 1123 at 1187, 56 CCC (3rd) 65 [*Sex Work Reference*].
2 See *R v Keegstra*, [1990] 3 SCR 697 at 731, 61 CCC (3rd) 1, citing *Irwin Toy Ltd v Quebec (Attorney General)*, [1989] 1 SCR 927, 58 DLR (4th) 577. See also *R v Khawaja*, 2012 SCC 69 at para 70, [2012] 3 SCR 555. Violence cannot constitute expression because it is inimical to the rule of law on which all other rights depend.
3 See *Irwin Toy*, supra note 2, 976.
4 See Patrick Monahan, Byron Shaw, and Padraic Ryan, *Constitutional Law*, 5th ed. (Toronto: Irwin Law, 2017), 452–53.
5 Supra note 1.
6 Ibid., reasons of Justices Dickson (1134–35), Lamer (1188–89), and Wilson (1206).
7 Ibid., 1134–35.
8 Ibid., 1135–36.
9 Ibid., 1138–39.
10 Ibid., 1194.
11 Ibid., 1195–1201.
12 Ibid., 1210–11.
13 Ibid., 1213–14.
14 Ibid.
15 2013 SCC 72, [2013] 3 SCR 1101. It is notable that the provisions, although renumbered as part of the reorganization of the *Criminal Code of Canada*, RSC 1985, c C-46, were identically worded.
16 Supra note 2.

17 Ibid., 714.
18 Ibid.
19 Ibid.
20 Ibid.
21 See *R v Keegstra,* 87 AR 200 at 268, 19 CCC (3rd) 254.
22 Ibid., 266–68.
23 Despite unanimity on the Charter breach, the court split 4–3 on whether the infringement of section 2(b) was justified under section 1.
24 See *Keegstra,* supra note 2, 732–33.
25 It is notable that uttering threats is prohibited under the *Criminal Code,* supra note 15, s 264.1.
26 See Kathleen Mahoney, "*R. v. Keegstra:* A Rationale for Regulating Pornography?," *McGill Law Journal* 37 (1992): 247–49. See also Lorraine Weinrib, "Hate Promotion in a Free and Democratic Society: *R. v. Keegstra,*" *McGill Law Journal* 36 (1991): 1419–25; and Richard Moon, "Drawing Lines in a Culture of Prejudice: *R. v. Keegstra* and the Restriction of Hate Propaganda," *University of British Columbia Law Review* 26 (1992): 104–13.
27 For a review of the purposive approach to Charter interpretation, see *Hunter v Southam,* [1984] 2 SCR 145, 11 DLR (4th) 641.
28 Justice McLachlin disagreed with the majority view that the law was justifiable under section 1 of the Charter but concurred with the majority's finding that the impugned law violated section 2(b).
29 See *Keegstra,* supra note 2, 833.
30 See Sanjeev Anand, "Beyond *Keegstra:* The Constitutionality of the Wilful Promotion of Hatred Revisited," *National Journal of Constitutional Law* 9 (1997–98): 128.
31 Ibid.
32 For academic commentary supporting this view, see Dino Bottos, "*Keegstra* and *Andrews:* A Commentary on Hate Propaganda and the Freedom of Expression," *Alberta Law Review* 27 (1989): 461–75; Arthur Fish, "Hate Promotion and Freedom of Expression: Truth and Consequences," *Canadian Journal of Law and Jurisprudence* 2 (1989): 111–38; Wayne MacKay, "Freedom of Expression: Is It All Just Talk?," *Canadian Bar Review* 68 (1989): 713–64; Naeem Rauf, "Freedom of Expression, the Presumption of Innocence and Reasonable Limits: An Analysis of *Keegstra* and *Andrews,*" *Criminal Reports* 65 (3rd) (1988): 356–71; and Alan Regel, "Hate Propaganda: A Reason to Limit Freedom of Speech," *Saskatchewan Law Review* 49 (1985): 303–18. Commentators who take the opposite view include Ronda Bessner, "The Constitutionality of the Group Libel Offences in the *Canadian Criminal Code,*" *Manitoba Law Journal* 17 (1988): 184–218; and Stefan Braun, "Social and Racial Tolerance and Freedom of Expression in a Democratic Society: Friends or Foes? *Regina v. Zundel,*" *Dalhousie Law Journal* 11 (1988): 471–513.
33 See *Keegstra,* supra note 2, 762.
34 Ibid., 763–64.

35 Ibid., 764.
36 Ibid.
37 [1992] 2 SCR 731, 95 DLR (4th) 202.
38 Ibid., 743–44.
39 Ibid., 754–55.
40 Ibid.
41 Ibid., 757–58.
42 Ibid., 744–46.
43 Ibid., 744–45.
44 Ibid., 763. For a detailed explanation of why the law's subsequent move to the nuisance provisions of the *Criminal Code* did not change its purpose, see Sanjeev Anand, "Beyond the Wilful Promotion of Hatred: The Other Criminal Code Provisions Proscribing Expressions of Racial Hatred," *Canadian Criminal Law Review* 3 (1998): 154–56.
45 Ibid., 764–66.
46 Ibid., 769–70.
47 Ibid. It is notable that the term "public interest" was found to be unconstitutionally vague in the bail context in *R v Morales*, [1992] 3 SCR 711, 77 CCC (3rd) 91.
48 Ibid., 771–72.
49 [1998] 1 SCR 439, 157 DLR (4th) 423.
50 Ibid., 447–48.
51 Ibid.
52 Ibid., 448.
53 Ibid., 448–49.
54 The accused were also charged under the *Criminal Code*, supra note 15, s 301, but that section was struck down at trial, and the ruling was not appealed. So the Supreme Court dealt only with the constitutionality of section 300.
55 See *Lucas*, supra note 49, 455. One intervenor did not make such a concession, arguing instead that defamatory libel is not worthy of constitutional protection. The Supreme Court, however, dismissed this argument based on its prior jurisprudence in *Keegstra*, supra note 2, *Zundel*, supra note 37, and *Libman c Québec (Procureur général)*, [1997] 3 SCR 569, 151 DLR (4th) 385, finding that freedom of expression is evaluated from a content-neutral vantage point. See *Lucas*, supra note 49, 455–56.
56 Ibid., 463.
57 Ibid., 467–70.
58 Ibid., 481. It is notable that a minor portion of section 299 was unjustifiable and therefore read out of the provision. See 476–78.
59 [1992] 1 SCR 452, 89 DLR (4th) 449.
60 Ibid., 461–62.
61 Ibid., 486–87.
62 Ibid., 487, citing *Irwin Toy*, supra note 2.

63 Ibid.
64 Ibid.
65 Ibid., 478. For the court's subsequent revision of this test, see, generally, *R v Labaye*, 2005 SCC 80, [2005] 3 SCR 728.
66 Ibid., 505–6.
67 Ibid., 479.
68 Ibid., 509.
69 2001 SCC 2, [2001] 1 SCR 45.
70 RSC 1985, c C-46.
71 See *Sharpe*, supra note 69, para 4. The appeal on the distribution offence was not heard.
72 Ibid., para 25.
73 The crown conceded as much. For an argument that mere possession is not "expression" under the Charter, see Jack Watson, "Case Comment: *R. v. Sharpe*," *National Journal of Constitutional Law* 10 (1999): 256:

> If "possession" is included within the scope of "expression," then one is put in mind of the old riddle about whether a tree falling in a forest makes any noise if no one is around to hear. Private conduct that is not intended to be, or even capable of being, shared or communicated with anyone would, by such a theory, have to be considered to be expressive. The idea is an oxymoron.

74 See *Sharpe*, supra note 69, para 30.
75 Ibid., paras 35–36, 38.
76 Ibid., paras 40–41.
77 Ibid., paras 35–36.
78 Ibid., paras 62–71, citing *Criminal Code*, supra note 15, s 163.1(6). Defences were available for pieces with artistic merit, those with educational/scientific purpose, and those that forward the "public good."
79 Ibid., paras 75–77.
80 Ibid., para 82.
81 Ibid., paras 85–94. For a critique of the evidentiary record with respect to the harm caused by possession of child pornography, see Watson, "Case Comment," supra note 73. This was consistent with the trial judge's findings as summarized in *R v Sharpe*, 1999 BCCA 416 at paras 23–29, 175 DLR (4th) 1.
82 Ibid., para 105.
83 Ibid., para 108.
84 See Wayne McKay, "*R. v. Sharpe:* Pornography, Privacy, Proportionality and the Protection of Children," *National Journal of Constitutional Law* 12 (2000–01): 117.
85 See *Sharpe*, supra note 69, para 110. For academic commentary supporting this conclusion, see Hamish Stewart, "A Judicious Response to Overbreadth: *R. v. Sharpe*," *Criminal Law Quarterly* 43 (2000): 159–80.
86 Ibid., para 114.

87 I add the qualifier "seriously" because in *Sharpe*, supra note 69, para 18, the Supreme Court addressed a section 7 challenge based on overbreadth found "wholly [to] replicate" the section 1 analysis. The court thus dealt with the constitutional issue under section 2(b), and the section 7 issue fell under section 1 to be decided.
88 2011 BCSC 1588, 279 CCC (3rd) 1.
89 Ibid., paras 1099–1105.
90 See Monahan et al., *Constitutional Law,* supra note 4, 453, citing *R v Big M Drug Mart*, [1985] 1 SCR 295 at para 116, 18 DLR (4th) 321.
91 See *Keegstra*, supra note 2, 728, 733–34.
92 See Chapter 3.
93 2020 ONCJ 103, 62 CR (7th) 402.
94 Ibid., para 128.
95 Ibid., para 133.
96 See David Lepofsky, "*Carter v. Canada (Attorney General)*, the Constitutional Attack on Canada's Ban on Assisted Dying: Missing an Obvious Chance to Rule on the Charter's Disability Equality Guarantee," *Supreme Court Law Review* 76 (2nd) (2016): 109.
97 See *R v Boudreault*, 2018 SCC 58 at para 45, [2018] 3 SCR 599, citing *R v Lloyd*, 2016 SCC 13 at para 24, [2016] 1 SCR 130; *R v Morrisey*, 2000 SCC 39 at para 26, [2000] 2 SCR 90; and *R v Ferguson*, 2008 SCC 6 at para 14, [2008] 1 SCR 96.
98 See Chapter 3.
99 See, for example, *R v Smith*, [1987] 1 SCR 1045, 40 DLR (4th) 435; *R v Luxton*, [1990] 2 SCR 711, 58 CCC (3rd) 449; *R v Goltz*, [1991] 3 SCR 485, 67 CCC (3rd) 481; *R v Latimer*, 2001 SCC 1, [2001] 1 SCR 3; *R v Nur*, 2015 SCC 15, [2015] 1 SCR 773; *Morrisey*, supra note 97; and *Ferguson*, supra note 97.
100 [1994] 3 SCR 761, 120 DLR (4th) 348.
101 Ibid., 824–25.
102 For a similar but undefended proposal, see Lepofsky, "Obvious Chance," supra note 96, 106.
103 See *Heywood*, supra note 101, 824–25.
104 See *Boudreault*, supra note 97, para 39, citing *R v KRJ*, 2016 SCC 31 at para 41, [2016] 1 SCR 906.
105 Recall that the prohibition was directed at protecting children but applied to those who posed no reasonable threat to children, such as those convicted of sexual assault against an adult.
106 2016 SCC 14, [2016] 1 SCR 180.
107 See *R v Safarzadeh-Markhali*, 2012 ONCJ 494, 265 CRR (2nd) 32; 2014 ONCA 627, 316 CCC (3rd) 87.
108 See *Criminal Code*, supra note 15, ss 515(9.1), 719(3.1).
109 [1985] 2 SCR 486, 512, 24 DLR (4th) 536.
110 For a detailed review, see Jamie Cameron, "Fault and Punishment under Sections 7 and 12 of the *Charter*," *Supreme Court Law Review* 40 (2nd) (2008): 553–92.

111 See *Criminal Code*, supra note 15, s 235(1). Parole eligibility for first-degree murder arises after twenty-five years, whereas for second-degree murder parole is possible after ten years.
112 [1994] 3 SCR 63, 118 DLR (4th) 469.
113 See *Criminal Code*, supra note 15, ss 271, 730. Sexual assault of adults qualifies for a discharge since its maximum penalty is ten years.
114 [1996] 1 SCR 683, 133 DLR (4th) 42.
115 Ibid., 708.
116 See *Criminal Code*, supra note 15, ss 235–36. Only manslaughter committed with the aid of a firearm carries a mandatory minimum punishment.
117 See *R v George*, [1960] SCR 871, 128 CCC 289.
118 See *Criminal Code*, supra note 15, s 344.
119 See *R v Aravena*, 2015 ONCA 250, 323 CCC (3rd) 54; and *R v Willis*, 2016 MBCA 113, 344 CCC (3rd) 443.
120 I have argued to the contrary in Colton Fehr, "(Re-)Constitutionalizing Duress and Necessity," *Queen's Law Journal* 42 (2017): 99–134. See also *Aravena*, supra note 119. However, the only other appellate court to rule on the issue determined that excluding murder does not violate the moral involuntariness principle. See *Willis*, supra note 119.
121 For a more detailed review of this argument, see Colton Fehr, "The Constitutionality of Excluding Duress as a Defence to Murder," *Manitoba Law Journal* 44 (2021): 109–33. See also *R v PC*, 2012 ONSC 5362, 99 CR (6th) 116.
122 See *Criminal Code*, supra note 15, s 267.
123 Ibid., s 730 (allowing for absolute and conditional discharges).
124 See *Motor Vehicle Act Reference*, supra note 109, 534.
125 See *Daviault*, supra note 113, 89–93.
126 See *Robinson*, supra note 115, 708.
127 [1987] 2 SCR 636, 47 DLR (4th) 399.
128 Ibid., 654–55.
129 See *Smith*, supra note 99.
130 See Kent Roach et al., *Criminal Law and Procedure: Cases and Materials*, 11th ed. (Toronto: Emond Montgomery, 2015), 1028–29.
131 Ibid., 1032.
132 See, generally, *Kahkewistahaw First Nation v Taypotat*, 2015 SCC 30 at paras 19–20, [2015] 2 SCR 548; and *Quebec (Attorney General) v Alliance du personnel professionnel et technique de la santé et des services sociaux*, 2018 SCC 17 at para 25, [2018] 1 SCR 464. See, most recently, *Fraser v Canada (Attorney General)*, 2020 SCC 28.
133 It is notable that the Supreme Court recently struck down a provincial regulation implementing the sex offender registry provisions of the *Criminal Code* under section 15 of the Charter. See *Ontario (Attorney General) v G*, 2020 SCC 38, striking down aspects of *Christopher's Law (Sex Offender Registry)*, SO 2000 c 1. At para 56,

the court explicitly chose to apply the equality provisions over section 7 of the Charter.
134 [1988] 1 SCR 30, 44 DLR (4th) 385.
135 Ibid., 156.
136 Ibid., explicitly adopting the reasoning of the Ontario Court of Appeal in *R v Morgentaler*, 22 DLR (4th) 641, 22 CCC (3rd) 353.
137 See *Morgentaler*, supra note 134, 171–72. The court's subsequent refusal to find that fetuses have any rights under the common/civil law or Quebec/Canadian Charter bolsters the equality claim since these competing interests are unlikely to outweigh women's equality claim. See Martha Shaffer, "Foetal Rights and the Regulation of Abortion," *McGill Law Journal* 39 (1994): 58–100, reviewing and critiquing the arguments presented in *Borowski v Canada (Attorney General)*, [1989] 1 SCR 342, 57 DLR (4th) 231; and *Tremblay v Daigle*, [1989] 2 SCR 530, 62 DLR (4th) 634. See also Joanna Erdman, "Constitutionalizing Abortion Rights in Canada," *Ottawa Law Review* 49 (2018): 221–61.
138 See *Morgentaler*, supra note 134, 171.
139 See Beverley Baines, "Abortion, Judicial Activism and Constitutional Crossroads," *University of New Brunswick Law Journal* 53 (2004): 179n62, citing various sources.
140 It is possible that the Supreme Court did not apply the equality provision because section 15 came into effect on 17 April 1985. Because the accused were charged between November 1982 and July 1983, applying the equality provision is tantamount, arguably, to a retroactive application of the right. The crown maintained as much at the Ontario Court of Appeal, but this argument was rejected. The Supreme Court also was willing to hear the argument, even if no set of judges applied the equality provision.
141 The Supreme Court has yet to find any positive rights in section 7 of the Charter, although it has not closed the door on that option. See, generally, *Gosselin v Quebec (Attorney General)*, 2002 SCC 84, [2002] 4 SCR 429.
142 See *Morgentaler*, supra note 134, 171.
143 Supra note 1.
144 2012 ONCA 186, 346 DLR (4th) 385.
145 Ibid., para 356, citing *New Brunswick (Minister of Health and Community Services) v G(J)*, [1999] 3 SCR 46, 177 DLR (4th) 124. See also *Canada (Attorney General) v Downtown Eastside Sex Workers United against Violence Society*, 2012 SCC 45, [2012] 2 SCR 524, in which the accused sought standing to argue breaches of sections 2, 7, and 15 of the same provisions challenged in *Bedford*.
146 See Jonathan Rudin, "Tell It Like It Is – An Argument for the Use of Section 15 over Section 7 to Challenge Discriminatory Criminal Legislation," *Criminal Law Quarterly* 64 (2017): 325.
147 [1993] 3 SCR 519, 107 DLR (4th) 342.
148 Ibid., 624.
149 Ibid., 613.

150 Ibid., 616.
151 Ibid., 550, 631.
152 Ibid., 557.
153 2012 BCSC 886, 287 CCC (3rd) 1; 2013 BCCA 435, 365 DLR (4th) 351.
154 See Maneesha Deckha, "A Missed Opportunity: Affirming the Section 15 Equality Argument against Physician-Assisted Death," *McGill Journal of Law and Health* 10 (2016): S74. See also Lepofsky, "Missing an Obvious Chance," supra note 96.
155 See *Carter v Canada (Attorney General)*, 2015 SCC 5 at para 93, [2015] 1 SCR 331.
156 See Deckha, "Missed Opportunity," supra note 154, S75.
157 See Lepofsky, "Missing an Obvious Chance," supra note 96, 98.
158 Ibid.
159 2004 SCC 4, [2004] 1 SCR 76.
160 Ibid., para 52.
161 Ibid., para 53.
162 Ibid., para 55.
163 Ibid., para 56.
164 Ibid.
165 Ibid., para 58.
166 Ibid. See also paras 60–62.
167 Ibid., para 59.
168 2004 SCC 46, [2004] 2 SCR 489.
169 Ibid., para 3.
170 Ibid., para 67.
171 See *R c Demers*, [2002] JQ No 590.
172 See *Demers*, supra note 168, para 92.
173 Ibid.
174 Unfortunately, Justice LeBel did not respond to the applicant's argument that the law violated section 15 of the Charter.
175 2020 ONCJ 429, 66 CR (7th) 382.
176 Ibid., para 4.
177 Ibid.
178 Ibid., paras 57–59.
179 Ibid., para 98.
180 Ibid., paras 99–100.
181 See *Lloyd*, supra note 97, para 15.
182 See *Turtle*, supra note 175, para 153.
183 2020 ONCA 478, 152 OR (3rd) 209.
184 SC 1996, c 19.
185 See *Criminal Code*, supra note 15, s 742.1(b).
186 Ibid., s 742.1(c).
187 Ibid., s 742.1(e).
188 See *Sharma*, supra note 183, para 21.

189 Ibid., paras 5–10.
190 Ibid., para 30.
191 Ibid., paras 31–37.
192 Ibid., para 52.
193 Ibid., paras 53–54.
194 Ibid., para 55.
195 Ibid., para 70.
196 Ibid.
197 Ibid., paras 73–86.
198 2013 ONCA 677, 117 OR (3rd) 401, upholding *R v Nur*, 2011 ONSC 4874, 275 CCC (3rd) 330.
199 See *Sharma*, supra note 183, paras 76–79.
200 Ibid., para 89. For discussions of the disparate impacts of mandatory minimum sentences on Indigenous people, see Larry Chartrand, "Aboriginal Peoples and Mandatory Sentencing," *Osgoode Hall Law Journal* 39 (2001): 449–68; and Faizal Mirza, "Mandatory Minimum Prison Sentencing and Systemic Racism," *Osgoode Hall Law Journal* 39 (2001): 491–512.
201 See *Sharma*, supra note 183, para 106.
202 Ibid., para 108.
203 Ibid., para 110.
204 Ibid., para 122, citing *R v Voong*, 2015 BCCA 285 at para 62, 325 CCC (3rd) 267.
205 Ibid., paras 116–20. It is notable that these factors are also relevant to whether a conditional sentence is imposed.
206 Ibid., paras 128–32.
207 Ibid., para 188, citing *Reference re Bowater's Pulp and Paper Mills Ltd*, [1950] SCR 608 at 640, [1950] 4 DLR 65 (per Justice Rand, concurring), and at 657 (per Justice Estey, concurring).
208 Ibid.
209 Ibid., para 84, citing *Alliance*, supra note 142, para 33.
210 Ibid., para 215, citing *Law v Canada (Minister of Employment and Immigration)*, [1999] 1 SCR 497 at para 51, 170 DLR (4th) 1.
211 Ibid., para 216.
212 Supra note 132.
213 Ibid., paras 220–23.
214 Ibid., para 224.
215 Ibid.
216 Ibid., paras 237–38.
217 Ibid., para 239.
218 Ibid.
219 Supra note 132.
220 Ibid., para 33.
221 Ibid., para 1, citing *Pay Equity Act*, SQ 1996, c 43.

222 Ibid., para 2, citing *Act to Amend the Pay Equity Act*, SQ 2009, c 9.
223 Ibid.
224 Ibid.
225 Ibid.
226 Ibid., para 33.
227 2011 SCC 44, [2011] 3 SCR 134.
228 Ibid., para 7.
229 Rudin, "Tell It Like It Is," supra note 146, 325.
230 *Sharma*, supra note 183, para 188.
231 Although I maintained in the previous chapter that those operating Insite could offer a justification-based defence if they were prosecuted for possession of drugs or trafficking, this claim assumed that the workers were still allowed to work at the safe injection site. Nothing in my reasoning would stop the government from simply closing the doors and preventing these employees from accessing the site.
232 See *Bedford*, supra note 15, para 86. See also Rudin, "Tell It Like It Is," supra note 146, 326, citing Wally Oppal, *Forsaken – The Report of the Missing Women Commission of Inquiry*, vol. 1 (Ottawa: Library and Archives Canada, 2012), 5. Rudin argues that this fact alone is sufficient to ground an equality violation.
233 2015 SCC 34, [2015] 2 SCR 602.
234 Ibid., para 24.
235 Ibid., para 25.
236 I will review this argument in greater detail in the next chapter.
237 Rudin, "Tell It Like It Is," supra note 146, 317–18. See also Lepofsky, "Missing an Obvious Chance," supra note 96, 91.
238 Ibid.
239 Deckha, "Missed Opportunity," supra note 154, S73.
240 Rosemary Cairns Way, "Attending to Equality: Criminal Law, the *Charter* and Competitive Truths," *Supreme Court Law Review* 57 (2nd) (2012): 40.
241 Ibid., 49.
242 Christine Boyle, "The Role of Equality in Criminal Law," *Saskatchewan Law Review* 58 (1994): 207.
243 Christine Boyle and John MacInnes, "Judging Sexual Assault Law against a Standard of Equality," *University of British Columbia Law Review* 29 (1995): 346.
244 Rudin, "Tell It Like It Is," supra note 146, 331–32.
245 Ibid.
246 Ibid.
247 Ibid.
248 See Cairns Way, "Competitive Truths," supra note 240, 49. See also Beverley McLachlin, "Equality: The Most Difficult Right," *Supreme Court Law Review* 14 (2nd) (2001): 18, citing Peter Westen, *Speaking of Equality: An Analysis of the Rhetorical Force of "Equality" in Moral and Legal Discourse* (Princeton, NJ: Princeton

University Press, 1990), 59 (describing equality analysis as "strange and difficult," "complex," "intricate," "ambiguous," "elusive," "slippery," and "mysterious").

249 Several commentators have observed the Supreme Court's clear preference for resolving a constitutional issue on any right other than equality. See Jennifer Koshan, "Redressing the Harms of Government (In)Action: A Section 7 versus Section 15 *Charter* Showdown," *Constitutional Forum constitutionnel* 22 (2013): 34; Elizabeth Sheehy, "Equality and Supreme Court Criminal Jurisprudence: Never the Twain Shall Meet," *Supreme Court Law Review* 50 (2nd) (2010): para 17; and Deckha, "Missed Opportunity," supra note 154, S98.

250 See Sheehy, "Equality," supra note 249, para 3.

251 Ibid., citing Donna Hackett, "Finding and Following the Road Less Travelled: Judicial Neutrality and the Protection and Enforcement of Equality Rights in Canadian Criminal Courts," *Canadian Journal of Women and the Law* 10 (1998): 131–32 (observing that litigants rarely raise equality concerns).

252 See *R v Ipeelee*, 2012 SCC 13 at paras 59–60, [2012] 1 SCR 433.

253 See Rudin, "Tell It Like It Is," supra note 146, 327.

254 Ibid. See, generally, sections 7–14 of the Charter.

255 The last major freedom of expression case was *Sharpe*, supra note 69, decided in 2001. The Supreme Court's instrumental rationality jurisprudence became prominent with its decision in *PHS*, supra note 227.

256 See Sarah Chaster, "Cruel, Unusual, and Constitutionally Infirm: Mandatory Minimum Sentences in Canada," *Appeal* 23 (2018): 116.

257 2016 SCC 13, [2016] 1 SCR 130.

258 Supra note 184.

259 See *Lloyd*, supra note 257, paras 29, 33.

260 See *Ipeelee*, supra note 252, para 37.

261 See *Keegstra*, supra note 2, 745–49, 755–58.

262 Ibid., 746–47.

263 Ibid.

264 See *Butler*, supra note 59, 496–97.

265 See Kerri Froc, "Constitutional Coalescence: Substantive Equality as a Principle of Fundamental Justice," *Ottawa Law Review* 42 (2012): 411–46; Suzy Flader, "Fundamental Rights for All: Toward Equality as a Principle of Fundamental Justice under Section 7 of the *Charter*," *Appeal* 25 (2020): 43–60; and *R v Appulonappa*, 2015 SCC 59 at para 78, [2015] 3 SCR 754.

266 See Froc, "Constitutional Coalescence," supra note 265, 428. For a more detailed description of this problem, see Margot Young, "Social Justice and the *Charter*: Comparison and Choice," *Osgoode Hall Law Journal* 50 (2013): 680–85.

267 Ibid.

268 Ibid., 429.

269 Froc recognizes that the Supreme Court arguably addressed the problem of "mirror comparators" in its then recent decision in *Withler v Canada (Attorney General)*,

2011 SCC 12 at para 58, [2011] 1 SCR 396. The court cited a variety of academic articles supporting its view that strict comparators can dull a court's ability to appreciate all harms relevant to the analysis. See Daphne Gilbert, "Time to Regroup: Rethinking Section 15 of the *Charter*," *McGill Law Journal* 48 (2003): 627–50; Nitya Iyer, "Categorical Denials: Equality Rights and the Shaping of Social Identity," *Queen's Law Journal* 19 (1993): 179–208; and Dianne Pothier, "Connecting Grounds of Discrimination to Real People's Real Experiences," *Canadian Journal of Women and the Law* 13 (2001): 37–73. Any doubt about the court's rejection of employing "mirror comparators" was recently confirmed in *Fraser*, supra note 132, para 94.

270 (1993), 14 OR (3rd) 321, 83 CCC (3rd) 210 (ONCA).
271 Ibid., 13.
272 See *Vaillancourt*, supra note 127, decided in 1987.

Chapter 5: A Normative Approach to Constitutionalizing Criminal Law

1 See *Canada (Attorney General) v Carter*, 2015 SCC 5 at para 72, [2015] 1 SCR 331.
2 See *United States v Carolene Products Co*, 304 US 144 (1938), n4 (laws that discriminate against "discrete and insular minorities" must be subject to strict constitutional review).
3 See, for example, Jeremy Waldron, "The Core of the Case against Judicial Review," *Yale Law Journal* 115 (2006): 1346–1407. For the most substantial response to these claims, see Ronald Dworkin, *Freedom's Law: The Moral Reading of the American Constitution* (Cambridge, MA: Harvard University Press, 1996), 1–38.
4 Alexander Bickel, *The Least Dangerous Branch: The Supreme Court at the Bar of Politics* (New York: Bobbs-Merrill, 1962).
5 Ibid., 16.
6 Ibid.
7 Waldron, "Judicial Review," supra note 3. For his most extensive, book-length discussion of the merits of judicial review, see Jeremy Waldron, *Law and Disagreement* (Oxford: Oxford University Press, 1999).
8 Ibid., 1354–59.
9 Ibid., 1355.
10 Ibid., 1354–55.
11 Ibid., 1354.
12 Ibid., 1356–57.
13 See Stephen Gardbaum, *The New Commonwealth Model of Constitutionalism: Theory and Practice* (Cambridge: Cambridge University Press, 2013).
14 See Waldron, "Judicial Review," supra note 3, 1356–57.
15 Ibid., 1360.
16 Ibid., 1361–62.
17 Ibid., 1362.
18 Ibid., 1363.
19 Ibid.

20 Ibid.
21 Ibid., 1363–64.
22 Ibid., 1364.
23 Ibid.
24 Ibid.
25 Ibid.
26 Ibid.
27 Ibid., 1365.
28 Ibid.
29 Ibid., 1366–67.
30 Ibid., 1367.
31 Ibid., 1368–69.
32 Ibid., 1369.
33 Ibid.
34 Ibid., 1372.
35 Ibid.
36 Ibid., 1373.
37 Ibid.
38 Ibid.
39 Ibid.
40 Ibid., citing Aileen Kavanagh, "Participation and Judicial Review: A Reply to Jeremy Waldron," *Law and Philosophy* 22 (2003): 466.
41 Ibid., 1387.
42 Ibid.
43 Ibid.
44 Ibid., 1387–88.
45 Ibid., 1388.
46 Ibid., 1389.
47 Ibid., 1390.
48 Ibid., 1391.
49 Ibid. For a similar point in the Canadian context, see Christopher Manfredi, *Judicial Power and the Charter: Canada and the Paradox of Liberal Constitutionalism*, 2nd ed. (Toronto: Oxford University Press, 2001), 33–35; F.L. Morton and Rainer Knopff, *The Charter Revolution and the Court Party* (Peterborough, ON: Broadview Press, 2000), 149; Andrew Petter, "The Politics of the Charter," *Canadian Bar Review* 8 (1986): 476; and Andrew Petter, *The Politics of the Charter: The Illusive Promise of Constitutional Rights* (Toronto: University of Toronto Press, 2010).
50 See Waldron, "Judicial Review," supra note 3, 1392.
51 Ibid., citing Marquis de Condorcet, *Essay on the Application of Mathematics to the Theory of Decision-Making* (1785).
52 Ibid.
53 Ibid., 1392–93.

54 See, for example, Abner Mikva, "How Well Does Congress Support and Defend the Constitution?," *North Carolina Law Review* 61 (1982): 609.
55 Ibid.
56 See Waldron, "Judicial Review," supra note 3, 1376.
57 Ibid., 1377–78, citing Joseph Raz, "Disagreement in Politics," *American Journal of Jurisprudence* 43 (1998): 46.
58 Ibid., 1378.
59 Ibid., 1379.
60 Ibid., citing Michael Moore, "Law as a Functional Kind," in *Natural Law Theory*, ed. Robert George (Oxford: Oxford University Press, 1992), 230.
61 Ibid., 1380.
62 Ibid.
63 Ibid.
64 See *Canada (Attorney General) v Bedford*, 2013 SCC 72 at paras 48–56, [2013] 3 SCR 1101.
65 See Waldron, "Judicial Review," supra note 3, 1381.
66 Ibid.
67 Ibid.
68 Ibid.
69 Ibid., 1382.
70 Ibid.
71 Ibid.
72 Ibid., 1383.
73 Ibid.
74 Ibid.
75 410 US 113 (1973).
76 See Waldron, "Judicial Review," supra note 3, 1383.
77 Ibid., 1384–85.
78 Ibid.
79 Ibid.
80 It is notable here that even some of those who disapprove of the practice of judicial review disagree with Waldron on this point. See, for example, Michael Walzer, "Philosophy and Democracy," *Political Theory* 9 (1981): 390:

> [Judges'] special role in the democratic community is connected ... to their thoughtfulness, and thoughtfulness is a philosophical posture ... For the discussions of judges among themselves really do resemble the arguments that go on in ... the mind of the philosopher ... much more closely than democratic debate can ever do. And it seems plausible to say that rights are more likely to be defined correctly in the *reflection* of the few than in the *votes* of the many.

81 Waldron, "Judicial Review," supra note 3, 1385n107, acknowledges this point but does not make much of it.
82 For other notable scholarship opposing judicial review, see Mark Tushnet, *Taking the Constitution Away from the Courts* (Princeton, NJ: Princeton University Press,

1999); Larry Kramer, *The People Themselves: Popular Constitutionalism and Judicial Review* (Oxford: Oxford University Press, 2004); and Richard Bellamy, *Political Constitutionalism: A Republican Defense of the Constitutionality of Democracy* (Cambridge: Cambridge University Press, 2007).
83 Supra note 2.
84 Ibid., n4.
85 See John Hart Ely, *Democracy and Distrust: A Theory of Judicial Review* (Cambridge, MA: Harvard University Press, 1980). For a similar work in Canada, see Patrick Monahan, *Politics and the Constitution: The Charter, Federalism and the Supreme Court of Canada* (Toronto: Carswell, 1987).
86 Ibid., 1–2.
87 Ibid., 4–5. Waldron does not necessarily support any strong form model of judicial review. When required to employ strong form review, however, the textualist approach is most clearly in line with his emphasis on majoritarian democracy.
88 Ibid., 8. Ely does recognize the illogicality of this argument in instances in which the relevant constitution has been in force for a significant amount of time. Ibid., 11.
89 Ibid., 13.
90 Ibid., 32.
91 Ibid., 38–41. For a contrary view, see Robert Bork, *The Tempting of America: The Political Seduction of the Law* (New York: Touchstone, 1990), 143–60.
92 Ibid., 44–48.
93 Ibid., 48–54, 56–60. As Ely observes, reason was used by both sides debating the scope of women's rights and the appropriateness of slavery.
94 Ibid., 54–55, replying to Herbert Wechsler, "Toward Neutral Principles of Constitutional Law," *Harvard Law Review* 73 (1959): 1–35. See also Bickel, *Least Dangerous Branch*, supra note 4, 55; Jan Ginter Deutsch, "Neutrality, Legitimacy, and the Supreme Court: Some Intersections between Law and Political Science," *Stanford Law Review* 20 (1968): 187–97; and Robert Bork, "Neutral Principles and Some First Amendment Problems," *Indiana Law Journal* 47 (1971): 7–8.
95 See Ely, *Democracy and Distrust*, supra note 85, 56–60, noting that lawyers, judges, and moral philosophers alike tend to come from upper-middle or upper classes. As Ely observes,

> the danger that upper-middle-class judges and commentators will find upper-middle-class values fundamental is obviously present irrespective of methodology. I think it's exacerbated when "reason" is the supposed value source, however, partly because the values we have mentioned are the values of the "reasoning class," and partly because "reason," being inherently an empty source, may lend itself unusually well to being filled in by the values of one's own kind (59n**).

96 Ibid., 60–63.
97 Ibid., 63–69, responding to Harry Wellington, "Common Law Rules and Constitutional Double Standards: Some Notes on Adjudication," *Yale Law Journal* 83 (1973): 284.

98 Ibid., 69–70, responding to Alexander Bickel's suggestion in *The Supreme Court and the Idea of Progress* (New York: Harper and Row, 1970) that the Warren Court's strong form of judicial review might be justified by the court's ability to predict progress. Although Bickel found this argument unpersuasive, others have supported this view. See, for example, Abram Chayes, "The Role of the Judge in Public Law Litigation," *Harvard Law Review* 89 (1976): 1316.
99 See Ely, *Democracy and Distrust*, supra note 85, 102–3.
100 Ibid., 103.
101 Ibid., 105–25.
102 Ibid., 103.
103 Ibid., 135.
104 Ibid., 153, citing Frank Goodman, "De Facto School Segregation: A Constitutional and Empirical Analysis," *California Law Review* 60 (1972): 315.
105 Ibid., 169.
106 Ibid., 164n93.
107 See Kent Roach, *The Supreme Court on Trial: Judicial Activism or Democratic Dialogue?* (Toronto: Irwin Law, 2016), 259.
108 See Ely, *Democracy and Distrust*, supra note 85, 87.
109 Ibid., 103.
110 Ibid.
111 See Dworkin, *Freedom's Law*, supra note 3.
112 Ibid., 2.
113 Ibid., 7.
114 Ibid.
115 Ibid., 15.
116 Ibid., 16.
117 Ibid., 17.
118 Ibid.
119 Ibid.
120 Ibid.
121 Ibid., 20.
122 Ibid., 22–23, 28–29.
123 Ibid.
124 Ibid., 23.
125 Ibid., 24.
126 Ibid., 24–25.
127 Ibid., 25.
128 Ibid., 25–26.
129 See Waldron, *Law and Disagreement*, supra note 7, chapter 10.
130 See Dworkin, *Freedom's Law*, supra note 3, 30.
131 Ibid.
132 Ibid., 30–31. Dworkin recognizes that the empirical evidence supporting either side of this argument is thin.

133 Ibid., 10. For his fullest discussion of integrity as a requirement of constitutional interpretation, see Ronald Dworkin, *Law's Empire* (Cambridge, MA: Harvard University Press, 1986), chapters 6–11.
134 See Dworkin, *Freedom's Law*, supra note 3, 10.
135 Ibid., 83.
136 Ibid.
137 Ibid., 11.
138 Ibid., 34.
139 See Ronald Dworkin, *Taking Rights Seriously* (Cambridge, MA: Harvard University Press, 1977), 143.
140 See Dworkin, *Law's Empire*, supra note 133, 375–76.
141 See Richard Fallon, "The Core of an Uneasy Case for Judicial Review," *Harvard Law Review* 121 (2008): 1705–6. Notably, Fallon's response does not follow Dworkin in arguing that courts are more likely to decide rights issues correctly because they are "forum[s] of principle." Ibid., 1695, citing Ronald Dworkin, *A Matter of Principle* (Cambridge, MA: Harvard University Press, 1985), 69–71.
142 See Roach, *Supreme Court*, supra note 107, 261–62.
143 Dworkin, *Freedom's Law*, supra note 3, 3, 18.
144 Christopher Manfredi and James Kelly, "Six Degrees of Dialogue: A Response to Hogg and Bushell," *Osgoode Hall Law Journal* 37 (1999): 524.
145 F.L. Morton, "Dialogue or Monologue?," in *Judicial Power and Canadian Democracy*, ed. Paul Howe and Peter Russell (Montreal and Kingston: McGill-Queen's University Press, 2001), 117.
146 Allan Hutchinson, *Waiting for CORAF* (Toronto: University of Toronto Press, 1995), 170. See also Petter, *Politics of the Charter*, supra note 49.
147 See Manfredi and Kelly, "Six Degrees," supra note 144 (one-third); and Emmett Macfarlane, "Dialogue or Compliance? Measuring Legislatures' Policy Responses to Court Rulings on Rights," *International Political Science Review* 34 (2012): 39–56 (below one-fifth). For those with broader definitions of dialogue, the numbers drastically increase. See Peter Hogg and Allison Bushell, "The *Charter* Dialogue between Courts and Legislatures (Or Perhaps the *Charter of Rights* Isn't Such a Bad Thing after All)," *Osgoode Hall Law Journal* 35 (1997): 75–124 (roughly two-thirds); and Peter Hogg, Allison Bushell, and Wade Knight, "*Charter* Dialogue Revisited: Or 'Much Ado about Metaphors,'" *Osgoode Hall Law Journal* 45 (2007): 1–66 (roughly two-thirds).
148 Roach, *Supreme Court*, supra note 107, 273.
149 Ibid.
150 Bickel, *Idea of Progress*, supra note 98, 91.
151 Ibid.
152 Alexander Bickel, *The Morality of Consent* (New Haven, CT: Yale University Press, 1975), 111.
153 Ibid., 79. See also Bickel, *Least Dangerous Branch*, supra note 4, 202–3.
154 Bickel, *Least Dangerous Branch*, supra note 4, 70.

155 Ibid., 70–71.
156 Ibid., 24.
157 See, for example, Michael Perry, *The Constitution in the Courts* (New York: Oxford University Press, 1994), 200.
158 See Bruce Ackerman, *We the People: Foundations* (Cambridge, MA: Harvard University Press, 1997), 13.
159 Section 33 applies to sections 2 and 7–15 of the Charter.
160 Roach, *Supreme Court*, supra note 107, 383–84.
161 Ibid., 393, responding to Jeremy Waldron, *Political Political Theory* (Cambridge, MA: Harvard University Press, 2016), 199.
162 Ibid., 395.
163 See, for example, Mark Tushnet, "Judicial Activism or Restraint in a Section 33 World," *University of Toronto Law Journal* 53 (2003): 94–97; Grégoire Webber, *The Negotiable Constitution* (Cambridge: Cambridge University Press, 2009), 10; and Manfredi, *Judicial Power*, supra note 49, 74.
164 See Mark Tushnet, "Weak Form Judicial Review and 'Core' Civil Liberties," *Harvard Civil Rights–Civil Liberties Law Review* 41 (2006): 6.
165 See Janet Hiebert, *Charter Conflicts* (Montreal and Kingston: McGill-Queen's University Press, 2002).
166 See Roach, *Supreme Court*, supra note 107, 404.
167 Andrew Petter, "Legalize This: The Chartering of Canadian Politics," in *Contested Constitutionalism: Reflections on the Canadian Charter of Rights and Freedoms*, ed. James Kelly and Christopher Manfredi (Vancouver: UBC Press, 2010), 33. See also Waldron, *Political Political Theory*, supra note 161, 354n30.
168 See Carissima Mathen, "Dialogue Theory, Judicial Review, and Judicial Supremacy," *Osgoode Hall Law Journal* 45 (2007): 128.
169 See Roach, *Supreme Court*, supra note 107, 267 (concluding that "it is a myth to think that there can be agreement on which theory is best supported by the constitution. It is also a myth to think that judges will reliably reach right answers that are themselves consistent with democracy").
170 Ibid., 246.
171 See Mark Carter, "Fundamental Justice," *Supreme Court Law Review* 78 (2nd) (2017): 259–60.
172 See *Perka v The Queen*, [1984] 2 SCR 232 at 248, 13 DLR (4th) 1.
173 See Alexander Kaufman and Michael Runnels, "The Core of an Unqualified Case for Judicial Review: A Reply to Jeremy Waldron and Contemporary Critics," *Brooklyn Law Review* 82 (2016): 169–70. Based on my reading of Waldron, "Judicial Review," supra note 3, little if any attention is paid to criminal law.
174 For a review of this commonly accepted rationale, see Donald Dripps, "Criminal Procedure, Footnote Four, and the Theory of Public Choice; or, Why Don't Legislatures Give a Damn about the Rights of the Accused?," *Syracuse Law Review* 44 (1993): 1079–1102.

175 The presumption of innocence found in section 11(d) of the Charter is interpreted, in my view, primarily as a procedural right pertaining to burden of proof and therefore does not significantly affect substantive criminal justice.

176 Since this is a book about the relationship between constitutional law and criminal law, I am hesitant to speak further to this issue. It seems, however, that an area such as immigration law is similarly plagued with majoritarian problems.

177 One exception would be *Canada (Attorney General) v PHS Community Services Society*, 2011 SCC 44, [2011] 3 SCR 134. However, for the reasons explained in Chapter 4, I think that case was wrongly decided.

178 Kent Roach, "Mind the Gap: Canada's Different Criminal and Constitutional Standards of Fault," *University of Toronto Law Journal* 61 (2011): 545–78.

179 [1994] 3 SCR 63, 118 DLR (4th) 469.

180 For a review of these cases, see Chapter 2.

181 As several authors have observed, the Supreme Court's development of section 7 is among the most significant forms of judicial overreach in a Western model of constitutionalism. See Hamish Stewart, *Fundamental Justice: Section 7 of the Canadian Charter of Rights and Freedoms* (Toronto: Irwin Law, 2019), 372, citing Michael Mandel, *The Charter of Rights and the Legalization of Politics in Canada* (Toronto: Wall and Thomson, 1989); Hutchinson, *Waiting for CORAF*, supra note 146; Petter, *Politics of the Charter*, supra note 49; Monahan, *Politics and the Constitution*, supra note 85; Manfredi, *Judicial Power*, supra note 49; and Morton and Knopff, *Court Party*, supra note 49.

182 Kent Roach, "American Constitutional Theory for Canadians (and the Rest of the World)," *University of Toronto Law Journal* 52 (2002): 510. For similar arguments that section 33 allows courts to be bolder in their interpretations of rights, see Paul Weiler, "Of Judges and Rights, or Should Canada Have a Constitutional Bill of Rights?," *Dalhousie Law Review* 60 (1980): 205–37; Paul Weiler, "Rights and Judges in a Democracy: A New Canadian Version," *University of Michigan Journal of Law Reform* 18 (1984): 51–92; and Lorraine Weinrib, "Canada's Constitutional Revolution: From Legislative to Constitutional State," *Israel Law Review* 33 (1999): 49.

183 See Richard Albert, "Advisory Review: The Reincarnation of the Notwithstanding Clause," *Alberta Law Review* 45 (2008): 1037–69; and Richard McAdam, "The Notwithstanding Taboo," *Federal Governance* 6 (2009): 1–20.

184 Ibid.

185 Ibid.

186 See Roach, *Supreme Court on Trial*, supra note 107, 318–19.

187 [1994] 3 SCR 63, 118 DLR (4th) 469.

188 See "Criminal Defence of Drunkenness an Offence to Reason," *Vancouver Sun*, 5 October 1994, A10.

189 See C.H. Farnsworth, "Use of Drunkenness Defense Prompts Outrage in Canada," *Houston Chronicle*, 13 November 1994, A38.

190 See the public reaction as reviewed in Don Stuart, *Canadian Criminal Law: A Treatise*, 6th ed. (Toronto: Thomson Carswell, 2011), 469–70; Isabelle Grant, "Second Chances: Bill C-72 and the *Charter*," *Osgoode Hall Law Journal* 33 (1995): 383n12; and Gerry Ferguson, "The Intoxication Defence: Constitutionally Impaired and in Need of Rehabilitation," *Supreme Court Law Review* 57 (2nd) (2012): 125n60.
191 2001 SCC 2, [2001] 1 SCR 45.
192 See Wayne McKay, "*R. v. Sharpe*: Pornography, Privacy, Proportionality and the Protection of Children," *National Journal of Constitutional Law* 12 (2000–01): 114.
193 Ibid.
194 For a review of the various media responses, see Jack Watson, "Case Comment: *R. v. Sharpe*," *National Journal of Constitutional Law* 10 (1999): 251.
195 2015 SCC 15, [2015] 1 SCR 773.
196 *Criminal Code of Canada*, RSC 1985, c C-46.
197 Ibid., s 95(2)(a).
198 See *Nur*, supra note 195, para 80, citing *R v MacDonald*, 2014 SCC 3, [2014] 1 SCR 37.
199 Ibid., paras 162–72.
200 See Angus Reid Institute, "Canadians Have a More Favourable View of Their Supreme Court Than Americans Have of Their Own," 17 August 2015, http://angusreid.org/supreme-court/ (40 percent agreed, whereas 37 percent did not; 7 percent were unsure; and 16 percent had not heard of the decision).
201 The criminal procedure context has also witnessed at least one law that was struck down and clearly subject to legislative override with public support. The Supreme Court's decision striking down the "rape shield" laws in *R v Seaboyer*, [1991] 2 SCR 577, 83 DLR (4th) 193, is illustrative. For a review of the evidence supporting public use of the override, see Lois MacDonald, "Promoting Social Equality through the Legislative Override," *National Journal of Constitutional Law* 4 (1994): 19.
202 See Angus Reid Institute, "Canadians," supra note 200.
203 Ibid.
204 Ibid.
205 Ibid.
206 See Angus Reid Institute, "Most Canadians Express Confidence in Police, but Those Levels Are Lower among Visible Minorities," 15 July 2016, http://angusreid.org/confidence-in-justice-system-police/; and Angus Reid Institute, "Half of Canadians Say Crime Is Rising in Their Communities, as Confidence in Police, Courts Wanes," 10 January 2020, http://angusreid.org/justice-system-confidence-2020/.
207 See Angus Reid Institute, "Supreme Court," supra note 200. See also Chris Wattie, "Politicized Supreme Court Fight One of Harper's Most Imprudent Acts," *Globe and Mail*, 26 May 2014, https://www.theglobeandmail.com/opinion/editorials/a-supreme-court-short-list-long-on-controversy/article18856513/ (52 percent agreed with this statement, whereas 20 percent disagreed with it).
208 [1985] 2 SCR 486, 512, 24 DLR (4th) 536 [*Motor Vehicle Act Reference*].

209 The Manitoba Court of Appeal came to this conclusion in *R v Willis*, 2016 MBCA 113, 344 CCC (3rd) 443. For a contrary view, see *R v Aravena*, 2015 ONCA 250, 323 CCC (3rd) 54. For my views on this question, see Colton Fehr, "The Constitutionality of Excluding Duress as a Defence to Murder," *Manitoba Law Journal* 44 (2021): 109–33.
210 See also Fehr, "Duress as a Defence to Murder," supra note 209.
211 See Alan Young, "Done Nothing Wrong: Fundamental Justice and the Minimum Content of Criminal Law," *Supreme Court Law Review* 40 (2nd) (2008): 482–83.
212 Ibid.

Chapter 6: Lessons from the Canadian Experience

1 Others have provided evidence of this phenomenon as well. As Matthew Hennigar observes in "Unreasonable Disagreement? Judicial-Executive Exchanges about *Charter* Reasonableness in the Harper Era," *Osgoode Hall Law Journal* 54 (2017): 1256, nineteen criminal justice laws were challenged under the Charter during the Harper years. Of these laws, only one did not include an argument made under section 7 of the Charter.
2 [1985] 2 SCR 486, 512, 24 DLR (4th) 536.
3 Ibid., 518.
4 See Victor Ramraj, "Four Models of Due Process," *International Journal of Constitutional Law* 2 (2004): 494–96. For a review of two other states, Germany and Israel, active in constitutionalizing principles of criminal law, see Miriam Gur-Arye and Thomas Wiegend, "Constitutional Review of Criminal Prohibitions Affecting Human Dignity and Liberty: German and Israeli Perspectives," *Israel Law Review* 44 (2011): 63–90. The constitutions discussed in these articles are illustrative, not exhaustive, of the states engaging in section 7–like judicial review.
5 See Singapore's Constitution, Art 9(1), and Malaysia's Constitution, Art 5(1) ("no person shall be deprived of his life or personal liberty save in accordance with law").
6 See India's Constitution, Art 21 ("no person shall be deprived of his life or personal liberty except according to procedure established by law").
7 See the US Constitution, Amendments Five ("no person ... shall be deprived of life, liberty, or property, without due process of law") and Fourteen ("no State shall ... deprive any person of life, liberty, or property, without due process of law").
8 See *Powell v Texas*, 392 US 514 (1968) at 535–37, 541, narrowly rejecting an earlier decision (*Robinson v California*, 370 US 660 (1962)), implying that the Fifth and Fourteenth Amendments might provide minimal requirements for standards of fault. The court has struck down, however, criminal prohibitions related directly to personal privacy and autonomy. See, for example, *Roe v Wade*, 410 US 113 (1973) (abortion); and *Lawrence v Texas*, 123 S CT 2472 (2003) (sodomy).
9 See South Africa's Constitution, s 12(1)(a) ("everyone has the right to freedom and security of the person, which includes the right ... (a) not to be deprived of freedom arbitrarily or without just cause").

10 Articles 9 and 5 of Singapore's and Malaysia's respective constitutions were initially found to provide for basic procedural protections in addition to constitutionalizing the principle of legality. However, this broader approach was later rejected in both countries. See *Jabar v Public Prosecutor*, [1995] 1 SLR 617 (CA) at 631; and *Ketua Pengarah Jabatan Alam Sekitar v Kajing Tubek*, [1997] 3 MLJ 23 at 43. Both cases overturned the Privy Council's decision in *Ong Ah Chuan v Public Prosecutor*, [1981] 1 MLJ 64 (PC).

11 The Supreme Court of India has recently found a general right to "privacy" in Article 21 of the Indian Constitution. See *Justice KS Puttaswamy (Retd) and Anr v Union of India and Ors* (2017). This rationale was then used as a basis to strike down a law criminalizing sodomy. See *Navtej Singh Johar v Union of India* (2018), overturning *Suresh Kumar Koushal v Naz Foundation* (2013).

12 See *Murarilal Jhunjhunwala v State of Bihar*, (1991) Supp 2 SCC 647. In the context of a prosecution imposing strict liability for carrying on a business without a licence, the court suggested at 649 that, since the accused was "not to be blamed ... [and had] done all that he could do under the law," the prosecution was contrary to the basic principles of Article 21.

13 1997 (3) SALR 527.

14 Ibid., 597.

15 George Fletcher, *The Grammar of Criminal Law: American, Comparative, and International*, vol. 1 (Oxford: Oxford University Press, 2007), 101.

16 Ibid.

17 Various Canadian criminal law professors have called on the government to update Canada's "embarrassingly bad" statutory criminal law. See Kathleen Harris, "Experts Urge Liberals to Update 'Embarrassingly Bad' *Criminal Code*," CBC News, 18 November 2016, https://www.cbc.ca/news/politics/criminal-code-outdated-justice-discrimination-1.3853810.

Bibliography

Jurisprudence

Canadian
Beaver v The Queen, [1957] SCR 531, 118 CCC 129.
Blencoe v British Columbia (Human Rights Commission), 2000 SCC 44, [2000] 2 SCR 307.
Borowski v Canada (Attorney General), [1989] 1 SCR 342, 57 DLR (4th) 231.
British Columbia Civil Liberties Association v Canada (Attorney General), 2019 BCCA 228, 377 CCC (3rd) 420.
Canada (Attorney General) v Bedford, 2012 ONCA 186, 109 OR (3rd) 1.
Canada (Attorney General) v Bedford, 2013 SCC 72, [2013] 3 SCR 1101.
Canada (Attorney General) v Downtown Eastside Sex Workers United against Violence Society, 2012 SCC 45, [2012] 2 SCR 524.
Canada (Attorney General) v PHS Community Services Society, 2011 SCC 44, [2011] 3 SCR 134.
Canadian Civil Liberties Association v Canada (Attorney General), 2019 ONCA 243, 144 OR (3rd) 641.
Canadian Foundation for Children, Youth and the Law v Canada (Attorney General), 2004 SCC 4, [2004] 1 SCR 76.
Carter v Canada (Attorney General), 2012 BCSC 886, 287 CCC (3rd) 1.
Carter v Canada (Attorney General), 2013 BCCA 435, 365 DLR (4th) 351.
Carter v Canada (Attorney General), 2015 SCC 5, [2015] 1 SCR 331.
Chiarelli v Canada (Minister of Employment and Immigration), [1992] 1 SCR 711, 90 DLR (4th) 289.

Fraser v Canada (Attorney General), 2020 SCC 28.
Gosselin v Québec (Attorney General), 2002 SCC 84, [2002] 4 SCR 429.
Hunter v Southam, [1984] 2 SCR 145, 11 DLR (4th) 641.
Irwin Toy Ltd v Quebec (Attorney General), [1989] 1 SCR 927, 58 DLR (4th) 577.
Kahkewistahaw First Nation v Taypotat, 2015 SCC 30, [2015] 2 SCR 548.
Krieger v Law Society of Alberta, 2002 SCC 65, [2002] 3 SCR 372.
Labatt Breweries of Canada Ltd v Attorney General of Canada, [1980] 1 SCR 914, 110 DLR (3rd) 594.
Latham v Canada (Solicitor General), 9 DLR (4th) 393, 12 CCC (3rd) 9.
Law v Canada (Minister of Employment and Immigration), [1999] 1 SCR 497, 170 DLR (4th) 1.
Lévis (City) v Tétreault; Lévis (City) v 2629-4470 Québec Inc, 2006 SCC 12, [2006] 1 SCR 420.
Libman c Québec (Procureur général), [1997] 3 SCR 569, 151 DLR (4th) 385.
M v H, [1999] 2 SCR 3, 171 DLR (4th) 577.
New Brunswick (Minister of Health and Community Services) v G(J), [1999] 3 SCR 46, 177 DLR (4th) 124.
Ontario (Attorney General) v G, 2020 SCC 38.
Perka v The Queen, [1984] 2 SCR 232, 13 DLR (4th) 1.
Philippines (Republic) v Pacificador (1993), 14 OR (3rd) 321, 83 CCC (3rd) 210 (ONCA).
Quebec (Attorney General) v Alliance du personnel professionnel et technique de la santé et des services sociaux, 2018 SCC 17, [2018] 1 SCR 464.
Rabey v The Queen, [1980] 2 SCR 513, 114 DLR (3rd) 193.
R c Demers, [2002] JQ No 590.
R c Lippé, [1991] 2 SCR 114, 61 CCC (3rd) 127.
Reference re Bowater's Pulp and Paper Mills Ltd, [1950] SCR 608, [1950] 4 DLR 65.
Reference re Firearms Act (Can), 2000 SCC 31, [2000] 1 SCR 783.
Reference re Section 94(2) of the Motor Vehicle Act, [1985] 2 SCR 486, 512, 24 DLR (4th) 536.
Reference re Section 293 of the Criminal Code, 2011 BCSC 1588, 279 CCC (3rd) 1.
Reference re ss 193 and 195.1(1)(c) of the Criminal Code (Man), [1990] 1 SCR 1123, 56 CCC (3rd) 65.
RJR-MacDonald Inc v Canada (Attorney General), [1995] 3 SCR 199, 127 DLR (4th) 1.
Rodriguez v British Columbia (Attorney General), [1993] 3 SCR 519, 107 DLR (4th) 342.
R v AB, 2015 ONCA 803, 342 OAC 346.
R v Allen, 2014 SKQB 402, 318 CCC (3rd) 335.
R v Ancio, [1984] 1 SCR 225, 6 DLR (4th) 577.
R v Anderson, 2013 NLCA 2, 331 Nfld and PEIR 308.
R v Anderson, 2014 SCC 41, [2014] 2 SCR 167.
R v Anwar, 2020 ONCJ 103, 62 CR (7th) 402.

R v Appulonappa, 2015 SCC 59, [2015] 3 SCR 754.
R v Aravena, 2015 ONCA 250, 323 CCC (3rd) 54.
R v Arkell, [1990] 2 SCR 695, 59 CCC (3rd) 65.
R v Beare, [1988] 2 SCR 387, 55 DLR (4th) 481.
R v Beatty, 2008 SCC 5, [2008] 1 SCR 149.
R v Big M Drug Mart, [1985] 1 SCR 295, 18 DLR (4th) 321.
R v Boodhoo, 2018 ONSC 7205.
R v Bouchard-Lebrun, 2011 SCC 58, [2011] 3 SCR 575.
R v Boudreault, 2018 SCC 58, [2018] 3 SCR 599.
R v Boutilier, 2017 SCC 64, [2017] 2 SCR 936.
R v Brenton, 180 DLR (4th) 314, [2000] 2 WWR 269 (NTSC).
R v Butler, [1992] 1 SCR 452, 89 DLR (4th) 449.
R v Charlie, 2015 YKCA 3, 366 BCAC 254.
R v Clay, 2003 SCC 75, [2003] 3 SCR 735.
R v Clay (2000), 49 OR (3rd) 577, 188 DLR (4th) 468 (ONCA).
R v Conception, 2014 SCC 60, [2014] 3 SCR 82.
R v Cribbin (1994), 18 CCC (3rd) 67, 28 CR (4th) 137.
R v Daley, 2007 SCC 53, [2007] 3 SCR 523.
R v Daviault, [1994] 3 SCR 63, 118 DLR (4th) 469.
R v DB, 2008 SCC 25, [2008] 2 SCR 3.
R v Demers, 2004 SCC 46, [2004] 2 SCR 489.
R v DeSousa, [1992] 2 SCR 944, 95 DLR (4th) 595.
R v Duke, [1972] SCR 917, 28 DLR (3rd) 129.
R v Dunn (1999), 28 CR (5th) 295, 44 WCB (2nd) 47 (ONCJ).
R v Durham (1992), 76 CCC (3rd) 219, 10 OR (3rd) 596.
R v Ferguson, 2008 SCC 6, [2008] 1 SCR 96.
R v Finlay, [1993] 3 SCR 103, 105 DLR (4th) 699.
R v Finta, [1994] 1 SCR 701, 112 DLR (4th) 513.
R v Fleming, 2010 ONSC 8022, 94 WCB (2nd) 252.
R v Fraser (1980), 26 AR 33, 15 Alta LR (2nd) 25 (ABCA).
R v Friesen, 2016 MBCA 50, 330 Man R (2nd) 32.
R v George, [1960] SCR 871, 128 CCC 289.
R v Gladue, [1999] 1 SCR 433, 171 DLR (4th) 385.
R v Goltz, [1991] 3 SCR 485, 67 CCC (3rd) 481.
R v Graf (1988), 42 CRR 146, 5 WCB (2nd) 167.
R v Hauser, [1979] 1 SCR 984, 98 DLR (3rd) 193.
R v Heywood, [1994] 3 SCR 761, 120 DLR (4th) 348.
R v Hibbert, [1995] 2 SCR 973, 99 CCC (3rd) 193.
R v Holman, 28 CR (3rd) 378, 16 MVR 225 affirmed 143 DLR (3rd) 748, 2 CCC (3rd) 19.
R v Hundal, [1993] 1 SCR 867, 79 CCC (3rd) 97.
R v Ipeelee, 2012 SCC 13, [2012] 1 SCR 433.

R v Jordan, 2016 SCC 27, [2016] 1 SCR 631.
R v JP, 2020 SKCA 52, 62 CR (7th) 328.
R v Keegstra, 87 AR 200, 19 CCC (3rd) 254.
R v Keegstra, [1990] 3 SCR 697, 61 CCC (3rd) 1.
R v Khawaja, 2012 SCC 69, [2012] 3 SCR 555.
R v King, [1962] SCR 746, 133 CCC 1.
R v KRJ, 2016 SCC 31, [2016] 1 SCR 906.
R v Labaye, 2005 SCC 80, [2005] 3 SCR 728.
R v Latimer, 2001 SCC 1, [2001] 1 SCR 3.
R v Leary, [1978] 1 SCR 29, 74 DLR (3rd) 103.
R v Lloyd, 2016 SCC 13, [2016] 1 SCR 130.
R v Logan, [1990] 2 SCR 731, 73 DLR (4th) 40.
R v Lucas, [1998] 1 SCR 439, 157 DLR (4th) 423.
R v Luxton, [1990] 2 SCR 711, 58 CCC (3rd) 449.
R v MacDonald, 2014 SCC 3, [2013] 1 SCR 37.
R v Malmo-Levine, 2000 BCCA 335, 145 CCC (3rd) 225.
R v Malmo-Levine, 2003 SCC 74, [2003] 3 SCR 571.
R v Martineau, [1990] 2 SCR 633, 58 CCC (3rd) 353.
R v Mason, 1 DLR (4th) 712, 7 CCC (3rd) 426.
R v McCaw, 2018 ONSC 3464, 48 CR (7th) 359.
R v Michaud, 2015 ONCA 585, 127 OR (3rd) 81.
R v Morales, [1992] 3 SCR 711, 77 CCC (3rd) 91.
R v Morgentaler, 22 DLR (4th) 641, 22 CCC (3rd) 353 (ONCA).
R v Morgentaler, [1988] 1 SCR 30, 44 DLR (4th) 385.
R v Moriarity, 2015 SCC 55, [2015] 3 SCR 485.
R v Morrisey, 2000 SCC 39, [2000] 2 SCR 90.
R v Murdock (2003), 173 OAC 171, 176 CCC (3rd) 232 (ONCA).
R v Naglik, [1993] 3 SCR 122, 105 DLR (4th) 712.
R v Nasogaluak, 2010 SCC 6, [2010] 1 SCR 206.
R v Nixon, 2011 SCC 34, [2011] 2 SCR 566.
R v Nova Scotia Pharmaceutical Society, [1992] 2 SCR 606, 74 CCC (3rd) 209.
R v Nur, 2011 ONSC 4874, 275 CCC (3rd) 330.
R v Nur, 2013 ONCA 677, 117 OR (3rd) 401.
R v Nur, 2015 SCC 15, [2015] 1 SCR 773.
R v Oakes, [1986] 1 SCR 103, 26 DLR (4th) 200.
R v Pappajohn, [1980] 2 SCR 120, 111 DLR (3rd) 1.
R v Paquette, [1977] 2 SCR 189, 70 DLR (4th) 129.
R v Parks, [1995] 2 SCR 836, 99 CCC (3rd) 1.
R v PC, 2012 ONSC 5362, 99 CR (6th) 116.
R v Penno, [1990] 2 SCR 865, 59 CCC (3rd) 344.
R v Polewsky (2005), 202 CCC (3rd) 257 (ONCA).
R v Potma, [1983] OJ No 9 (ONCA).

R v Power, [1994] 1 SCR 601, 89 CCC (3rd) 1.
R v Preston (1990), 47 BCLR (2nd) 273, 79 CR (3rd) 61 (BCCA).
R v Ramsay, 2012 ABCA 257, 536 AR 174.
R v Rees, [1956] SCR 640, 4 DLR (2nd) 406.
R v Robinson, [1996] 1 SCR 683, 133 DLR (4th) 42.
R v Roy, 2012 SCC 26, [2012] 2 SCR 60.
R v Ruzic, 2001 SCC 24, [2001] 1 SCR 687.
R v Ryan, 2013 SCC 3, [2013] 1 SCR 14.
R v Safarzadeh-Markhali, 2012 ONCJ 494, 265 CRR (2nd) 32.
R v Safarzadeh-Markhali, 2014 ONCA 627, 316 CCC (3rd) 87.
R v Safarzadeh-Markhali, 2016 SCC 14, [2016] 1 SCR 180.
R v Sault Ste Marie, [1978] 2 SCR 1299, 85 DLR (3rd) 161.
R v Seaboyer, [1991] 2 SCR 577, 83 DLR (4th) 193.
R v Sharma, 2020 ONCA 478, 152 OR (3rd) 209.
R v Sharpe, 1999 BCCA 416, 175 DLR (4th) 1.
R v Sharpe, 2001 SCC 2, [2001] 1 SCR 45.
R v Skalbania, [1997] 3 SCR 995, 120 CCC (3rd) 217.
R v Smith, [1987] 1 SCR 1045, 40 DLR (4th) 435.
R v Smith, 2015 SCC 34, [2015] 2 SCR 602.
R v SN, 2012 NUCJ 2, 99 WCB (2nd) 841.
R v Solowan, 2008 SCC 62, [2008] 3 SCR 309.
R v Stone, [1999] 2 SCR 290, 173 DLR (4th) 66.
R v Sullivan, 2020 ONCA 333, 151 OR (3rd) 353.
R v Summers, 2014 SCC 26, [2014] 1 SCR 575.
R v Tatton, 2015 SCC 33, [2015] 2 SCR 574.
R v TBJ, 2000 SKQB 572, 200 Sask R 42.
R v Théroux, [1993] 2 SCR 5, 100 DLR (4th) 624.
R v Turtle, 2020 ONCJ 429, 66 CR (7th) 382.
R v Vaillancourt, [1987] 2 SCR 636, 47 DLR (4th) 399.
R v Vickberg (1998), 16 CR (5th) 164, 18 CPC (4th) 357 (BCSC).
R v Voong, 2015 BCCA 285, 325 CCC (3rd) 267.
R v WALD, 2002 SKPC 37, 53 WCB (2nd) 441.
R v Wholesale Travel Group Inc, [1991] 3 SCR 154, 84 DLR (4th) 161.
R v Willis, 2016 MBCA 113, 344 CCC (3rd) 443.
R v Wilmott, [1966] 2 OR 654, 58 DLR (2nd) 33 (ONCA).
R v Zundel, [1992] 2 SCR 731, 95 DLR (4th) 202.
R v 1260448 Ontario Inc (2003), 68 OR (3rd) 51 (ONCA).
Suresh v Canada (Minister of Citizenship and Immigration), 2002 SCC 1, [2002] 1 SCR 3.
Tremblay v Daigle, [1989] 2 SCR 530, 62 DLR (4th) 634.
Truchon c Procureur général du Canada, 2019 QCCS 3792, 158 WCB (2nd) 246.
Withler v Canada (Attorney General), 2011 SCC 12, [2011] 1 SCR 396.

International

Attorney General v Bradlaugh (1885), 14 QBD 667.
Director of Public Prosecutions v Majewski, [1977] AC 443.
DPP v Beard, [1920] AC 479.
Jabar v Public Prosecutor, [1995] 1 SLR 617 (CA).
Justice KS Puttaswamy (Retd) and Anr v Union of India and Ors, (2017).
Ketua Pengarah Jabatan Alam Sekitar v Kajing Tubek, [1997] 3 MLJ 23.
Lawrence v Texas, 123 S CT 2472 (2003).
Murarilal Jhunjhunwala v State of Bihar, (1991) Supp 2 SCC 647.
Navtej Singh Johar v Union of India, (2018).
Ong Ah Chuan v Public Prosecutor, [1981] 1 MLJ 64 (PC).
Powell v Texas, 392 US 514 (1968).
Robinson v California, 370 US 660 (1962).
Roe v Wade, 410 US 113 (1973).
Shaw v Director of Public Prosecutions, [1962] AC 220 (HL).
Suresh Kumar Koushal v Naz Foundation (2013).
S v Coetzee, 1997 (3) SALR 527.
United States v Carolene Products Co, 304 US 144 (1938).

Books and Articles

Ackerman, Bruce. *We the People: Foundations*. Cambridge, MA: Harvard University Press, 1997.
Albert, Richard. "Advisory Review: The Reincarnation of the Notwithstanding Clause." *Alberta Law Review* 45 (2008): 1037–69.
Anand, Sanjeev. "Beyond *Keegstra*: The Constitutionality of the Wilful Promotion of Hatred Revisited." *National Journal of Constitutional Law* 9 (1997–98): 117–53.
–. "Beyond the Wilful Promotion of Hatred: The Other Criminal Code Provisions Proscribing Expressions of Racial Hatred." *Canadian Criminal Law Review* 3 (1998): 141.
Angus Reid Institute. "Canadians Have a More Favourable View of Their Supreme Court Than Americans Have of Their Own." 17 August 2015. Online: http://angusreid.org/supreme-court/.
–. "Half of Canadians Say Crime Is Rising in Their Communities, as Confidence in Police, Courts Wanes." 10 January 2020. Online: http://angusreid.org/justice-system-confidence-2020/.
–. "Most Canadians Express Confidence in Police, but Those Levels Are Lower among Visible Minorities." 15 July 2016. Online: http://angusreid.org/confidence-in-justice-system-police/.
Archibald, Bruce. "The Constitutionalization of the General Part of Criminal Law." *Canadian Bar Review* 67 (1988): 403–54.

–. "The General Part of Canadian Criminal Law and Criminal Law Reform." Unpublished paper, n.d.

Bailey, Ian. "Vancouver Police Urge Drug Addicts to Use Insite following Deaths." *Globe and Mail*, 16 September 2013. Online: https://www.theglobeandmail.com/news/british-columbia/vancouver-police-warn-drug-addicts-to-use-insite/article14366192/.

Baines, Beverley. "Abortion, Judicial Activism and Constitutional Crossroads." *University of New Brunswick Law Journal* 53 (2004): 157–84.

Bala, Nicholas. "Changing Professional Culture and Reducing Use of Courts and Custody for Youth: *The Youth Criminal Justice Act* and Bill C-10." *Saskatchewan Law Review* 78 (2015): 127–80.

Beck, Ulrich. *Risk Society: Toward a New Modernity*. London: Sage, 1992.

Bellamy, Richard. *Political Constitutionalism: A Republican Defense of the Constitutionality of Democracy*. Cambridge: Cambridge University Press, 2007.

Bender, Paul. "The *Canadian Charter of Rights and Freedoms* and the United States Bill of Rights: A Comparison." *McGill Law Journal* 28 (1983): 811–66.

Berger, Benjamin. "The Abiding Presence of Conscience: Criminal Justice against the Law and the Modern Constitutional Imagination." *University of Toronto Law Journal* 61 (2011): 579–616.

–. "Constitutional Principles in Substantive Criminal Law." In *The Oxford Handbook of Criminal Law*, edited by Markus Dubber and Tatjana Hörnle, 422–46. Oxford: Oxford University Press, 2014.

–. "Emotions and the Veil of Voluntarism: The Loss of Judgment in Canadian Criminal Defences." *McGill Law Journal* 51 (2006): 99–130.

Bessner, Ronda. "The Constitutionality of the Group Libel Offences in the Canadian Criminal Code." *Manitoba Law Journal* 17 (1988): 184–218.

Bickel, Alexander. *The Least Dangerous Branch: The Supreme Court at the Bar of Politics*. New York: Bobbs-Merrill, 1962.

–. *The Morality of Consent*. New Haven, CT: Yale University Press, 1975.

–. *The Supreme Court and the Idea of Progress*. New York: Harper and Row, 1970.

Binder, Guyora. "The Culpability of Felony Murder." *Notre Dame Law Review* 83 (2008): 965–1060.

Bondy, Susan. "Self-Induced Intoxication as a Defence in the Criminal Code of Canada: Issues and Discussion around *Daviault v. R.*" *Contemporary Drug Problems* 23 (1996): 571–82.

Bork, Robert. "Neutral Principles and Some First Amendment Problems." *Indiana Law Journal* 47 (1971): 1–35.

–. *The Tempting of America: The Political Seduction of the Law*. New York: Touchstone, 1990.

Bottos, Dino. "*Keegstra* and *Andrews*: A Commentary on Hate Propaganda and the Freedom of Expression." *Alberta Law Review* 27 (1989): 461–75.

Boyle, Christine. "The Role of Equality in Criminal Law." *Saskatchewan Law Review* 58 (1994): 203–16.

Boyle, Christine, and John MacInnes. "Judging Sexual Assault Law against a Standard of Equality." *University of British Columbia Law Review* 29 (1995): 341–82.

Braun, Stefan. "Social and Racial Tolerance and Freedom of Expression in a Democratic Society: Friends or Foes? *Regina v. Zundel.*" *Dalhousie Law Journal* 11 (1988): 471–513.

Brudner, Alan. "Constitutionalizing Self-Defence." *University of Toronto Law Journal* 61 (2011): 867–97.

–. "Guilt under the *Charter:* The Lure of Parliamentary Supremacy." *Criminal Law Quarterly* 40 (1998): 287–325.

–. "Proportionality, Stigma and Discretion." *Criminal Law Quarterly* 38 (1996): 302–21.

Burstein, Paul. "What's the Harm in Having a 'Harm Principle' Enshrined in Section 7 of the *Charter?*" *Supreme Court Law Review* 24 (2nd) (2004): 159–94.

Cairns Way, Rosemary. "Attending to Equality: Criminal Law, the *Charter* and Competitive Truths." *Supreme Court Law Review* 57 (2nd) (2012): 39–56.

–. "Constitutionalizing Subjectivism: Another View." *Criminal Reports* 79 (3rd) (1990): 260.

Cameron, Jamie. "Fault and Punishment under Sections 7 and 12 of the *Charter.*" In *The Charter and Criminal Justice Twenty-Five Years Later,* edited by Jamie Cameron and James Stribopoulos. Toronto: LexisNexis, 2008.

–. "Fault and Punishment under Sections 7 and 12 of the *Charter.*" *Supreme Court Law Review* 40 (2nd) (2008): 553–92.

Campbell, Angela. "Sex Work's Governance: Stuff and Nuisance." *Feminist Legal Studies* 23 (2015): 27–45.

Carter, Mark. "Fundamental Justice." *Supreme Court Law Review* 78 (2nd) (2017): 259.

Catterick, Maria, and Liam Curran. *Understanding Fetal Alcohol Spectrum Disorder: A Guide for Parents, Carers, and Professionals*. London: Jessica Kingsley Publishers, 2014.

Chartrand, Larry. "Aboriginal Peoples and Mandatory Sentencing." *Osgoode Hall Law Journal* 39 (2001): 449–68.

Chaster, Sarah. "Cruel, Unusual, and Constitutionally Infirm: Mandatory Minimum Sentences in Canada." *Appeal* 23 (2018): 89–120.

Chayes, Abram. "The Role of the Judge in Public Law Litigation." *Harvard Law Review* 89 (1976): 1281–1316.

Choudhry, Sujit. "The Lochner Era and Comparative Constitutionalism." *International Journal of Constitutional Law* 2 (2004): 1–55.

Christian, Timothy. "Section 7 of the *Charter of Rights and Freedoms:* Constraints on State Action." *Alberta Law Review* 22 (1984): 222–46.

Coenen, Michael. "Rules against Rulification." *Yale Law Journal* 124 (2014): 644–715.

Cohen, Stanley. "Safeguards in and Justifications for Canada's New Anti-Terrorism Act." *National Journal of Constitutional Law* 14 (2002–03): 99–123.

Colvin, Eric. "Section Seven of the *Canadian Charter of Rights and Freedoms*." *Canadian Bar Review* 68 (1989): 560–85.

Condorcet, Marquis de. *Essay on the Application of Mathematics to the Theory of Decision-Making.* 1785.

Coughlan, Stephen. "Duress, Necessity, Self-Defence, and Provocation: Implications of Radical Change." *Canadian Criminal Law Review* 7 (2002): 147–208.

Crump, David. "Reconsidering the Felony Murder Rule in Light of Modern Criticisms: Doesn't the Conclusion Depend upon the Particular Rule at Issue?" *Harvard Journal of Law and Public Policy* 32 (2009): 1155–86.

Cumming, Tom. "Fundamental Justice in the *Charter*." *Queen's Law Journal* 11 (1985): 134–65.

Deckha, Maneesha. "A Missed Opportunity: Affirming the Section 15 Equality Argument against Physician-Assisted Death." *McGill Journal of Law and Health* 10 (2016): S69–S122.

Devlin, Patrick. *The Enforcement of Morals*. Oxford: Oxford University Press, 1965.

Dripps, Donald. "Criminal Procedure, Footnote Four, and the Theory of Public Choice; or, Why Don't Legislatures Give a Damn about the Rights of the Accused?" *Syracuse Law Review* 44 (1993): 1079–1102.

Duff, R.A. *Intention, Agency and Criminal Liability: Philosophy of Action and the Criminal Law*. Oxford: Basil Blackwell, 1990.

Dufraimont, Lisa. "*Canada (Attorney General) v. Bedford* and the Limits on Substantive Criminal Law under Section 7." *Supreme Court Law Review* 67 (2014): 483–503.

Dworkin, Ronald. *Freedom's Law: The Moral Reading of the American Constitution*. Cambridge, MA: Harvard University Press, 1996.

–. *Law's Empire*. Cambridge, MA: Harvard University Press, 1986.

–. *A Matter of Principle*. Cambridge, MA: Harvard University Press, 1985.

–. *Taking Rights Seriously*. Cambridge, MA: Harvard University Press, 1977.

Ely, John Hart. *Democracy and Distrust: A Theory of Judicial Review*. Cambridge, MA: Harvard University Press, 1980.

Erdman, Joanna. "Constitutionalizing Abortion Rights in Canada." *Ottawa Law Review* 49 (2018): 221–61.

Fallon, Richard. "The Core of an Uneasy Case for Judicial Review." *Harvard Law Review* 121 (2008): 1693–1736.

Farnsworth, C.H. "Use of Drunkenness Defense Prompts Outrage in Canada." *Houston Chronicle*, 13 November 1994, A38.

Fehr, Colton. "Consent and the Constitution." *Manitoba Law Journal* 42 (2019): 217–48.

–. "The Constitutionality of Excluding Duress as a Defence to Murder." *Manitoba Law Journal* 44 (2021): 109–33.

–. "The 'Individualistic' Approach to Arbitrariness, Overbreadth, and Gross Disproportionality." *University of British Columbia Law Review* 51 (2018): 55–74.

–. "Infusing Reconciliation into the Sentencing Process." *Constitutional Forum constitutionnel* 28 (2019): 25–30.
–. "Instrumental Rationality and General Deterrence." *Alberta Law Review* 57 (2019): 53–68.
–. "The (Near) Death of Duress." *Criminal Law Quarterly* 62 (2015): 123–49.
–. "(Re-)Constitutionalizing Duress and Necessity." *Queen's Law Journal* 42 (2017): 99–134.
–. "Re-Thinking the Instrumental Rationality Principles of Fundamental Justice." *Alberta Law Review* 58 (2020): 133–52.
–. "Self-Defence and the Constitution." *Queen's Law Journal* 43 (2017): 85–122.
Feinberg, Joel. *The Moral Limits of the Criminal Law*. Oxford: Oxford University Press, 1984.
Ferguson, Gerry. "Causation and the *Mens Rea* for Manslaughter: A Lethal Combination." *Criminal Reports* 99 (6th) (2013): 351.
–. "The Intoxication Defence: Constitutionally Impaired and in Need of Rehabilitation." *Supreme Court Law Review* 57 (2nd) (2012): 111–48.
Fine, Sean, and Laura Stone. "In Absence of Federal Law, Assisted Dying Enters Era of Uncertainty." *Globe and Mail*, 6 June 2016. Online: https://www.theglobeandmail.com/news/national/leading-constitutional-expert-says-assisted-dying-law-unconstitutional/article30283048/.
Fish, Arthur. "Hate Promotion and Freedom of Expression: Truth and Consequences." *Canadian Journal of Law and Jurisprudence* 2 (1989): 111–38.
Flader, Suzy. "Fundamental Rights for All: Toward Equality as a Principle of Fundamental Justice under Section 7 of the *Charter*." *Appeal* 25 (2020): 43–60.
Fletcher, George. *The Grammar of Criminal Law: American, Comparative, and International*. Oxford: Oxford University Press, 2007.
–. "Human Dignity as a Constitutional Value." *University of Western Ontario Law Review* 22 (1984): 171–82.
–. *Rethinking Criminal Law*. Oxford: Oxford University Press, 2000.
–. "The Theory of Criminal Negligence: A Comparative Analysis." *University of Pennsylvania Law Review* 119 (1971): 401–38.
Frickey, Philip, and Daniel Farber. *Law and Public Choice: A Critical Introduction*. Chicago: University of Chicago Press, 1992.
Friedland, Martin. "Criminal Justice and the *Charter*." *Manitoba Law Journal* 13 (1983): 549–72.
Froc, Kerri. "Constitutional Coalescence: Substantive Equality as a Principle of Fundamental Justice." *Ottawa Law Review* 42 (2012): 411–46.
Gardbaum, Stephen. *The New Commonwealth Model of Constitutionalism: Theory and Practice*. Cambridge: Cambridge University Press, 2013.
Gardner, John. *Offences and Defences*. Oxford: Oxford University Press, 2007.
Garland, David. *The Culture of Control*. Chicago: University of Chicago Press, 2001.

Gilbert, Daphne. "Time to Regroup: Rethinking Section 15 of the *Charter*." *McGill Law Journal* 48 (2003): 627–50.

Ginter Deutsch, Jan. "Neutrality, Legitimacy, and the Supreme Court: Some Intersections between Law and Political Science." *Stanford Law Review* 20 (1968): 169–261.

Goodman, Frank. "De Facto School Segregation: A Constitutional and Empirical Analysis." *California Law Review* 60 (1972): 275–437.

Grant, Isabel. "Second Chances: Bill C-72 and the *Charter*." *Osgoode Hall Law Journal* 33 (1995): 379–410.

Gur-Arye, Miriam, and Thomas Wiegend. "Constitutional Review of Criminal Prohibitions Affecting Human Dignity and Liberty: German and Israeli Perspectives." *Israel Law Review* 44 (2011): 63–90.

Hackett, Donna. "Finding and Following the Road Less Travelled: Judicial Neutrality and the Protection and Enforcement of Equality Rights in Canadian Criminal Courts." *Canadian Journal of Women and the Law* 10 (1998): 129–48.

Harcourt, Bernard. "The Collapse of the Harm Principle." *Journal of Criminal Law and Criminology* 90 (1999): 109–94.

Harcourt, Bernard, and Jens Ludwig. "Broken Windows: New Evidence from New York City and a Five-City Social Experiment." *University of Chicago Law Review* 73 (2006): 271–320.

Harris, Kathleen. "Experts Urge Liberals to Update 'Embarrassingly Bad' *Criminal Code*." CBC News, 18 November 2016. Online: https://www.cbc.ca/news/politics/criminal-code-outdated-justice-discrimination-1.3853810.

Hart, H.L.A. *Law, Liberty, and Morality*. Stanford, CA: Stanford University Press, 1977.

–. *Punishment and Responsibility*. New York: Oxford University Press, 1968.

Hennigar, Matthew. "Unreasonable Disagreement? Judicial-Executive Exchanges about *Charter* Reasonableness in the Harper Era." *Osgoode Hall Law Journal* 54 (2017): 1245–74.

Hiebert, Janet. *Charter Conflicts*. Montreal and Kingston: McGill-Queen's University Press, 2002.

Hogg, Peter. "The Brilliant Career of Section 7 of the *Charter*." *Supreme Court Law Review* 58 (2nd) (2012): 195–210.

–. *Canada Act 1982: Annotated*. Toronto: Carswell, 1982.

–. "Legal and Constitutional Affairs: June 6, 2016." CPAC, 6 June 2016. Online: https://www.cpac.ca/en/programs/in-committee-from-the-senate-of-canada/episodes/47941576.

Hogg, Peter, and Allison Bushell. "The *Charter* Dialogue between Courts and Legislatures (Or Perhaps the *Charter of Rights* Isn't Such a Bad Thing after All)." *Osgoode Hall Law Journal* 35 (1997): 75–124.

Hogg, Peter, Allison Bushell, and Wade Wright. "*Charter* Dialogue Revisited: Or 'Much Ado about Metaphors.'" *Osgoode Hall Law Journal* 45 (2007): 1–66.

Horder, Jeremy. "Self-Defence, Necessity and Duress: Understanding the Relationship." *Canadian Journal of Law and Jurisprudence* 11 (1998): 143–66.
Hutchinson, Allan. *Waiting for CORAF*. Toronto: University of Toronto Press, 1995.
Iftene, Adelina, Kim Pate, and Debra Parkes. "Solitary Confinement and the Supreme Court." *Vancouver Sun*, 10 May 2020. Online: https://vancouversun.com.
Iyer, Nitya. "Categorical Denials: Equality Rights and the Shaping of Social Identity." *Queen's Law Journal* 19 (1993): 179–208.
Kahn, Paul. "Comparative Constitutionalism in a New Key." *Michigan Law Review* 101 (2003): 2677–2705.
Kaplow, Louis. "Rules versus Standards: An Economic Analysis." *Duke Law Journal* 42 (1992): 557–629.
Kaufman, Alexander, and Michael Runnels. "The Core of an Unqualified Case for Judicial Review: A Reply to Jeremy Waldron and Contemporary Critics." *Brooklyn Law Review* 82 (2016): 163–216.
Kavanagh, Aileen. "Participation and Judicial Review: A Reply to Jeremy Waldron." *Law and Philosophy* 22 (2003): 451–86.
Kelling, George, and James Wilson. "Broken Windows: The Police and Neighbourhood Safety." *Atlantic*, March 1982. Online: https://www.theatlantic.com/magazine/archive/1982/03/broken-windows/304465/.
Kennedy, Duncan. "Form and Substance in Private Law Adjudication." *Harvard Law Review* 89 (1976): 1685–1778.
Klein, Alana. "The Arbitrariness in 'Arbitrariness' (and Overbreadth and Gross Disproportionality): Principle and Democracy in Section 7 of the *Charter*." *Supreme Court Law Review* 63 (2nd) (2013): 377–402.
Koren, Gideon, et al. "Fetal Alcohol Spectrum Disorder." *Canadian Medical Association Journal* 169 (2003): 1181–85.
Koshan, Jennifer. "Redressing the Harms of Government (In)Action: A Section 7 versus Section 15 *Charter* Showdown." *Constitutional Forum constitutionnel* 22 (2013): 31–46.
Kramer, Larry. *The People Themselves: Popular Constitutionalism and Judicial Review*. Oxford: Oxford University Press, 2004.
Lawrence, Michelle. "Voluntary Intoxication and the *Charter*: Revisiting the Constitutionality of Section 33.1 of the Criminal Code." *Manitoba Law Journal* 40 (2017): 391–424.
Lepofsky, David. "*Carter v. Canada (Attorney General)*, the Constitutional Attack on Canada's Ban on Assisted Dying: Missing an Obvious Chance to Rule on the Charter's Disability Equality Guarantee." *Supreme Court Law Review* 76 (2nd) (2016): 89–110.
MacDonald, Lois. "Promoting Social Equality through the Legislative Override." *National Journal of Constitutional Law* 4 (1994): 1–27.

Macfarlane, Emmett. "Dialogue or Compliance? Measuring Legislatures' Policy Responses to Court Rulings on Rights." *International Political Science Review* 34 (2012): 39–56.

–. "Dialogue, Remedies, and Positive Rights: *Carter v Canada* as a Microcosm for Past and Future Issues under the *Charter of Rights and Freedoms*." *Ottawa Law Review* 49 (2017): 107–30.

MacIntosh, Constance. "*Carter*, Medical Aid in Dying, and Mature Minors." *McGill Journal of Law and Health* 10 (2016): S1–S34.

MacKay, Wayne. "Fairness after the *Charter*: A Rose by Any Other Name?" *Queen's Law Journal* 10 (1985): 263–335.

–. "Freedom of Expression: Is It All Just Talk?" *Canadian Bar Review* 68 (1989): 713–64.

–. "*R. v. Sharpe:* Pornography, Privacy, Proportionality and the Protection of Children." *National Journal of Constitutional Law* 12 (2000–01): 113–31.

MacKinnon, Catharine. *Only Words*. Cambridge, MA: Harvard University Press, 1993.

–. *Toward a Feminist Theory of the State*. Cambridge, MA: Harvard University Press, 1989.

MacMillan-Brown, Heather. "No Longer '*Leary*' about Intoxication: In the Aftermath of *R v Daviault*." *Saskatchewan Law Review* 59 (1995): 311–34.

Magnet, Joseph. "The Presumption of Constitutionality." *Osgoode Hall Law Journal* 18 (1980): 87–145.

Mahoney, Kathleen. "*R. v. Keegstra:* A Rationale for Regulating Pornography?" *McGill Law Journal* 37 (1992): 242–69.

Mandel, Michael. *The Charter of Rights and the Legalization of Politics in Canada*. Toronto: Wall and Thomson, 1989.

Manfredi, Christopher. "The Day the Dialogue Died: A Comment on *Sauvé v Canada*." *Osgoode Hall Law Journal* 45 (2007): 105–24.

–. *Judicial Power and the Charter: Canada and the Paradox of Liberal Constitutionalism*. 2nd ed. Toronto: Oxford University Press, 2001.

Manfredi, Christopher, and James Kelly. "Six Degrees of Dialogue: A Response to Hogg and Bushell." *Osgoode Hall Law Journal* 37 (1999): 513–28.

Manikis, Marie. "Towards Accountability and Fairness for Aboriginal People: The Recognition of *Gladue* as a Principle of Fundamental Justice That Applies to Prosecutors." *Canadian Criminal Law Review* 21 (2016): 173–94.

Manning, Morris. *Rights, Freedoms and the Courts*. Toronto: Emond Montgomery, 1983.

Mathen, Carissima. "Dialogue Theory, Judicial Review, and Judicial Supremacy." *Osgoode Hall Law Journal* 45 (2007): 125–46.

McAdam, Richard. "The Notwithstanding Taboo." *Federal Governance* 6 (2009): 1–20.

McLachlin, Beverley. "Equality: The Most Difficult Right." *Supreme Court Law Review* 14 (2nd) (2001): 17–26.

McMorrow, Thomas. "MAID in Canada? Debating the Constitutionality of Canada's New Medical Assistance in Dying Law." *Queen's Law Journal* 44 (2018): 69–120.

Menchynski, Andrew, and Jill Presser. "A Withering Instrumentality: The Negative Implications of *R. v. Safarzadeh-Markhali* and Other Recent Section 7 Jurisprudence." *Supreme Court Law Review* 81 (2nd) (2017): 75–96.

Mikva, Abner. "How Well Does Congress Support and Defend the Constitution?" *North Carolina Law Review* 61 (1982): 587–612.

Mill, John Stuart. *On Liberty and Considerations on Representative Government*. Oxford: Basil Blackwell, 1946.

Mirza, Faizal. "Mandatory Minimum Prison Sentencing and Systemic Racism." *Osgoode Hall Law Journal* 39 (2001): 491–512.

Monahan, Patrick. *Politics and the Constitution: The Charter, Federalism and the Supreme Court of Canada*. Toronto: Carswell, 1987.

Monahan, Patrick, Byron Shaw, and Padraic Ryan. *Constitutional Law*. 5th ed. Toronto: Irwin Law, 2017.

Moon, Richard. "Drawing Lines in a Culture of Prejudice: *R. v. Keegstra* and the Restriction of Hate Propaganda." *University of British Columbia Law Review* 26 (1992): 99–144.

Moore, Marcus. "*R. v. Safarzadeh-Markhali*: Elements and Implications of the Supreme Court's New Rigorous Approach to Construction of Statutory Purpose." *Supreme Court Law Review* 77 (2nd) (2017): 223–53.

Moore, Michael. "Law as a Functional Kind." In *Natural Law Theory*, edited by Robert George, 188–242. Oxford: Oxford University Press, 1992.

Morton, F.L. "Dialogue or Monologue?" In *Judicial Power and Canadian Democracy*, edited by Paul Howe and Peter Russell, 111–17. Montreal and Kingston: McGill-Queen's University Press, 2001.

Morton, F.L., and Rainer Knopff. *The Charter Revolution and the Court Party*. Peterborough, ON: Broadview Press, 2000.

Mueller, Denis. *Public Choice III*. Cambridge: Cambridge University Press, 2003.

Nicolaides, Eleni, and Matthew Hennigar. "*Carter* Conflicts: The Supreme Court of Canada's Impact on Medical Assistance in Dying Policy." In *Policy Change, Courts, and the Canadian Constitution*, edited by Emmett Macfarlane, 313–35. Toronto: University of Toronto Press, 2018.

Nussbaum, Sarah-jane. "Diminishing Protection of Subjective Fault? A Case Comment on *R. v. A.D.H.*" *Saskatchewan Law Review* 77 (2014): 279–300.

Oppal, Wally. *Forsaken – The Report of the Missing Women Commission of Inquiry*. Vol. 1. Ottawa: Library and Archives Canada, 2012.

Paciocco, David. "Death by *Stone*-ing: The Demise of the Defence of Simple Automatism." *Criminal Reports* 26 (5th) (1999): 273–85.

Perry, Michael. *The Constitution in the Courts*. New York: Oxford University Press, 1994.

Petter, Andrew. "Legalize This: The Chartering of Canadian Politics." In *Contested Constitutionalism: Reflections on the Canadian Charter of Rights and Freedoms*, edited by James Kelly and Christopher Manfredi, 33–49. Vancouver: UBC Press, 2010.

–. "The Politics of the Charter." *Canadian Bar Review* 8 (1986): 473–505.

–. *The Politics of the Charter: The Illusive Promise of Constitutional Rights*. Toronto: University of Toronto Press, 2010.

Pothier, Dianne. "Connecting Grounds of Discrimination to Real People's Real Experiences." *Canadian Journal of Women and the Law* 13 (2001): 37–73.

Ramraj, Victor. "Four Models of Due Process." *International Journal of Constitutional Law* 2 (2004): 492–524.

Rauf, Naeem. "Freedom of Expression, the Presumption of Innocence and Reasonable Limits: An Analysis of *Keegstra* and *Andrews*." *Criminal Reports* 65 (3rd) (1988): 356–71.

Raz, Joseph. "Disagreement in Politics." *American Journal of Jurisprudence* 43 (1998): 25–52.

Read, Piers Paul. *Alive*. New York: Avon Books, 1974.

Regel, Alan. "Hate Propaganda: A Reason to Limit Freedom of Speech." *Saskatchewan Law Review* 49 (1985): 303–18.

Roach, Kent. "American Constitutional Theory for Canadians (and the Rest of the World)." *University of Toronto Law Journal* 52 (2002): 503–22.

–. "The Changed Nature of the Harm Debate." *Criminal Law Quarterly* 60 (2014): 321–23.

–. "Dialogue between the Court and Parliament: A Recent *Charter* Trilogy." *Criminal Law Quarterly* 63 (2016): 251–54.

–. "Mind the Gap: Canada's Different Criminal and Constitutional Standards of Fault." *University of Toronto Law Journal* 61 (2011): 545–78.

–. "The New Terrorism Offences and the Criminal Law." In *The Security of Freedom: Essays on Canada's Anti-Terrorism Bill*, edited by Ronald Daniels, Patrick Macklem, and Kent Roach, 151–72. Toronto: University of Toronto Press, 2001.

–. *The 9/11 Effect*. Cambridge: Cambridge University Press, 2011.

–. *The Supreme Court on Trial: Judicial Activism or Democratic Dialogue?* Toronto: Irwin Law, 2016.

–. "Terrorism Offences and the *Charter*: A Comment on *R v Khawaja*." *Canadian Criminal Law Review* 11 (2007): 271–300.

Roach, Kent, and Andrea Bailey. "The Relevance of Fetal Alcohol Spectrum Disorder and the Criminal Law from Investigation to Sentencing." *University of British Columbia Law Review* 42 (2009): 1–68.

Roach, Kent, et al. *Criminal Law and Procedure: Cases and Materials*. 11th ed. Toronto: Emond Montgomery, 2015.

Room, Robin. "Drinking, Violence, Gender and Causal Attribution: A Canadian Case Study in Science, Law and Policy." *Contemporary Drug Problems* 23 (1996): 649–86.

Rosenberg, Marc. "The *Mens Rea* Requirements of Criminal Negligence: *R. v. Waite* and *R. v. Tutton.*" *Journal of Motor Vehicle Law* 2 (1990): 243–59.

Rudin, Jonathan. "Tell It Like It Is – An Argument for the Use of Section 15 over Section 7 to Challenge Discriminatory Criminal Legislation." *Criminal Law Quarterly* 64 (2017): 317–33.

Scalia, Antonin. "The Rule of Law as a Law of Rules." *University of Chicago Law Review* 56 (1989): 1175–88.

Schlag, Pierre. "Rules and Standards." *UCLA Law Review* 33 (1985): 379–430.

Schwartz, Hart. "Circularity, Tautology and Gamesmanship: 'Purpose' Based Proportionality-Correspondence Analysis in Sections 15 and 7 of the *Charter.*" *National Journal of Constitutional Law* 35 (2016): 105–29.

Shaffer, Martha. "Foetal Rights and the Regulation of Abortion." *McGill Law Journal* 39 (1994): 58–100.

–. "Scrutinizing Duress: The Constitutional Validity of Section 17 of the *Criminal Code.*" *Criminal Law Quarterly* 40 (1998): 444–75.

Shain, Martin. "The *Charter* and Intoxication: Some Observations on Possible *Charter* Challenges to an Act to Amend the *Criminal Code* (Self-Induced Intoxication) 1995, C-72." *Contemporary Drug Problems* 23 (1996): 731–34.

Sheehy, Elizabeth. "Equality and Supreme Court Criminal Jurisprudence: Never the Twain Shall Meet." *Supreme Court Law Review* 50 (2nd) (2010): 329–48.

–. "The Intoxication Defense in Canada: Why Women Should Care." *Contemporary Drug Problems* 23 (1996): 595–630.

Sinel, Zoë. "The Duress Dilemma: Potential Solutions in the Theory of Right." *Appeal: Review of Current Law and Legal Reform* 10 (2005): 56–69.

Skolnik, Terry. "Objective *Mens Rea* Revisited." *Canadian Criminal Law Review* 22 (2017): 307–40.

Stalker, Anne. "The Fault Element in Recodifying Criminal Law: A Critique." *Queen's Law Journal* 14 (1989): 119–32.

Standing Senate Committee on Legal and Constitutional Affairs. "Bill C-14, *An Act to Amend the Criminal Code and to Make Related Amendments to Other Acts (Medical Assistance in Dying).*" *Proceedings of the Standing Senate Committee on Legal and Constitutional Affairs* 42–1, no. 10 (6 June 2016). Online: https://sencanada.ca/en/committees/report/33275/42-1.

Stephens, Michael. "Fidelity to Fundamental Justice: An Originalist Construction of Section 7 of the *Canadian Charter of Rights and Freedoms.*" *National Journal of Constitutional Law* 13 (2002): 183–253.

Stewart, Hamish. "*Bedford* and the Structure of Section 7." *McGill Law Journal* 60 (2015): 575–94.

–. "The Constitution and the Right of Self-Defence." *University of Toronto Law Journal* 61 (2011): 899–919.

–. "The Constitutionality of the New Sex Work Law." *Alberta Law Review* 54 (2016): 69–88.
–. *Fundamental Justice: Section 7 of the Canadian Charter of Rights and Freedoms.* Toronto: Irwin Law, 2012.
–. *Fundamental Justice: Section 7 of the Canadian Charter of Rights and Freedoms.* 2nd ed. Toronto: Irwin Law, 2019.
–. "A Judicious Response to Overbreadth: *R. v. Sharpe.*" *Criminal Law Quarterly* 43 (2000): 159–80.
–. "*R. v. Khawaja:* At the Limits of Fundamental Justice." *Supreme Court Law Review* 63 (2nd) (2013): 403–16.
Stone, Alec Sweet, and Jud Mathews. "Proportionality Balancing and Global Constitutionalism." *Columbia Journal of Transnational Law* 47 (2008): 72–164.
Stribopoulos, James. "The Constitutionalization of 'Fault' in Canada: A Normative Critique." *Criminal Law Quarterly* 42 (1999): 227–85.
Strike, Carol, et al. "Increasing Public Support for Supervised Injection Facilities in Ontario, Canada." *Addiction* 109 (2014): 946–53.
Stuart, Don. *Canadian Criminal Law.* 3rd ed. Toronto: Carswell, 1995.
–. *Canadian Criminal Law.* 6th ed. Toronto: Thomson Carswell, 2011.
–. *Canadian Criminal Law.* 7th ed. Toronto: Carswell, 2014.
–. *Charter Justice in Canadian Criminal Law.* 3rd ed. Scarborough, ON: Carswell, 2001.
–. "Criminal Negligence: Deadlock and Confusion in the Supreme Court." *Criminal Reports* 69 (3rd) (1989): 331–36.
–. "Progress on the Constitutional Requirement of Fault." *Criminal Reports* 64 (3rd) (1988): 352.
Sullivan, Kathleen. "The Supreme Court, 1991 Term – Foreword: The Justices of Rules and Standards." *Harvard Law Review* 106 (1992): 22–123.
Sunstein, Cass. "Problems with Rules." *California Law Review* 83 (1995): 953–1026.
Tadros, Victor. *Criminal Responsibility.* Oxford: Oxford University Press, 2005.
Tough, Suzanne, and Monica Jack. "Frequency of FASD in Canada, and What This Means for Prevention Efforts." In *Fetal Alcohol Spectrum Disorder: Management and Policy Perspectives of FASD,* edited by Edward Riley et al., 27–43. Weinheim: Wiley-Blackwell, 2011.
Tremblay, Luc. "Section 7: Substantive Due Process?" *University of British Columbia Law Review* 18 (1984): 201–54.
Tushnet, Mark. "Judicial Activism or Restraint in a Section 33 World." *University of Toronto Law Journal* 53 (2003): 89–100.
–. *Taking the Constitution Away from the Courts.* Princeton, NJ: Princeton University Press, 1999.
–. "Weak Form Judicial Review and 'Core' Civil Liberties." *Harvard Civil Rights–Civil Liberties Law Review* 41 (2006): 1–22.

United Kingdom. House of Commons. "Report of the Committee on Homosexual Offences and Prostitution." Cmnd 247 in *Sessional Papers* 14 (1956–57): 85.

Vancouver Sun. "Criminal Defence of Drunkenness an Offence to Reason." *Vancouver Sun*, 5 October 1994, A10.

Waldron, Jeremy. "The Core of the Case against Judicial Review." *Yale Law Journal* 115 (2006): 1346–1407.

–. *Law and Disagreement*. Oxford: Oxford University Press, 1999.

–. *Political Political Theory*. Cambridge, MA: Harvard University Press, 2016.

Walzer, Michael. "Philosophy and Democracy." *Political Theory* 9 (1981): 379–99.

Watson, Jack. "Case Comment: R. v. Sharpe." *National Journal of Constitutional Law* 10 (1999): 251.

Wattie, Chris. "Politicized Supreme Court Fight One of Harper's Most Imprudent Acts." *Globe and Mail*, 26 May 2014. Online: https://www.theglobeandmail.com/opinion/editorials/a-supreme-court-short-list-long-on-controversy/article18856513/.

Webber, Grégoire. *The Negotiable Constitution*. Cambridge: Cambridge University Press, 2009.

Wechsler, Herbert. "Toward Neutral Principles of Constitutional Law." *Harvard Law Review* 73 (1959): 1–35.

Weiler, Paul. "Of Judges and Rights, or Should Canada Have a Constitutional Bill of Rights?" *Dalhousie Law Review* 60 (1980): 205–37.

–. "Rights and Judges in a Democracy: A New Canadian Version." *University of Michigan Journal of Law Reform* 18 (1984): 51–92.

Weinrib, Lorraine. "Canada's Constitutional Revolution: From Legislative to Constitutional State." *Israel Law Review* 33 (1999): 13–50.

–. "Hate Promotion in a Free and Democratic Society: R. v. Keegstra." *McGill Law Journal* 36 (1991): 1416–49.

–. "Human Dignity as a Rights-Protecting Principle." *National Journal of Constitutional Law* 17 (2004): 325–45.

Wellington, Harry. "Common Law Rules and Constitutional Double Standards: Some Notes on Adjudication." *Yale Law Journal* 83 (1973): 221–311.

Westen, Peter. *Speaking of Equality: An Analysis of the Rhetorical Force of "Equality" in Moral and Legal Discourse*. Princeton, NJ: Princeton University Press, 1990.

Whyte, John. "Fundamental Justice: The Scope and Application of Section 7 of the Charter." *Manitoba Law Journal* 13 (1983): 455–76.

Woo, Andrea. "Bill C-2 Could Impede Harm-Reduction Sites." *Globe and Mail*, 24 March 2015. Online: https://www.theglobeandmail.com.

Yeo, Stanley. "Revisiting Necessity." *Criminal Law Quarterly* 56 (2010): 13–50.

Young, Alan. "Done Nothing Wrong: Fundamental Justice and the Minimum Content of Criminal Law." *Supreme Court Law Review* 40 (2nd) (2008): 441–511.

–. "Fundamental Justice and Political Power: A Personal Reflection on Twenty Years in the Trenches." *Supreme Court Law Review* 16 (2002): 121–59.

Young, Margot. "Social Justice and the *Charter*: Comparison and Choice." *Osgoode Hall Law Journal* 50 (2013): 669–98.

Legislation

Canadian

Statutes

An Act to Amend the Controlled Drugs and Substances Act and to Make Related Amendments to Other Acts, SC 2017, c 7.
An Act to Amend the Criminal Code and the Department of Justice Act and to Make Consequential Amendments to Another Act, SC 2018, c 29.
An Act to Amend the Criminal Code and to Make Related Amendments to Other Acts (Medical Assistance in Dying), SC 2016, c 3.
An Act to Amend the Criminal Code (Mental Disorder) and to Make Consequential Amendments to Other Acts, SC 2005, c 22.
An Act to Amend the Criminal Code, the Youth Criminal Justice Act and Other Acts and to Make Consequential Amendments to Other Acts, SC 2019, c 25.
Act to Amend the Pay Equity Act, SQ 2009, c 9.
Canadian Bill of Rights, SC 1960, c 44.
Canadian Charter of Rights and Freedoms, Part I of the *Constitution Act, 1982*, being schedule B to the *Canada Act 1982* (UK), 1982, c 11.
Cannabis Act, SC 2018, c 16.
Christopher's Law (Sex Offender Registry), SO 2000 c 1.
Competition Act, RSC 1970, c C-23.
Competition Act, RSC 1985, c C-34.
Constitution Act, 1867 (UK), 30 & 31 Vict, c 3, reprinted in RSC 1985, Appendix II, No 5.
Controlled Drugs and Substances Act, SC 1996, c 19.
Corrections and Conditional Release Act, SC 1992, c 20.
Criminal Code of Canada, RSC 1985, c C-46.
Highway Traffic Act, RSO 1990, c H8.
Highway Traffic Act Regulations, RRO 1990, Reg 587.
Marihuana for Medical Purposes Regulations, SOR/2013–119.
Motor Vehicle Act, RSBC 1977, c 288.
Motor Vehicle Act, RSBC 1996, c 318, s 95.
Pay Equity Act, SQ 1996, c 43.
Protecting Canada's Immigration System Act, SC 2012, c 17.
Public Hospitals Act, RSO 1960, c 322.
Respect for Communities Act, SC 2015, c 22.
Traffic Safety Act, RSA 2000, c T-6, s 160(3).
Truth in Sentencing Act, SC 2009, c 29.
Youth Criminal Justice Act, SC 2002, c 1.

Bills

Bill C-36, *Protection of Communities and Exploited Persons Act*, SC 2014, c 25.
Bill C-83, *An Act to Amend the Corrections and Conditional Release Act and Another Act*, SC 2019, c 27.

International

Texas Penal Code, s 19.02(b)(3) (2008).
United Nations Standard Minimum Rules for the Treatment of Prisoners (the Nelson Mandela Rules), 70/175 (8 January 2016).

Index

absolute liability, 26–27, 33, 115, 117
abuse of process, 168
actus reus, 18; the harm principle, 21–25; intoxication and physical voluntariness, 18–20; overlap with *mens rea*, 54; respect for human dignity, 20–21; symmetry with *mens rea*, 31–32
American Constitution, 95, 151, 153, 157, 175
Anand, Sanjeev, 105
arbitrariness, 6, 46, 58–59, 61; abortion, 61–62; euthanasia, 62–63; individualistic conception, 65; medical marijuana, 64–65; possession/distribution of marijuana, 63, 131; safe injection sites, 64
automatism, 19, 53, 115; rules, 117

Beard Rules, 33
Beaver v The Queen, 26
Berger, Benjamin, 42
Bickel, Alexander, 142, 157–58,
Bill C-83, 90

bill of rights, 144, 148; moral reading, 153
Boyle, Christine, 132–33
bright-line rule, 73–75
Brudner, Alan, 35–36
burden of proof, Charter proceedings, 60, 81, 101, 111
Bushell, Allison, 9, 86

Cameron, Jamie, 55–56, 115
Canada (Attorney General) v Bedford, 35, 60; bawdy house and communication prohibitions, 78–79; equality, 120, 130–31; instrumental rationality and judicial dialogue, 92; living on the avails of sex work, 69–70; overbreadth, 65, 72; overlap with principles of criminal law theory, 98–99; Parliament's response, 85, 87–88
Canada (Attorney General) v PHS Community Services Society, arbitrariness, 64; gross disproportionality, 77–78; instrumental rationality and legislative

dialogue, 85–87; equality 129–30; and judicial dialogue, 92; overlap between overbreadth and gross disproportionality, 80–81; overlap with principles of criminal law theory, 100
Canadian Bill of Rights, 4–5
Canadian Charter of Rights and Freedoms, 3, 158; section 1: 11, 13, 34, 137, 158–59; section 2(b): 103; section 7: 3–7, 9, 13, 15, 17, 20–21, 27, 34, 59, 135, 137–38, 165, 170; section 12: 44, 46, 113, 118, 135; section 15: 119–32, 137–38; section 27: 105; section 33: 11, 13, 159. *See also* Constitution, the
Canadian Foundation for Children, Youth and the Law v Canada (Attorney General), 122–23
Carter v Canada (Attorney General): equality, 12; instrumental rationality and legislative dialogue, 85, 89; judicial dialogue, 92–93; overbreadth, 70, 75; overlap with gross disproportionality, 79–82; overlap with principles of criminal law theory 97; parity in sentencing, 47–48
Chaster, Sarah, 135
Chief Justice Dickson, 61, 103, 105, 111
child pornography, possession of, 109–10
Competition Act, 29
Condorcet's jury theorem, 146
Conservative Party, 45, 64, 87, 126, 169
Constitution, the, 150–56
Constitution Act, 1867, 25, 123
constitutional conception, 153
constructive murder, 28
Controlled Drugs and Substances Act, 64, 92, 124, 135–36
coordinate interpretation, 86–87, 157

Corrections and Conditional Release Act, 86, 90
counter-majoritarian: critique, 9–10, 163; difficulty, 142, 157
Criminal Code of Canada, 177; Part XX. 1: 66; section 8(3): 38; section 17: 38–39, 54; section 21(2): 28; section 33.1: 20, 84, 166; section 43: 122; section 83.18: 67–69; section 86(2): 31; section 96(2)(a): 167; section 150.1(1): 75; section 163(8): 108; section 163.1(3): 109; section 163.1(4): 109; section 175(1)(c): 97; section 179(1)(b): 66, 97–98; section 181: 106; section 193: 103; section 195.1(1)(c): 103; section 210: 69; section 212(1)(j): 69; section 213(a): 28; section 213(1)(c): 69; section 213(d): 27–28; section 241: 47; section 241(b): 20, 62; section 251(4): 61; section 286.4: 112; section 298: 107; section 300: 107; section 319(2): 104–5; section 672.54: 67; section 672.81(1): 67; section 718.2(e): 49, 125, 136; section 719(3.1): 45, 71–72; section 732: 124; section 742.1: 124
custodial sentences, 127

de scandalis magnatum, 106
Deckha, Maneesha, 121, 132
defamatory libel, 107–8
defences, 37; moral blamelessness, 40–41; moral innocence, 41–42; moral involuntariness, 38–39; moral involuntariness, proportionality, and the role of blamelessness, 42–44
democracy, 153–54, 162, 177
democratic dialogue, 86, 150
Devlin, Lord Patrick, 22
dialogue theory, 89

Did Six Million Really Die?, 106
dignity interest, 22, 121
diminished moral blameworthiness, 44–45, 171
DPP v Beard, 33
duress: cruel and unusual punishment, 116–17, 171; fairness, 54–55; moral blamelessness, 40–41; moral innocence, 42–43; moral involuntariness, 38–39
Dworkin, Ronald, 153–56

Ely, John Hart, 150–52
enumerated rights 7, 10–12, 15, 118, 131–32, 141, 163–64, 174
equality, 119; abortion, 119–20; child spanking, 122–23; conditional sentence orders, 124–29; euthanasia, 120–22; fitness to stand trial, 123; intermittent sentences, 123–24; sex work, 120
excuse, 38–44, 50–51

Fallon, Richard, 155
false news, 106–7
fault, 33–36; objective, 29–32, 36; proportionality with stigma, 161; subjective, 26–29, 56
Feinberg, Joel, 24
felony murder, 28, 54, 118
fetal alcohol syndrome disorder, 36–37
Fletcher, George, 17, 37–38, 43, 177
Froc, Kerri, 137

Gardbaum, Stephen, 142
general intent offence, 18–20, 84, 117
Germany, 176
Gladue principle, 50
Goodman, Frank, 152
Gosselin v Quebec (Attorney General), 96
gross disproportionality, 6, 58, 76; bawdy house and communication prohibitions, 78; overlap with overbreadth, 78–82; possession/distribution of marijuana, 76–77; safe injection sites, 77–78

Hansard debates, 148
harm principle, 21–24
Harper, Prime Minister, 169. See also Conservative party
Hart, H.L.A., 22–23
hate speech, 104–6
high stigma offences, 27–28, 51
Highway Traffic Act (Ontario), 74
Hogg, Peter, 4, 9, 49, 86, 89
human dignity, respect for, 20–21, 97
hybrid offence, 167

Iftene, Adelina, 90
Immigration and Refugee Protection Act, 71, 86
incapacity to form intent, 33, 53, 116
India, 175
Indigenous status, 48–50, 55
institutional elitism, 164
instrumental rationality, 6, 9–10, 12, 14–15, 173–74; blended approach, 82; holistic approach 58–61, 74–75; individualistic conception, 65–75, 80–81, 173; judicial dialogue, 91–94; legislative dialogue, 83–91; overlap with principles of criminal law theory, 94–100
interpretivism, 150–51
intrinsic rationality, 134

Judge Whelan, 37
judicial: consensus, 15; elite, 156, 165; notice, 134; overreach, 13, 173–74
judicial review, 9, 13, 141; counter-majoritarian difficulty, 142–50; dialogue 156–59; justifications, 150–53; moral reading, 153–56
Justice Abella, 128–29

Justice Arbour, 25, 31, 96
Justice Beetz, 62
Justice Cartwright, 26
Justice Cory, 121,
Justice Doherty, 137
Justice Gibson, 124
Justice Gonthier, 113
Justice Lamer, 4–5, 27, 29, 56, 103, 121
Justice Lauwers, 74
Justice LeBel, 45, 98, 123
Justice McKay, 112
Justice McLachlin, 62–63, 105, 120–21
Justice Miller, 127–28, 130, 134
Justice Moldaver, 49
Justice Quigley, 104
Justice Stone, 150–51
Justice Wilson, 62, 95–96, 104, 119
justification, 41–44, 53, 100, 161
Juvenile Delinquents Act, 31–32

leave to intervene, 134–35
legal moralism, 22, 25, 27
legal rights, 135
legislative: displacement, 26–27; process, 93, 128, 163; reform, 11
legislative-judicial dialogue, 84, 156, 164, 173
legislators, 145–47, 149
Lepofsky, David, 112, 121–22,
Liberal Party, 89–90

MacLellan, Anne, 167
majoritarianism, 153–54, 162, 165, 169, 177
majority: decision making, 145; rule, 142–43, 157
Malaysia, 175
mandatory minimum sentences, 48, 115–18, 136
Mandela Rules, 90
Manikis, Marie, 49
marked departure, 20, 31, 36–37

McKay, Wayne, 167
mens rea, 19, 25; absolute liability, 26–27; constitutionalization, 34–37; high-stigma offences, 27–29; intoxication, 33; objective fault, 29–31; overlap with *actus reus*, 54; proportionality principle, 51, 161, 172; symmetry with *actus reus*, 31–32
Mill, John Stuart, 18, 21
minority interests, 83, 136, 152
Monahan, Patrick, 111
Moore, Marcus, 93–94
moral blamelessness, 40–41; involuntariness, 38–39, 42–44, 98–99, 161, 171; members, 154; philosophy, 173–74; reading, 153–56
morally innocent, 5–6, 27, 29–30, 41–42, 115
Motor Vehicle Act Reference, 27, 55, 85, 115, 117, 170–72, 174

natural justice, 4
natural law, 151
necessity, 38–41
negative right, 120
negligence, 30–31
neutral principles, 151
non-clause-based approach, 151
non-interpretivism, 150–51
notwithstanding clause, 142, 159, 165–70. *See also Canadian Charter of Rights and Freedoms*, section 33

objective: fault, 29–31, 35–37; foreseeability, 28
obscenity, 108–9
offence principle, 24
Opium and Narcotic Drug Act, 26
over-constitutionalizing, 155, 165, 176
overbreadth, 6, 58, 65; euthanasia, 70–71; fitness to stand trial, 66–67; human smuggling, 71; individualistic

conception, 75; overlap with gross disproportionality, 78–82; sentencing credit, 71–72; sex work, 69; terrorism, 67–69; vagrancy, 66
overincarceration, 125–26

parity, 47–48
Parliament, 25, 163; approval rating, 169–70; conditional sentences, 125–27; instrumental rationality and legislative dialogue, 84–91; notwithstanding clause, 166–68; residual power, 25
Perka v The Queen, 38–39
permanently unfit accused persons, 98, 123
Petter, Andrew, 159
Philippines (Republic) v Pacificador, 137
precedential system of rule, 143
presumption of innocence, 117–18
principles of fundamental justice, 3, 12, 173; fundamental criteria, 22–23; interpretation, 4–6;
procedural protections, 4
proportionality analysis, 158–59. See also *Canadian Charter of Rights and Freedoms*, section 1
proportionality principle, 35, 43, 161, 172; coherence, 50–52; ordinal, 36; sentencing, 45–48, 50, 114, 136
proportionality test, 14
public choice, 84
public solicitation, 103–4
punishment principles, 117

Quebec (Attorney General) v Alliance du personnel professionnel et technique de la sante et des services sociaux, 128–29

R v Anderson, 48–50, 55
R v Anwar, 112
R v Appulonappa, 71

R v Boodhoo, 88
R v Butler, 108, 136
R v Clay, 79
R v Creighton, 30, 32, 35, 51–52
R v Daviault, 19–20, 53, 84, 90–91, 115, 166
R v DB, 44
R v Demers, 66, 98, 123
R v DeSousa, 30, 32, 56
R v Durham, 31
R v Finlay, 31
R v Graf, 97
R v Heywood, 66, 97, 113
R v Hundal, 31
R v Ipeelee, 45
R v Kahkewistahaw First Nation v Taypotat, 128
R v Keegstra, 104–5, 136
R v Khawaja, 67, 78
R v Leary, 19
R v Lloyd, 135–36
R v Logan, 28–29, 56
R v Lucas, 107
R v Malmo-Levine, 21–22, 25, 63, 76
R v Martineau, 28, 35
R v Michaud, 74–75, 81
R v Morgentaler, 61, 95, 119
R v Nova Scotia Pharmaceutical Society, 30
R v Nur, 126, 167
R v Rees, 31–32
R v Robinson, 33, 53, 116
R v Ruzic, 38–39, 41, 44
R v Safarzadeh-Markhali, 45, 50, 71–72, 86, 100, 114
R v Sault Ste Marie, 26
R v Sharma, 124, 126, 129–30, 134
R v Sharpe, 109, 167
R v Smith, 64, 100, 131
R v Turtle, 123
R v Vaillancourt, 27, 29, 116, 118
R v WALD, 37

R v Wholesale Travel Group Inc, 29, 84
R v Zundel, 106
racial prejudice, 152
Ramraj, Victor, 8
Read, Piers Paul, 40
reasonable foreseeability of death, 89
Reference re Section 293 of the Criminal Code, 110
Reference re Section 94(2) of the Motor Vehicle Act, 3, 5
Reference re ss 193 and 195.1(1)(c) of Criminal Code (Man), 103, 112, 120, 130–31
Respect for Communities Act, 87
Roach, Kent, 33–34, 55–56, 86–87, 158, 164–65
Rodriguez v British Columbia (Attorney General), 20–21, 62, 97, 120–21
Roe v Wade, 95, 149
Rudin, Jonathan, 130, 132–33, 135

S v Coetzee, 175
Schwartz, Hart, 92
self-induced intoxication, 18–19
Singapore, 175
social science facts, 134
societal consensus, 23–34, 35, 49
solitary confinement, 90
South Africa, 175–76

specific intent offence, 18–19, 33, 116–17
statutory interpretation, 94
Stewart, Hamish, 48, 65, 69, 87–88
strict liability, 26–27
structured intervention units, 90
subjective fault, 26–29, 33–35; foresight, 28–29; intent, 30; *mens rea*, 29, 31
substantive criminal justice, 162
Supreme Court of Canada, 168–69, 176
suspended sentences, 126–27
symmetry, 32

thin skull principle, 31, 54

under-constitutionalizing, 155–56
United States, 175
United States v Carolene Products Co, 150

vagrancy, 66, 97–98, 113–14
victim surcharge, 77
voluntary intoxication rule, 19

Waldron, Jeremy, 142–49, 162
Way, Rosemary Cairns, 132

Yeo, Stanley, 42
Young, Alan , 171
Youth Criminal Justice Act, 44–45, 55